The Lives of
Justine Johnstone

The Lives of Justine Johnstone

Follies Star, Research Scientist, Social Activist

KATHLEEN VESTUTO

McFarland & Company, Inc., Publishers
Jefferson, North Carolina

ISBN (print) 978-1-4766-7276-2
ISBN (ebook) 978-1-4766-3131-8

LIBRARY OF CONGRESS CATALOGUING DATA ARE AVAILABLE

BRITISH LIBRARY CATALOGUING DATA ARE AVAILABLE

© 2018 Kathleen Vestuto. All rights reserved

No part of this book may be reproduced or transmitted in any form or by any means, electronic or mechanical, including photocopying or recording, or by any information storage and retrieval system, without permission in writing from the publisher.

Front cover image of Justine Johnstone, photograph by James Abbe (courtesy of David S. Shields Broadway Photographs Collection, University of South Carolina / colorization by Olga Shirina)

Printed in the United States of America

McFarland & Company, Inc., Publishers
Box 611, Jefferson, North Carolina 28640
www.mcfarlandpub.com

To the memory of my mother

Table of Contents

Acknowledgments   ix

Preface   1

1. From the Forest of Funnels   5
2. Talent Counts Only 10 Percent   12
3. Patience Rejoices in Hardship   20
4. Ziegfeld's American Beauty   26
5. *Oh, Boy!*   38
6. The Land of Frocks and Frills   46
7. The Most Awful, Cheap Trash   60
8. Some Change   67
9. Real Art   77
10. Actress-Manager   90
11. The Two-a-Day   98
12. A Tissue of Lies   109
13. The Wife of Justine Johnstone's Husband   116
14. Influence of Velocity   123
15. Like Paradise   133
16. Hollywood Snapshots at Random   139
17. Medical Arts   145

18 The Bliss of Uncertainty	151
19 Her Name Is News	156
20 The Most Elementary Emotions	163
21 Women's Activities	168
22 Walter, My Dear	173
23 Producer, Agent, Dramaturg and She Still Looks Lovely	179
24 Her Own Woman	187
Chapter Notes	195
Bibliography	204
Index	207

Acknowledgments

While conducting some online research for a work project one weekend, I wandered into tangential territory, for which I have a peculiar talent, and wound up reading a history of the Mount Sinai Medical Center. I came across a name that intrigued me: Mrs. Justine O. Wanger, who had co-authored a 1933 scientific paper on the slow-drip method of drug delivery, which established the modern IV unit. A woman scientist in 1933 was interesting enough, but I was curious as to why she had no academic title. I wondered if she had ever become an MD or PhD, and what had become of her. A quick search unveiled the startling discovery about who this Mrs. Wanger actually was. I had to find out more. Unfortunately there seemed to be no full biography of her. So I decided to write one.

Easy for me to say. My quest to find Justine Johnstone proved more challenging than I imagined, and I'm deeply indebted to a number of extraordinary people who guided me.

I spent some very happy hours in the beautiful Shubert Archive in the delightful and most helpful company of Sylvia Wang, Maryann Chach and Mark Swartz. Barbara Niss and Nicholas Webb at the Archives and Records Management at the Mount Sinai Medical Center were extremely kind and enthusiastic. As always, the amazing curators at the Billy Rose Theatre Collection of the New York Public Library for the Performing Arts at Lincoln Center were very gracious and accommodating.

I'm also very grateful to Andrea Felder and Thomas Lisanti in the Permissions Office at the New York Public Library; Meredith Mann and her staff at the Brooke Russell Astor Reading Room for Rare Books and Manuscripts at the New York Public Library; Lauren Robinson at the Museum of the City of New York; Jocelyn Wilk of the University Archives and Columbiana Library at Columbia University; Stephen Novak of the Augustus C. Long Health Sciences Library at Columbia University; Cait Miller in the Music Division of the Library of Congress; Alexis Valentine, Office of Business Enterprises of the Library of Congress; Mary K. Huelsbeck of the Wisconsin Center for

Acknowledgments

Film and Theater Research; Cristina Meisner at the Harry Ransome Center, University of Texas at Austin; Jessica Guardado and Cynthia Becht in the William H. Hannon Library at Loyola Marymount University; Dr. David Shields of the University of South Carolina; Claude Zachary of the University of Southern California Libraries Special Collections; and Louise Smith of the USC Digital Imaging Laboratory.

Mr. Bill Marx, executor of the estate of his father, Harpo Marx, has been a delightful acquaintance and guide on several issues.

Justine removed herself from public view in 1926 and lived the rest of her long life in contented privacy, so details about her later life often proved as elusive as she could be. I'm therefore enormously grateful to Justine's son, Mr. Justin Wanger, and her granddaughter, Justine Wanger Nutter, RN, for their kindness and generosity with their time and their memories. I am especially indebted to Mr. Wanger for his astonishing and quite rare family photos.

I'm very lucky to know some very special people who offered encouragement, advice, information and their invaluable friendship: editor extraordinaire Mike Schermerhorn, Neila Ruben Lee; Jennifer Lauren Lee; Emilio A. Emini, PhD; Michael Hotopp; Jack MacBean; Bob Osman; Lynn Sterling; Jan Stuart; Sam Viverito; and my incomparable, supportive family.

And I'm forever grateful to my mother, the late Marjorie Inglish Vestuto, for so many things, including being a role model for a woman's second and third acts in life. You can take the girl out of the theatre, but...

Preface

Ask any theatre or film buff, "Who was Justine Johnstone?," and you may get one of several answers. Justine Johnston? Great Broadway character actress from the 1970s. Julanne Johnston? Wasn't she in silent films with Douglas Fairbanks? *Justine Johnstone?* Never heard of her.

All those answers would have been perfectly fine to Justine Johnstone.

But there was a time when everyone knew who she was. "The most beautiful woman in the world," she was usually called. A Broadway show was produced for her, songs were written about her, a dance and a nightclub were named for her. H. L. Mencken and Lee Shubert were besotted by her. *Vanity Fair* caricaturist Ralph Barton included her in a famous illustration of film-world elite. F. Scott Fitzgerald dropped her name in his works and had his fiancée, Zelda Sayre, replace her unstylish wardrobe with French couture, à la Justine. "The thing was to look like Justine Johnstone at the time," Zelda Fitzgerald later wrote, "and it still seems like a fine way to have looked."[1] Justine's name was splashed above the titles of her films and twirled in flashing red lights on a Broadway theatre rooftop. In 1919, Florenz Ziegfeld called her "my American Beauty."

Ten years later, she was ensconced in a medical laboratory at Columbia University, experimenting with resuscitation techniques, developing a method for intravenous drug delivery and co-authoring scientific papers. Nobody noticed.

When word eventually got out that former Ziegfeld Follies girl and film star Justine Johnstone was now a lady scientist who had contributed to the cure for syphilis, journalists tumbled over each other for an interview. She politely refused them. She wasn't being coy. She simply didn't think she had anything interesting to say. She was simply a single mom raising two boys and working on cancer cures.

Even more than Hedy Lamarr, the glamorous actress and inventor who did not leave acting for scientific pursuits, Justine Johnstone defied popular expectations of what actresses and "show girls" were supposed to be. Those expectations were a hyperbole of the ideal female of the time: basically, very pretty, intellectually unchallenging to men, and someone who took no action on anything of much importance.

By the time Justine Johnstone made her Broadway debut at age 15 in 1910, theatrical producers and press agents had long been making a cult of female performers known as "show girls." Initially a "show girl" was simply a girl who appeared in the chorus or small role of a Broadway show or vaudeville. In 1900, the British import *Floradora* featured a chorus of six "English Girls" who became known as "the Floradora Girls." Daintily dressed in prim frocks, hats and parasols, the girls created a sensation by winking at the audience and, supposedly, establishing the phenomenon of "stage door johnnies," wealthy men lined up after the show to take them out.

As musical productions became more elaborate and producers more daring, the show girl could be dressed in either elegant contemporary clothing or extravagant period costumes, or, especially if hired for a revue, something that emphasized her body as much as New York Society for the Suppression of Vice would allow. Sometimes she danced, more or less, but dancers were a separate category of performer. Sometimes—especially if the costumes were particularly revealing—a show girl didn't move at all, but simply appeared motionless in tableaux to accommodate decency laws.

Thus show girls were, by and large, hired for their looks over their talent. After all, producers marketed to those with the most buying power: men (with the general assumption of heterosexuality). Male theatregoers' obsession with show girls was such a thing that Justine's onetime employer Florenz Ziegfeld famously capitalized on it with his self-proclaimed commitment to "glorifying the American girl." By Ziegfeld's definition, such glorification meant promoting physical beauty, objectification and the fantasy of subjection. It was considered the highest form of flattery.

Not so much to Justine. To her, "the most beautiful woman in the world" tag was meaningless except as a publicity hook generated by her own press agent. It was great when it could get her a job, not so great when it was the only reason she'd get a job.

At 5'7", Justine was a photogenic beauty. Even before she became a show girl, she was one of the most successful artist's models in the business. "Tall and soulful" is how *Boston Post* drama critic Edward Harold Crosby described her.[2] Her light Nordic looks were considered a beauty ideal at the time. She was blonde, with large, heavily-lidded blue eyes, a generous bow-shaped mouth, a soft oval face and a resonant contralto speaking voice sometimes compared to Ethel Barrymore's. "Every flapper in New York," according to a 1921 magazine, "seems to be imitating either Justine Johnstone's or Anna Q. Nilsson's [voice]. Justine's is very deep and husky.... But their imitators are terrible!"[3]

She also had, according to her son, a "cultivated accent"[4] which may have been acquired during her studies at the Emma Willard School and/or picked up from other actors. Sometimes known as Stage Standard, Mid-Atlantic or Aristocratic speech, the dialect is a learned mix of American and Received British pronunciation that is indigenous to nowhere but early to mid–20th century stage and prep schools.

P. G. Wodehouse, who seemed to have an odd love-hate attitude toward Justine, referred to her Scandinavian "aloofness and faintly haughty carriage."[5] That's perhaps not surprising: aloofness can be used as a protective device, one that could come in handy for a woman who began receiving constant attention from besotted men at an early age. It was also a quality that worked well for Justine professionally. Aloof is good for model shots. A degree of reserve can be interpreted as sophisticated, and for a Ziegfeld girl, "haughty carriage" was essential: a sophisticated attitude elevated his productions several notches above basic burlesque.

But Justine's success as a model and show girl had its downside. At the time, a "model" was literally referred to as a "manikin." Ziegfeld show girls were also referred to as mannequins. A mannequin is inhuman: it poses, doesn't speak, and has no brain. Art critic John Berger famously said in the 1970s, "men act, women appear."[6] The Ziegfeld mannequin "appeared." She took little to no action, was generally silent (and therefore non-threatening), and how she looked was more important than who she was. A mannequin with ideas was an oxymoron at best, a joke at worst.

Justine certainly had ideas. She wasn't even tremendously aloof. Her earliest head shots as a teenager reveal a youthful exuberance. She delighted in posing for offbeat photos, such as smoking a pipe or imitating her friend Harpo Marx. Friends knew her to be quite warm and casual, wearing little to no makeup in public. Her personality could be described as "sweet" but "quiet."[7] She had a wry sense of humor and wasn't shy about using it. Generally, she wasn't shy about anything. She had a distaste for rudeness and vulgarity, but never for voicing her considerable opinions.

She sought out challenges and enjoyed hard work. According to a 1918 news article, she felt that "doing something, and doing it well ... is a joy."[8] What she wanted to do was get out of the chorus and act. Her plan was to use work in musicals as a stepping stone, as it had been for several dramatic actresses, such as Marguerite Clark, Elsie Ferguson and other stars of the day. She was clearly ambitious, but deplored the stereotypical definition of getting ahead that was attached to her close friend Marion Davies.

This wouldn't be the only trait that separated her from the show girl cliché. She was also curious, clever, well read, and too focused to be distracted by anything she considered inconsequential—such as being stereotyped as a show girl. She walked out on three of the most powerful producers on Broadway, including Ziegfeld himself. When she was ousted from a play to make room for a backer's girlfriend, she sued.

She was, according to her son, a feminist, and her brand of feminism was an interesting combination of first- and second-wave. She saw no reason why a woman could not have her own career. Striving against gender bias, she negotiated her own contracts, selected her own scripts, and publicly decried film depictions of women as brainless, submissive cyphers. Even as a *Follies* star, she spoke out against preconceived notions of "beautiful women" and their supposed inability to think.

She continued to work after she married a producer who became her manager. He was not a feminist. At a time when only her closest friends were aware that her marriage was in trouble, she publicly expressed dismay about the challenges of what would become known as work-life balance. After the marriage ended, she had lovers, but she never again became anyone's wife.

But she did not, as many former Ziegfeld girls did, dissolve into misfortune or tragedy. By her early 30s, she was happily living out of public view. She did not disappear, she re-appeared, but only to those who were not looking at a show girl. Not only did she "appear," she did in fact "act," in the Berger sense. She entered a male-dominated field, where she thrived; a *Follies* girl—one of those creatures not expected to think much—who authored peer-reviewed, published scientific papers. She spent the rest of her long life immersed in tasks designed to help others: science, medicine, and social causes.

What makes Justine's story unique is her persistence, endurance, intelligence and creativity, and her ability to achieve success within the confines of her time. She was also exceptionally resilient. Once she left her theatrical career, the one for which everyone knew her, she found something else to do. She did it well, and found joy in it.

1

From the Forest of Funnels

Gustina Sophia Olive Johnson, called Justine by her friends, was born on January 31, 1895, in Englewood, New Jersey, to Gustav Johnson, a 26-year old Swedish immigrant, and his 25-year-old Norwegian wife, Sophia Ommundson Johnson. The family name may have been Anglicized, but public records only indicate Gustav and Sophia as "Johnson." They were never "Johnstone." That would come later for Justine.

Very little is known about Sophia, and even less about Gustav (sometimes seen as Gustave). The couple, who may have met after emigrating some years earlier, had married in Englewood on May 20, 1893. According to the 1910 U.S. census, Justine was one of two children in the family, and the only one to have survived. In spite, or because, of the financial struggles the immigrant couple faced, they managed to raise their one child into a creative, well-balanced woman with superb survival skills.

Gustav and Sophia entered the United States during a peak tide of Swedish immigration, many escaping poverty and political uncertainty. Farmers or tradesmen, migrated west to middle America. Gustav was a maritime worker, and he and Sophia lived their lives in America on the East Coast. He operated a "lighter" or flat-bottomed covered barge on the Hudson, transporting goods up and down river. A barge captain wasn't necessarily a captain per se, as barges were pulled by tugboats. That may have been too prosaic for some press agents, who would refer to Gustav as a "Swedish sea captain," and that Justine "had the royal blood of the Bernadottes in her veins."[1]

Other than the Johnsons' marriage date and Justine's birth, there is no information about the Johnson family in Englewood. Some barge families did not live in traditional accommodations, but on the river. Barge captains applied for vessels with living quarters—two or three rooms with a stove at the bow—and could thus live with their families on the boats rent-free. At docks up and down the Hudson, barge children would watch in fascination as longshoremen loaded good from ships onto their homes through sliding-door hatches in the roof. When the barge holds were filled with burlap-bagged cargo, the barge would shove off to Hoboken, West New York, or Brooklyn for unloading and transporting to railroad cars. Barge captains worked ten hours a day, six days a week, for about $60 per month, just slightly more than the average New Jerseyan's income.

The Johnsons' first known home was about twelve miles south of Englewood in Hoboken, nestled between the Hudson River and the Jersey bluffs. The move may have been prompted by a desire to be closer to Hoboken residents Peter Nielsen, a Dane, and his Norwegian wife Louise, who was probably Sophia's sister. The Nielsen children, Lester and Evelyn, are known to have been Justine's cousins and lifelong friends.

Hoboken was a major port with piers for steamship lines, including Scandinavian-American, Hamburg-American, North German Lloyd, and Holland-America. The Johnsons rented an apartment, which may have in fact been a tenement, at 1029 Washington Street, "dwelling number 40," between 10th and 11th Streets. The large brick building was just steps from Elysian Park (location of the first baseball game some sixty years prior) and a five-minute walk to the river. Justine recalled that her Hoboken home was "within a stone's throw from its docks with their forest of funnels."[2] With the streets only one to five feet above high tide, the summertime dock smells were probably also quite memorable, and bitter winters near the river unbearable.

In 1910, Hoboken was comprised of about 260,000 residents, largely German, Scandinavian, Italian and Irish immigrants, along with a smattering of native New Jerseyans, all crammed into the "mile-square city." Washington Street was, and is, a major commercial hub. Horses clopped and trolleys chimed up and down the cobblestoned boulevard past a line of densely-packed, multi-unit, buildings, many boasting first-floor shops for dry goods, meat, baked goods and books. Neighboring streets housed silk, pencil, cork, and iron works, clothing stores, and film development factories. It was a gritty, hard-working town.

If Hoboken had a comparable neighborhood in Manhattan at the time, it probably would have been a combination of the ethnicities of the Lower East Side, Upper East Side and Little Italy. Hoboken was certainly less expensive than Manhattan, where rents could be as high as $40 a month. In any town, tenement life in the early 20th century was crowded, meager, and often cold, and dirty. In the 1910 U.S. census, both Gustav and Sophia listed that they were currently unemployed. Justine rarely spoke about her childhood to the press, except to confide to drama critic Ashton Stevens, "As a child, I was poor. More than romantically poor."[3]

Sophia took in sewing as a ladies' dressmaker, a potentially lucrative addition to the family income. Dressmakers could make $1 to $3 per garment at a time when the average income for New Jerseyans was about $9.50 a week.

Norwegian dressmakers were known for their elaborate detail and vibrant colors, and all immigrant dressmakers adapted quickly to American fashions, combining their own taste with that of their clients, many of whom were wealthy enough to pay someone else to make their clothes.

This seems to have had an impact on Justine. At the time, what one wore indicated one's status. She would equate fashion and good taste with power, and cultivated a sophisticated style throughout her life.

Justine would attribute a number of her personal qualities to her parents. One was her appreciation of hard work and discipline. Another was perspective. This was especially true whenever Justine was complimented on her looks. She was always a pretty child, even beautiful, or so everyone always told her. She knew it. She found it difficult to thank people who complimented her on her looks. Not because she was shy. She just didn't consider it an accomplishment, so she had nothing to thank them for. With what may be considered Scandinavian pragmatism, she always acknowledged her looks as a gift from her parents, not a personal achievement.

Yet another trait influenced by her parents was Justine's joy of words. Whereas many European immigrants of the late 19th century could barely read or write, most Scandinavians, including Gustav and Sophia, were literate. A seeming contradiction that would baffle journalists about Justine was the fact that such a beautiful girl had such intelligence and voracious, eclectic reading habits.

Justine probably attended Public School Number 2 on Garden Street, two blocks from her home, where she would have learned German (as did all Hoboken public school children, regardless of ethnicity, until World War I). The school was a large, sturdy lump of a building, but apparently it did not have an auditorium. Graduation exercises for many Hoboken elementary schools at the time took place at the Gayety Theatre.

Ah—the Gayety Theatre. It was Justine's neighbor, right next door, a four-story, castle-like vaudeville theatre with pillars, a wrought-iron terrace, three huge arched doorways, a bright yellow façade and buzzing marquee lights that would have bedazzled any child who passed by every day.

Hoboken had dozens of theatres, many having grown from immigrants' social and cultural societies to grand-scale legit, music, vaudeville and variety houses. Some of the larger venues were on Washington and Hudson Streets, with others sprinkled throughout the city. Theatres drew capacity crowds from all over town as well as from Manhattan—particularly on Sundays, when New York's strict no-alcohol blue laws were ignored in Hoboken. The jewels in Hoboken's theatrical crown were Soulier's Lyric, offering Broadway-caliber musicals on Hudson Street, about a three-minute walk away from the Johnsons, and the high-class vaudevillian Empire, formerly known as the Germania Garden, just a few clangs downtown on the Washington Street trolley. The cheapest gallery seats for the better theatres were as high as fifteen cents—about the price of three loaves of bread—so theatergoing was an event.

Justine became hooked on theatre—dramas, musicals, variety shows. "When I was a child," she said in 1919, "I used to write plays which my little chums and I acted. I hoped someday to write a real play," starring herself, of course. She based her scenarios on plays, novels, histories, magazine articles, anything else she could get her hands on. Reading and performing were usually, but not always, compatible passions. "A cherished wish was to become— what do you think?—a librarian!"[4] Her preference, she said, was to be "a Belle Green sort of librarian,"[5] referring to J. P. Morgan's special book collections archivist, a brilliant, stylish African American woman who, during her lifetime, "passed" for white. "But librarians can't jump and dance all the time the way I like to do."[6]

For Justine, the reason for her love of theatre was simple. "I am Scandinavian," she said. "I have always loved the theatre in the way all the Northern peoples love it."[7] It was actually also a way she could be transported out of Hoboken and its "forest of funnels." Her early foray into theatre was actually not so much for the love of it, but for her love of a decent wardrobe.

The story of how Justine began working in the theatre depends on who is telling it. According to a 1919 feature article purportedly written by Florenz Ziegfeld, the showman told the story of how, a decade earlier, the stage-struck girl was appearing with an acting company in Union Hill (now Union City), about three miles north of Hoboken from the Washington Street "stage line" trolley route. The best-known stock company in the area at the time was the Hudson Theatre Stock Company, which served as a training ground for many actors. But exactly which stock company, at which Union Hill theatre, and how she got the job, were never mentioned.

Ziegfeld claimed that she was "doing small bits in drama and comedy, and doing them well, let it be said, but there was no future in it."[8] How he knew that she was doing them well is unclear, since Ziegfeld never saw her on stage at this time. But the fact that "there was no future in it" is presumably in reference to Justine's looks. Apparently she was too pretty to be a good actress.

One of his press agents, Ziegfeld said, spotted her in the show. The man introduced himself to Justine and her mother. He suggested that Justine could make some decent money as a "manikin," or model, which could lead to a career on Broadway. Modeling was how many girls got their foot in the door because managers (producers), particularly of musical shows, held beauty at a premium. "And with your looks and personality," the agent reportedly told her, "you could make New York sit up and take notice."[9]

It's a great story, but when Justine told it, she never mentioned being in a theatre company in Union Hill or anywhere else. Plus, she was already working as a model.

1. From the Forest of Funnels

At age 13, Justine answered a newspaper ad for showroom models at Harry Kitzinger and Company on 14th Street just off Fifth Avenue in Union Square. The neighborhood had once been New York's theatre district, which had since moved uptown. Union Square was now a cacophony of shops, restaurants, needle trade offices, socialist rallies in the park, a smattering of vaudeville and Yiddish theatres, and corporate headquarters for various producers in the fledgling film industry. Not terribly glamorous, but more cosmopolitan and faster-paced than Hoboken.

Kitzinger was a manufacturer of misses' and children's coats who supplied goods to department stores and other retailers. It wasn't a difficult job: trying on coats. If they fit, she'd walk around the showroom and pose for potential buyers and sales personnel. And she got to wear stylish pre-season fashions for a whopping $7 a week. That was a pair of shoes, or one of Kitzinger's coats if she saved for three weeks.

Plus, the job was short trip on the newly-constructed Hudson tube (now the PATH train) or, in good weather, on the ferry. Perhaps, if her dad was headed to Lower Manhattan, she could have even hitched a ride on his barge.

It was while working for Kitzinger that Justine made her move from the showroom to the stage and, according to her, the process was relatively simple. A salesman to whom she was showing a coat happened to know a man named Walter Kingsley. The salesman introduced Justine to Kingsley, Kingsley introduced her to a Broadway manager, and the manager gave Justine a small role in a show. It was a no-brainer: she was offered more than double her current salary. Kingsley "got me eighteen dollars playing one of the children for Winthrop Ames in *The Blue Bird*."[10]

The show was a hit 1910 mystical drama that played two elegant and gargantuan theatres built during attempts to expand the theatre district uptown: the New Theatre on 62nd Street and Central Park West, and a few months later, the Majestic in Columbus Circle. The producers included the Shubert brothers, Lee and J. J.

Written by Belgian playwright Maurice Maeterlinck, *The Blue Bird* had premiered at the Moscow Art Theatre in 1908. That sort of cred appealed to manager Winthrop Ames, who with his partners was trying to create a popular yet artistic theatre company at the New Theatre. The story concerns a brother and sister (played by two teenaged actresses Justine's age, Gladys Hulette and Ilene Brown) who are sent by the fairy Bérylune to search for the blue bird of happiness. Along the way, they have adventures in the past, in a scary forest with talking animals and trees, and in the future, where they encounter children waiting to be born. That's where Justine came in.

It's unclear if Justine was in the opening night cast, as her name does not seem to appear in any reviews. It's also unclear if she even had any lines, other than group cries of "Look! Live children!"; "Here we are, here we are!";

and so on. But she could now consider herself a legitimate theatre actress. Considering how she was fulfilling a childhood dream, it actually wasn't that big a deal to her. Naturally, she said years later, she was excited, but not so much because she was doing a great, big Broadway show. She was basically an extra. The main selling point of *The Blue Bird* for Justine was that now she could afford the types of clothes she was modeling.

She said nearly a decade later that "one day I walked down Fifth Avenue and saw all the beautiful clothes. I decided to have those clothes—somehow. But how? The stage was the only quick way."[11] The daughter of the sometimes-employed barge captain and the dressmaker knew what she wanted, and why, and how to get it.

The man who introduced Justine to manager Ames, Walter Kingsley, was indeed press agent and wrangler for Florenz Ziegfeld and several other Broadway musical producers. A slight, balding man with round-framed glasses, Kingsley was a former newspaper reporter from upstate New York with a talent for hyperbole. He is credited with having coined the phrase

The New Theatre (later the Century Theatre), Central Park West and 62nd Street, site of Justine's first professional appearance in *The Blue Bird,* 1910. Frances Benjamin Johnston Collection, Library of Congress Prints and Photographs Division.

"You haven't arrived until you've played the Palace!"[12] He is also noted for his 1917 essay in the *New York Sun*, "Whence Comes Jass? Facts from the Great Authority on the Subject,"[13] which he wasn't, but his bizarre claims about the origins of the term "jazz," racist overtones and all, were taken at face value for decades.

By the time Justine met him, Kingsley was considered the "king of Broadway" and "the godfather of struggling actresses" who specialized in finding "talent" for pretty-girl chorus lines. He was married to actress Alma Hanlon but soon abandoned her and their baby daughter (future screenwriter Dorothy Kingsley), supposedly due to a relationship with one of his clients.

Kingsley knew how to sell a product. He would take an unknown chorine in one of his employers' shows and call her Broadway's latest sensation to boost box office receipts. He took complete control over a girl's publicity, creating a marketable public persona that would sell. Justine's later admission about *The Blue Bird* being a purely monetary decision never surfaced under Kingsley's watch.

But with Justine, Kingsley hit pay dirt. The Justine Johnstone who became a household name was Kingsley's creation. He would often call Justine his "proudest discovery."[14] He would also say that she was eleven years old when he found her. Actually, she was 15. In Kingsley's world, there was apparently no limit on how young a beautiful young girl could be.

2

Talent Counts Only 10 Percent

In a time before photographs were widely used in print advertising, artists constantly sought new young faces as models for lithographs. There were dozens of such artists in New York at the time, and Kingsley knew them all. He also knew he could get some decent commissions by introducing them to Justine.

For a model, the pay could be quite good: some artists paid their models up to $20 a week, which beat even Justine's *Blue Bird* salary. To Gustav and Sophia's dismay, Justine dropped out of high school and made contact with artists recommended by Kingsley.

Reportedly her first "manikin" assignments were for Henry Hutt, who painted women in everyday situations that would appeal to readers of magazines such as *Life*, *Harper's* and *The Saturday Evening Post*. The Hutt jobs led to other jobs. Justine's image began appearing in advertisements, posters, calendars, and books. She logged hours for some of the most successful commercial illustrators of the day, including Howard Chandler Christy, James Montgomery Flagg, Coles Phillips and A. B. Wenzell. Phillips, cover artist *for Good Housekeeping* and famous for his unique "fade-away" styles, gushed over her "youth, freshness and coloring" and called her mouth "a perfect cupid's bow."[1]

Kingsley managed to move Justine out of her walk-on part in *The Blue Bird* to an assignment as a chorus replacement in *Madame Sherry*. The show was a popular operetta produced by A. H. Woods at the regal, narrow New Amsterdam on 42nd Street. This was a great credit for a newcomer: the theatre was owned by two powerful impresarios, A.L. (Abe) Erlanger and Marcus Klaw, members of the Theatrical Syndicate, which essentially owned Broadway. In terms of venue, it was a step up: the New Amsterdam was the type of theatre people thought of when one mentioned "The Great White Way."

2. Talent Counts Only 10 Percent 13

The New Amsterdam Theatre on 42nd Street, home of the Ziegfeld *Follies*. Courtesy The Shubert Archive.

There had been a "theatre district" in New York since before there was a United States of America. The first theatre in the city was possibly a playhouse Nassau Street, which opened in 1753, although theatrical performances had been staged in converted stores and warehouses as much as twenty years earlier. Theatre was concentrated in Lower Manhattan for the next forty or fifty years, but as people and commerce moved north, so did the playhouses: to the Bowery, Union Square, through the red-light Tenderloin, past genteel

Madison Square and finally reaching Longacre Square, a onetime horse carriage hub centered around 42nd Street and Broadway. In 1904, when *The New York Times* moved into a towering new structure at the 42nd Street crossroad of Broadway and Seventh Avenue, Longacre Square became Times Square. The area became a media center, the media center became an entertainment center, and the entertainment center became an advertising center. "The Great White Way" originally referred not to the dazzling lights of the Broadway theatres, but to the enormous animated electric signs emblazoned on Times Square buildings, pitching beer, gloves, coats, gum, underwear, and everything else. The district grew fast: from 1903 to 1918 more than a dozen new theatres were built, primarily on the side streets just west or east of Broadway. Most of the theatres were controlled either by the Syndicate or by its upstart rivals, the Shubert brothers.

Madame Sherry was straightforward ensemble work for Justine, with no lines. The size of the role was immaterial: she was proving eminently hirable as a chorus girl in a chorus girl-loving culture. Kingsley wanted to make sure the public connected the name with the face. He sent her to the renowned White Studio at 1546 Broadway, a soon-to-be dwarfed, three-story office building on the northwest corner of 46th Street. The White Studio was the premier Broadway photographer for all major theatrical managers including Ziegfeld,

Above and opposite: **Early modeling shots of Justine by the renowned White Studio, ca. 1911. Courtesy Mr. Justin Wanger.**

David Belasco, Daniel Frohman, the Shuberts and others. The photographers' specialties were both studio portraits and rehearsal shots taken from theatre balconies.

Actor portraits aren't cheap, and in 1911 ran about $6 (over $100 in contemporary dollars) for 12 9 × 12 enlargements. They could have been part of a production's advertising budget as long as they were used to promote the show. But whoever paid for Justine's portraits got their money's worth. She proved a natural camera model: poised, relaxed, natural, unaffected and, of course, extremely photogenic. She mastered the type of model poses still utilized today: the "smiling eyes" shot, gazing intently into the camera (thus the viewer), relaxed face, sometimes with a slight, lip-parted smile, sometimes looking at something apparently fascinating in the distance.

Studio shots of young Justine began appearing regularly in rotogravure sections. The studio photographers dressed her in various costumes, some perhaps having nothing to do with her shows, simply because they made for gorgeous pictures. A photo of Justine in a cute ribbon-trimmed bonnet was captioned as "Miss Johnson, of *Madame Sherry*."[2] Another in a Bo-Beep outfit was "Miss Johnson, one of the Mist Maidens in *The Blue Bird*, an English beauty."[3] The Broadway trade paper *Dramatic Mirror* began receiving letters addressed to Justine until the editors begged readers to contact the White Studio instead.

That "English beauty" may have been an editor's assumption, but Kingsley, who had once reported for the London *Daily Mail*, picked up on it. He decided that her name should be changed from Johnson to the more British-sounding Johnstone. "Among the new girls on Broadway, none has received more adulation than Justine Johnstone," ran one story. "She is one of the most talked-about beauties of the season. A dozen prominent artists have pronounced her the ideal American girl."[4] "Her face has brightened many covers of the best sellers and has popped refreshingly out from magazines without number,"[5] noted the *Boston Sunday Post*. Kingsley knew his business.

By the spring of 1911, Justine had graduated to one of the biggest productions of the season, the premiere offering of an elaborate new theatre at

210 West 46th Street called the Folies-Bergère, built by California-born vaudeville manager Jesse L. Lasky and Boston impresario Henry B. Harris.

Lasky and Harris envisioned a revolutionary theatrical offering based on French cabaret, an entertainment form which Lasky claimed (incorrectly) to introduce to New York. Audience members were served dinner at 6:30 p.m. at round tables throughout the theatre as a live band played. At 8:30 p.m., the first portion of the show began. This consisted of three one-acts, all with multiple scenarists and song writers, including the young Irving Berlin. The acts were *Hell*, a "profane burlesque," basically a vaudeville offering a series of innuendo gags and songs; *Temptations*, an erotic ballet about a young swain surrounded by sylphs; and a satire, *Gaby*, rather blatantly based on French chanteuse Gaby Deslys' romantic involvement with the king of Portugal. The last sketch starred Ethel Levy, ex-wife of George M. Cohan, and popular actor Taylor Holmes.

After intermission, more food. The audience was served supper while watching ten vaudeville acts, which included Olga Petrova, a British actress whom Lasky had discovered and changed her name (from Muriel Harding) to fit her "exotic" looks; Ina Claire, with whom Justine would work in the *Follies*; the Pender Troupe, an English acrobatic team featuring a seven-year-old stilt-walker named Archie Leach (later Cary Grant); and a young actress named Elda Furry, who would change her name to Hedda Hopper.

The production was called either *Hell/Temptations/Gaby* or simply "the Folies-Bergère show." The most expensive tickets to the show were $2.50, the highest cost for any entertainment except the Metropolitan Opera. But essentially, it was dinner theatre that went on until 1 a.m.

As a chorus girl, Justine was not even mentioned by name in the reviews. She was one of many, and they were all apparently commendable for what they needed to do. "A word should be added for the chorus," wrote the *Dramatic Mirror*. "They can dance, sing, and wear clothes—all with much éclat."[6]

It's difficult to pinpoint all the numbers in which Justine appeared, but she reportedly had a noticeable bit early in the show as one of eight girls playing messenger boys, dressed in snappy caps, white tunics and pants. The "boys" were sent out into the audience to retrieve messages supposedly written by the playgoers to the chorus girls. The "boys" would then return to the stage and read the fake messages, which invariably involved digs at the better-known society people and politicians in the audience. This shtick was initially built around a number called "The Messenger Boy," which was dropped during an Atlantic City tryout and replaced with "Don't Keep the Taxi Waiting, Dearie," written by Berlin: "Dearie, don't keep the taxi waiting / Dearie, don't be so hesitating / There'll be just you and me / And if your wife comes buzzin' / Tell her that I'm your cousin / Please keep it waiting, dear, for me."[7] This number has the distinction of being an Irving Berlin song never to be copyrighted or published. (Lasky approved this piece, but for some reason refused Berlin's request to include his recently-published "Alexander's Ragtime Band," a huge hit tune which Berlin may or may not have poached from Scott Joplin.)

But at least the messenger boy bit gave Justine her first solo lines on stage. They were probably stupid lines, but they were lines. And even though she was one of reportedly 200 cast members, she made an impression. Lasky would later remember, a bit creepily, that 16-year-old Justine (he said she was 15) was "already as luscious as Marilyn Monroe."[8]

The "chorus girl culture" of the day is well illustrated by Justine's experience at the Folies-Bergère: pretty young girl, small role, big show, many admirers. One was the

Jesse Lasky's Folies-Bergère Theatre (later the Fulton, later the first Helen Hayes Theatre), 210 West 46th Street, where Justine first became a "show girl,"1911. Courtesy The Shubert Archive.

enormous, rather decrepit financier "Diamond" Jim Brady, who reportedly took up a couple of seats on various nights to gawk at Justine. Another was playwright Owen Johnson, a young widower at the time. Still another was a 40-year-old social-climbing bachelor stockbroker named Ralph Ranlet, who had an eye for stage beauties (he would later marry English operetta star Kitty Gordon). Justine, with one of the most unspectacular of roles, got the orchids, the notes backstage, the dinner invitations, boxes of chocolates (which she said she gave to her father), everything chorus girls usually got from stage-door Johnnies.

Her popularity had nothing to do with anything except her ability to look pretty. It didn't matter to anyone but Justine. She knew she was being hired for her looks, as she expected, but she hadn't expected that would be an end in itself. As she would later admit, the attention was flattering and enjoyable at first. "But heavens, how it palled!"[9]

She wasn't the only one experiencing disillusionment. Her friend and fellow Folies-Bergère chorine Margaret Adair wrote a scathing overview of chorus girl life that was syndicated by Scripps newspapers. Under the headline "Truth About the Chorus Girl," Margaret wrote:

> The chorus girl is the tiniest and least important cog in the whole theatrical machine. There are so many of us, that we don't count as an individual. There are hundreds of girls, newer, fresher, younger than we are, always ready to take our places. A tidal wave of youthful girlhood is always sweeping into Broadway.
>
> Shall I say it is all a tragedy?
>
> A girl who enters the chorus soon finds that all who enter must leave hope behind. The girl who makes good and becomes a prima donna is infinitely rare. Talent counts only 10 per cent. Looks count the other 90 per cent. And in 10 years the looks are gone....
>
> Her career is so full of uncertainties that she becomes discouraged and hopeless. She finds out that fame too often goes hand-in-hand with what the old-fashioned folks back home would call ruin. She becomes the prey of beasts in human and male form, who seek not only her person but also her money. She is not respected; she is only a tiny dot.
>
> Why, only the other day 75 chorus girls rehearsed a piece for five weeks in New York, on no pay. At the end of that time the manager told them he wasn't going to put on the piece and he dismissed them all, even without saying thank you. They were only chorus girls.
>
> I had a chum who paid a theatrical agent five dollars to get her a job. He put her in a musical show that opened at Norfolk, Va. It ran two nights and then the managers took the money, closed the show and left my chum stranded.
>
> There is a manager right here in New York who, only a few years ago,

Interior of the Folies-Bergère. Audience members were given two meals and a vaudeville-dinner theatre show until 1 a.m. Courtesy The Shubert Archive.

left a company of 40 girls stranded in Colorado. It took some of them six months to get back to New York. And yet this manager took back the male members of the company with him. The others were only chorus girls....

A manager can fire her at a minutes' notice. Everything is uncertainty; even her bread and butter isn't sure.[10]

It's a fascinating description of life for a specialized, uncountable population at that time: female theatrical professionals working in a world (aside from being pre-union) where success was defined by those in power. In this case, the power was held by white males making money off their employees' looks. The appeal for many women was limited, or became so.

For many readers at the time, Margaret's story would have been interpreted as simply amusing. It was illustrated with photographs of both her and Justine, posing prettily. Above their photos, an ink-sketched man ogles them wide-eyed through binoculars.

3

Patience Rejoices in Hardship

The Folies-Bergère show flopped rather spectacularly, closing on July 8, 1911, after a run of little more than two months and at a loss to Lasky of $150,000. Margaret Adair moved on to another show. The next two productions at the theatre also tanked, including a burlesque called *A La Broadway*, which brought attention to 18-year-old Mae West but closed in a week. Jesse Lasky and Henry Harris ripped out the cabaret tables, renamed the theatre the Fulton (later to become the first Helen Hayes Theatre), and sold it to another producer. Then Harris went down with the *Titanic*. (Harris' wife Renée, who survived the sinking, gathered the reins of his business to become Broadway's first woman producer.)

Lasky began considering a recommendation made by his brother-in-law, Sam Goldfish (Gelbfisz), who would later change his last name to Goldwyn. A successful glove manufacturer, Goldfish was bedazzled by the movies and suggested that Lasky might consider getting out of the theatre business and create a "film play" company to showcase his vaudeville acts.

Justine was reconsidering her own priorities. "My stage experience in *The Blue Bird* and subsequent engagement at the ill-fated Folies-Bergère convinced me that something besides mere beauty is necessary to achieve success," she said in 1915. "I was woefully deficient in many ways."[1] As a first step toward achieving success, she chucked Broadway to finish high school.

It may not have been her idea, despite her awareness of being "woefully deficient." According to a 1918 story in the *New York Sun*, the decision to return to school was made for her by her "stern parents of Viking ancestry" in an attempt "to keep her from mischief."[2] Be that as it may, Justine was up for the change.

She opted for a private boarding school. Apparently she had a backer. "A charming, benevolent gentleman was instrumental in my going there," she said in 1918. "And I was very grateful to him—oh, very! But he was forty-two—and I was sixteen."[3] She didn't elaborate beyond that, unfortunately, but it seems the benevolent gentleman was hoping for a reciprocity that never materialized. She never named him, but he appears to have been the infatuated stockbroker Ralph Ranlet.

She first enrolled in the exclusive Manor Girls' School in Larchmont, a small conservatory with twenty live-in students and an emphasis on art and music. Although she said she wasn't "fired"[4] from the school, she didn't last long. She then transferred to the prestigious Emma Willard School, one the country's oldest prep schools for girls and the first to offer curriculum similar to that of boys' schools.

Located near the Hudson River in Troy, New York, Emma Willard prepared students for Bryn Mawr, Radcliffe and Barnard. Its graduates were admitted by certificate "without further examination" to Vassar, Wellesley, Smith and Mount Holyoke.[5] With its collegiate Gothic architecture and scenic surroundings, the school has also proven a photogenic and versatile film location (the institution played a boys' school in the 1992 Al Pacino film, *Scent of a Woman*).

At 17, Justine was older than most of her school mates and probably more sophisticated after three years of working in and around Broadway. This was not unnoticed by her chums' parents. "My photograph presently appeared in the Green Book," Justine said, "and anxious mothers wanted to know if I was the sort of girl to be going to the same school with their daughters."[6]

It was also not unnoticed by the staff. "We have been grieved and annoyed at the numerous pictures of Justine appearing in all sorts of papers and magazines, advertising articles of every description," wrote headmistress Eliza Kellas. "I have closed my eyes and ears to everything in my effort to help Justine."[7] What Justine needed help with isn't made clear, but the letter was addressed to Ralph Ranlet.

Justine thrived at Emma, easily making friends who called her "JuJo." She welcomed the challenging curriculum of algebra, geometry, Latin, Greek (French or German were mere electives), composition, literature, biology, chemistry, and physics. The gymnasium had barbells and pulleys, and exercises were "based on the Swedish system" of rigorous calisthenics. With the discipline and focus she developed at Emma, Justine developed a lifelong habit of physical exercise and a joy of eclectic, consequential reading.

She became president of the dramatic club, athletic editor of the school yearbook, played on the basketball team and sang in the glee club and choir. In the weeks before her 1914 graduation—the school's 100th, thus a gala affair—Justine performed a featured role in a school operetta, sang the "Habanera" from *Carmen* in a musicale (nice showpiece for a contralto), and played Orlando in *As You Like It*. She even got invited to the Hamilton College junior prom.

Justine's theatrical performance experiences at Emma Willard were something of a revelation. For the first time, she was on stage in quality pieces a few cuts above the average show girl musical. It didn't take her long to realize that this was the type of work she wanted to do. Even before graduating, she began devising a plan.

She would start with jobs she knew she could get and eventually transform that career into a dramatic one. Thus Justine would leverage her looks—at the moment, her currency—into something more legitimate. She knew enough about the business to know that there would be no guarantees. It would be tough. But she was an Emma girl. The school's motto was "Gaudet Patientia Duris" (Patience rejoices in hardship).

Her first step was to reconnect with Walter Kingsley, the connoisseur of pretty girls and, more importantly, the man of many connections.

Press stories mentioning Justine at this time were primarily local. She was merely listed among her fellow classmates in various activities, and nothing was ever said about her having been a show girl. Kingsley's hyperventilating presence was nowhere. That would change.

Weeks after graduation, Justine was back in professional theatre. She was cast in an out-of-town tryout run of a romantic farce called *Are You My Wife?* at the Broadway Theatre in Long Branch, New Jersey, about 50 miles south of Hoboken. The play was co-written by and starring comic actor Roy Atwell (later known as a radio actor and the voice of "Doc" in Disney's *Snow White and the Seven Dwarfs*). Justine played a small role as a society girl. The play was supposedly to open that fall at Maxine Elliot's Theatre, co-owned by Lee Shubert, a producer of *The Blue Bird*. But the reviews in Long Branch were not great, and *Are You My Wife?* closed after three performances. Rewrites postponed the Broadway opening for another three years as *Here Comes the Bride* (later made into a movie with John Barrymore), but without Justine.

No matter. She got a film. Almost certainly through Kingsley, Justine met two of his high-profile clients, theatrical producer Daniel and Charles Frohman. With wealthy furrier Adolph Zukor, the Frohman brothers were co-founders of the new Famous Players film company. Daniel Frohman cast Justine in his production of *The Crucible,* a melodrama based on a popular novel and co-directed by film pioneer Edwin S. Porter. Billed as Justina Johnstone, she played Amalia, the spoiled-brat sister of Jean (Marguerite Clark), a misunderstood tomboy who is sent to a reform school.

Marguerite, two years older than Justine, had the type of career path that Justine wished to follow. With the help of Winthrop Ames, Justine's *Blue Bird* producer, Marguerite had transformed a backlog of musicals and comedies into an impressive resume of serious work. It would not have escaped Justine's notice that this was possible. She may not have considered that Marguerite had been a soubrette, not a show girl. There was a difference.

The Crucible was shot in Brooklyn and at Famous Players' West 26th Street Studio. It wasn't exactly a turning point in Justine's career. The *Canton*

3. Patience Rejoices in Hardship 23

Daily News noted that "Justina Johnstone has a rather a weak part, but makes the most of it."[8] It was all anyone could do. Film acting at the time was viewed as a quick, relatively painless paycheck. "Don't quit your night job," was the actors' joke about filmmaking. Broadway ruled.

Within a few months, Justine and her parents left Hoboken for an apartment on West 105th Street in Manhattan, a quiet, tree-shaded neighborhood of rocky terrain, row houses and primarily German and Irish immigrants. According to the 1915 New York State census, Gustav was still working as a "boatsman," Sophia as a dressmaker, and 20-year-old Justine's occupation was listed as "actress." Interestingly, Sophia was listed as the "head" of the family—possibly because her income exceeded her husband's (income is not listed on this census), or because, as Justine would mention later, Sophia took an active role in her daughter's career and was her de facto manager.

Their home was just steps away from to the recently-constructed IRT local subway train station, which meant a mere 25-minute ride to the theatre district. Justine began building the groundwork for the career she wanted.

The Alviene School of Stage Arts, a theatre students' factory similar to the American Academy of Dramatic Arts, was located at the time just north of the theatre district at 225 West 57th Street. Alviene offered courses in both drama and musical comedy, and boasted a large "stage dancing" department (earlier dance students had included sibling child performers Fred and Adele Astaire). Stage dancing at the time could include tap, rhythmic gymnastics, military-type drills and expressionistic or "modern" styles, as utilized by such choreographers as Ziegfeld's flamboyant Ned Wayburn. (The term "choreographer," as opposed to "dance director" or "dances by," did not actually appear in a Broadway program until 1936, when applied to George Balanchine for *On Your Toes*.) It was athletic and tough work. But Alviene's advertisements proclaimed, "Failure impossible, if we accept you as a student."[9] Justine was accepted. She didn't exactly emerge an Astaire, but she developed a sense of poise, as well as superb posture that would be a hallmark for her.

She also began a serious study of the classics: Shakespeare, Ibsen, and Molière. Her ultimate ambition, she said, was to do Norwegian dramas such as Ibsen's *Peer Gynt*—preferably playing Peer; otherwise, Solveig would do, or even Peer's mother Åse. She wasn't picky. She just wanted a very good role in a very good play.

Her intellectual curiosity created tangential pathways. She became fascinated with the monkeys in the Central Park Zoo and incorporated their movements into her own dance exercises. She became a devotee of Darwin and developed an interest in physiology. Even Kingsley was in awe of how well-read she was. But he wouldn't mention that until years after Justine had left the business. It wouldn't have fit her image.

By December 1914, Justine was back on Broadway. She accepted an offer from one of Kingsley's employers, Charles Dillingham, a manager who had been influential in the early career of Elsie Ferguson, who, like Marguerite Clark, had been able to restructure her career from musicals to dramas.

A former newspaper reporter and sometime Ziegfeld collaborator, Dillingham was a dapper, gentle, jovial man, known for his trademark derby hats. His friends knew, or assumed, that he was the longtime lover of popular manager Charles Frohman, brother of Daniel, the producer of Justine's film *The Crucible*. Dillingham was an unusual theatrical producer: refined, paternal towards his actors, and socially very well-connected. He would take players under his wing and bring them to parties hosted by his friends, such as the Astors and Vanderbilts. It was possibly through Dillingham that Justine became acquainted with some of the most blue-blooded names in society.

Dillingham is noted for installing the first moving electric sign in front of a Broadway theatre, a revolving windmill at the Knickerbocker for his 1908 hit *The Red Mill*. His shows were similar to Ziegfeld's, but on a smaller scale. They were typical "musical comedies" of the era: basically, a revue, a series of songs strung tenuously together by the thinnest of plots performed by vaudevillians and pretty chorus girls who appealed to the "TBM" (tired businessman). Like Ziegfeld's, Dillingham's shows were more or less "legit vaudeville."[10]

Watch Your Step featured a number of vaudeville stars but was basically a showcase for the popular fox-trotting dance team of Vernon and Irene Castle. The show's feeble plot revolved around an inheritance left by a millionaire to any of his relatives who did not fall in love. A naïve boy and his girl cousin turn out to be the only family members who have not, and others spend the show trying to introduce them to people they could fall for. Irving Berlin, in his first full Broadway assignment, wrote an all-ragtime score, including the delightful syncopated duet "Play a Simple Melody." The big finale was a ragtime opera parody that sounds faintly like a nightmare, with Giuseppe Verdi arising from the dead to scold the cast for jazzing up his scores.

The hours were long and the pace was breakneck. A tryout in Syracuse resulted in multiple script changes and elimination of an entire scene, which meant that vaudeville juggler W. C. Fields was out. But the show opened to an appreciative, packed house at the New Amsterdam on December 8, 1914. The ragtime opera finale was such a huge hit that Berlin was brought onstage for a curtain speech. The *Clipper* called the show "one of the sure-fire hits of the New York season,"[11] and *Theatre* magazine said, "Berlin is now a part of America."[12]

Justine's role wasn't a large one, but at least her character had a name, Estelle, described as a "hesitating typewriter." She joined a line of other "office girls" in singing of the drudgery of work after a night dancing on the town, and performed in the "Trovatore" segment of the ragtime opera finale. Despite, or because of, having little to do, *Vanity Fair* found a rather bizarre reason to mention her: "While not listed among the stars, Miss Johnstone furnishes proof of the care that has been taken in 'Watch Your Step' to select a sound cast throughout. The heavy work in her role consists of being kissed by Vernon Castle."[13]

Still, it was a hit Broadway show. Not a bad start for someone just a few months out of high school. And as such, it seems she still had a few things to learn. "You spoiled a good performance at the Saturday matinee,"[14] Dillingham wrote to her on January 25, 1915. The note does not elaborate on what Justine did—a forgotten line, a missed cue, a fit of giggles—but she straightened up enough to finish the run. Her part may have been small, but she was capable of an infraction large enough for the boss to consider a show-spoiler. As long as she could stay in the show and move on, her plan might work reasonably well.

Kingsley was doing his job by regularly getting her name in the papers. In fact, he was helping so well that he was about to brand her in a way that would ultimately haunt her.

4

Ziegfeld's American Beauty

A few months into the run of *Watch Your Step*, press agent Kingsley hit PR gold. It probably started as just another stunt for him, but it turned Justine into one of the most talked-about young women of the era.

Kingsley learned that a Troy photographer named Philip Conklin had entered his portrait of Justine in a photo contest sponsored by the Ansco Camera Company of Binghamton, New York. The contest, called "Ansco's Loveliest Woman," was judged by actress Minnie Maddern Fiske, artist Harrison Fisher and photographer Alfred Stieglitz. Conklin was awarded the $500 first prize, and his photo of Justine then became part of Ansco exhibits at the Grand Central Palace (an exhibit hall near Grand Central Terminal) and at the Panama-Pacific Exposition in San Francisco.

Even though the company clearly promoted the winning photo as its own "loveliest woman," not necessarily anyone else's, Kingsley figured Justine could now legitimately be called the loveliest something, and ran with it.

Headlines splashed across papers nationwide claimed that Justine Johnstone had officially been proclaimed the "most beautiful" woman in America. Or the world; the stories varied. Some claimed that she had won a beauty contest, or several, or that she'd won the $500 or even $5,000. The details didn't seem important: she was The Most Beautiful Woman.

She actually wasn't much of a woman when the winning photo had been taken. It was a graduation picture dating more than a year earlier, but her parents had not granted permission for use until after she had left school. The artistic, soft-focus shot makes it difficult to tell how old she is, or even much of what she looks like. Justine is positioned in an over-the-shoulder pose with her face in a three-quarter profile. She's wearing what seems to be a fur jacket and a broad-brimmed hat decorated with a peacock feather that swoops down and curls up her back. The hat casts a shadow over the upper portion of her face, and her downcast eyes are barely visible. It's indeed a lovely portrait, as no doubt all the entries were, but it was the only one flacked by Kingsley.

4. Ziegfeld's American Beauty

Reporters scrambled to interview the newly-crowned Most Beautiful Justine. Many were surprised to find not a giggly, compliant show girl, but a frank, level-headed young woman. She told *The New York Times* that of course she knew what she looked like, "but what does it matter? If I am pretty, it is no fault of mine, and if I am not, I am equally blameless. I would much rather be considered intelligent than handsome. I am more ambitious to do something on the stage than win beauty prizes."[1]

A much-quoted statement from Justine in 1915—"If I had my choice between being the prettiest girl in America and the most talented, I would unhesitatingly choose the latter"[2]—was generally met with bemusement. A syndicated opinion piece fairly summed up the usual response to that idea:

> Do you suppose Miss Johnstone really, truly, down deep in her heart means this?... For a good many thousands of years being beautiful has been one of the big ambitions of women. In recent years there has been a lot of talk about sex equality and such, but despite their new demands and new hopes women are still as anxious to be beautiful as ever.
>
> If exceptionally beautiful girls are rarely superlatively talented, it usually is not altogether their fault. The men attracted by their beauty flatter them and take up their time until they have no chance to become talented.... [The women] are acting perfectly logical and in line with the demands and expectations in life.[3]

The 1914 "Ansco's Loveliest Woman" contest-winning portrait taken as a high school graduation photograph, used by Justine's publicist to proclaim her "the world's most beautiful woman." *American Photography* magazine, May 1915.

(This offers a couple of interesting ideas: that even though all that talk of "sex equality and such" was going on, a woman's number one priority is to be beautiful because she's drawn that way. If she never develops her talent, we can understand: her time is completely consumed by admiring men. One wonders if the writer actually knew any women.)

Justine's time was in fact being consumed by looking for work. To her dismay, nobody was offering her *Peer Gynt*. Through a friend, she managed an introduction to popular actor John Drew, Jr., a star for producer Charles Frohman and the uncle of John, Lionel and Ethel Barrymore. Drew offered her a small role in a non-musical comedy for $25 a week as long as she provided her own costumes. Not great. It matched her Folies-Bergère salary four years earlier. And although some managers provided costumes for actors, many did not. But Justine figured she could do worse in an entry-level job out of the chorus.

Then Kingsley's boss Florenz Ziegfeld called Justine to his office.

Ziegfeld was preparing his new *Follies*, the latest incarnation of his "girl show," as he called it. Since Justine had achieved a level of fame as the most-beautiful, he wanted her for his "beauty chorus." She would be featured as a mannequin: one of those spectacularly-gowned creatures who didn't do much but appear. Was she interested?

It was precisely the type of thing she was hoping to avoid. But Ziegfeld was one of the most financially generous managers on Broadway. His going rate for the "beauty chorus," Justine would later say, was $50 a week, twice what Drew was offering. But this was not her job of choice. She negotiated for $75 a week, and got it. "So I went into the *Follies* chorus," she said, "and Ziggy furnished the costumes."[4] She didn't reveal her salary to her dressing roommate, Kay Laurell, who was getting the standard $50.

Florenz Ziegfeld, legendary glorifier. Billy Rose Theatre Division, The New York Public Library. "Florenz Ziegfeld." New York Public Library Digital Collections. Accessed May 16, 2017.

Ziegfeld was delighted to have her. He called her "my American beauty."[5] "She was not spoiled with compliments," he said, "although there must have been many in her young life."[6]

Justine had all the qualities Ziegfeld considered perfect: Caucasian, large blue eyes, natural blonde hair, tall, wore clothes well, and under 22 years of age. He had a particular penchant for "Nordic" types. "The Swedish race," he once wrote, "is a race of beauty.... The Swedish type, of course, is usually blonde, statuesque, dignified, queenly-looking. They have rather less temperament than their bewitching sister-type, the Irish."[7]

4. Ziegfeld's American Beauty

Follies girl: left, as a member of the "beauty chorus" and as Columbia in the 1915 production; right, an unusually young and beautiful Nurse in the 1916 *Romeo and Juliet* sketch. Courtesy Billy Rose Theatre Division, New York Public Library for the Performing Arts, Astor, Lenox and Tilden Foundations.

Ziegfeld pretty much had the perfect woman all figured out, from her "straight" nose to her "white teeth" to the color of her eyes. "They must be blue or brown. Green eyes cannot be beautiful. They are too hard, too intellectual. They are the eyes of the typical college girl. Black eyes are seldom beautiful. They have an opaque quality that is repellant."[8] He was Ziegfeld, so of course he was right about all this, according to Ziegfeld. The secret of his success, he claimed, was his instinct about these things. "I am governed by what I regard as beautiful,"[9] he said.

French-German Florenz Ziegfeld, Jr., was born to an upper middle-class Chicago family in 1867. Legend has it that he developed his appreciation for spectacle as a fascinated four-year-old watching as Chicago burned in the Great Fire of 1871, and his taste for the erotic inspired by cooch dancers at the 1893 Chicago World's Fair. Unlike his film portrayers—debonair William Powell in the 1936 *The Great Ziegfeld* or distinguished Walter Pidgeon in 1968's *Funny Girl*—Ziegfeld had a rather character-y, pugnacious face, an "odd, whiny voice,"[10] and was privately rather shy. But he learned early in his career that sex was money. He'd had his first success presenting a vaudevillian bodybuilder named The Great Sandow, charging a nominal fee for women to meet the strongman backstage and feel his muscles.

Like any good showman, Ziegfeld knew how to promote. In 1896, he discovered a petite, coquettish cabaret singer in London named Anna Held, a Pole who passed herself off Parisian. With a clever bombardment of imaginative press features, Ziegfeld sold her to New York audiences even before he had brought her to the States. Anna became a star and Ziegfeld's longtime lover, occasionally referred to as his wife, although they never legally married.

The "follies" concept was actually Anna's idea, based on the Parisian cabaret combination of sexual allure and comedy acts. It was a formula that Jesse Lasky had tried unsuccessfully with his Folies-Bergère Theatre, although Lasky's concept was probably more vaudeville than cabaret. One thing that Lasky had left out of the mix was fashion, which, as Anna knew, elevated the French productions to a certain level of sophistication. Whether or not American audiences would be as sophisticated was a gamble, but Ziegfeld was a gambler, and it paid off. Beginning with his first *Follies* in 1907, he created increasingly lavish and daring fashion-comedy-musical shows that unashamedly "glorified" the American (white) female, or at least her physical attributes. The productions were spectacular, the music often great and many of the Ziegfeld comedians would become entertainment legends, but Ziegfeld's priority was always to glorify. He was certainly not the first man to set arbitrary standards for female

Dapper theatrical manager Charles Dillingham, right, for whom Justine performed in three musicals, pictured with his lover, manager Charles Frohman. Billy Rose Theatre Division, The New York Public Library. "Charles Frohman and Charles Dillingham." New York Public Library Digital Collections. Accessed May 16, 2017.

beauty, but he was one of the most prominent in the 20th century to sanctify objectification, a practice adopted by the media and the film industries and exploited for decades. Ziegfeld's legacy is grand spectacle, but it is certainly also idealization, subjugation, and body shaming.

A seeming contradiction was that the man who was marketing women as sex objects prided himself in promoting his girls as "chaste." It was good for his image, allowed him to rise above any assumptions of pimpdom, and kept the women under a nice glass jar, like hothouse flowers. If, however, he was especially attracted to any of them, all bets were off, and the old double-standard and *droit du seigneur* kicked in. There are plenty of stories of Ziegfeld's affairs, some considered valid, some not. Lillian Lorraine, a chorine Ziegfeld first hired in 1909, began an affair with him in 1910 and was set up by the impresario in an apartment at the Ansonia Hotel two floors above his and Anna's.

How well Justine and Ziggy (usually called Flo by friends, but Ziggy to Dillingham and the "help")[11] got along, if at all, is subject to some speculation. One interesting tidbit comes from Ziegfeld's daughter, Patricia Ziegfeld, in her 1964 autobiography *Confessions of an Abnormally Happy Childhood*. She relates a second-hand story that happened when her mother, actress Billie Burke, was under contract to Charles Dillingham's lover Charles Frohman. Billie had met Ziegfeld at a 1914 New Year's Day party at the Astor Hotel, and fell hopelessly in love. A few months later, much to Frohman's displeasure, Billie and Ziegfeld became engaged. Frohman and his business partner Al Hayman paid Billie a visit and begged her to reconsider.

"Anna Held. Lillian Lorraine. Justine Johnstone. Shall I go on with the list?" Frohman supposedly asked. "Do you," demanded Hayman, "want to toss away everything for the sake of this—this—Lothario?" Patricia Ziegfeld writes that her mother Billie was both angry and frightened: "Were they telling her the truth? she wondered, panic-stricken. Was she throwing away her career? Or were they simply two meddlesome old gossips trying to scare her?"[12]

It's interesting that Justine got tossed in with these high-profile Ziegfeld lovers. The timing may be a bit off, however. The story is set prior to the April 1914 Ziegfeld-Burke wedding (in Hoboken, no less), while Justine was still at Emma Willard. If Ziegfeld and Justine ever had a tryst prior to her return to high school, the story makes her 1915 entry into the *Follies* seem a curiously delayed payoff.

The Ziegfeld Follies of 1915 is considered the vehicle that established the look for which the Ziegfeld productions would become known, due in large part to the lavish sets created by Viennese designer-architect Joseph Urban, who had initially sniffed to Ziegfeld that he would not demean himself to work on a girlie show. (The impresario handed him a check for $10,000.

Urban essentially responded, when do I start?) Another new standard set by this *Follies* were the magnificent costumes designed by innovative British couturier Lady Duff Gordon (Lucile), a *Titanic* survivor whose husband, according to rumor, paid lifeboat crew members not to turn back and pick up more passengers.

The stars that season included Bert Williams, the gifted, resilient but tragic black comedian, considered one of the greatest of his time. Ed Wynn, clown master of puns, goofy props, and audience interaction, signed on. Ziegfeld snatched up W. C. Fields after Dillingham let him go. Also in the cast were dancer George White, who would become a producer and Ziegfeld competitor, and several women who would have film careers, including Ina Claire, Mae Murray, Olive Thomas and Justine's friend Kay Laurell (who would, three years later, volunteer to be the first Ziegfeld girl to appear bare-breasted).

Each Lucile costume was custom-made. Ziegfeld thought nothing of paying $50 a yard for fabric. Gowns were trimmed in genuine fur. The girls wore silk stockings: Ziegfeld considered bare legs unseemly. For a Ziegfeld girl, the aura of elegance and mystery was so essential he insisted on a strict dress code, even for the girls' own clothing worn in their private lives: a Ziegfeld girl could only be seen in heels, never flats; tasteful dresses, with hats and gloves, always. It may be one reason why he paid so well.

Rehearsals were grueling, sometimes going past midnight (the two-year-old actors' labor union, Actors Equity, had yet to develop a standard contract, which Ziegfeld and most managers would ignore anyway). Songs and scenes were rehearsed, abandoned and re-written; costumes were created and re-designed; complex production numbers were precariously choreographed within gigantic set pieces, including an opening number featuring enormous automated gold elephants spewing real water into a Roman bath.

The entire cast had a 7:30 a.m. call one morning for a trek to a Fort Lee film studio to create one of the more innovative sketches: a movie projected onto a stage screen as "director" Ed Wynn wandered about the audience shouting directions to the filmed actors, resulting in comedic chaos. After the morning shoot, the cast was driven back to the theatre for 11am rehearsal. By midnight, girls were napping on the floor backstage and the actor playing the Kaiser fell asleep in the arms of the actor playing the King of France. The final dress rehearsal lasted almost 48 hours as Ziegfeld attempted to cut the four-hour run down to two.

Justine took it all seriously. "And how that girl did work!"[13] an awed Ziegfeld said of her. She was "glorified" with eleven other "beauty chorines," including Kay and Olive, in a number called "I Want a Girl for Every Month," sung to the ladies by star Bernard "Bunny" Granville (father of 1930s film ingénue Bonita Granville). Justine was "Mazie," the "May" girl in a white taffeta dress with a bouquet at the waist. Her pointed cap was apparently meant to symbolize a Maypole, and Justine made graceful use of its streamers wrapped around her arms.

She also appeared in one of the most popular sketches in the show, "Hallway of the Bunkem Court Apartment," as one of the tenants of a woman's apartment hotel for which a harried Bert Williams was entrusted to keep out gentlemen callers.

But her *piece de resistance* was in a pageant number, "America." She portrayed Columbia, a recurring Ziegfeld character in patriotic scenes. Draped in a flowing, sleeveless American flag costume with a form-fitting bodice and topped with gold-starred tiara, Justine and an actor portraying President Wilson appeal to the Kaiser for peace. A winged Kay Laurell, as Peace herself, flies in from the heavens to present them all with an olive branch to cheers and applause.

The show was a smash but, unsurprisingly, did little to advance Justine's career in the direction she wanted. Everyone simply wanted to know what it was like to be "the most beautiful." Justine always answered that she didn't know. Her candor piqued the interest of noted theatre critic Burns Mantle, who wanted to meet the girl who "faced a steadily-poised battery of opera glasses that questioned her right to the reputation she had gained."[14]

Justine was characteristically blunt. "As soon as a girl is called a beauty," she told Mantle backstage at the New Amsterdam, "it is assumed she has no brains." A bemused Mantle referred to her as "pouty." He asked her what she wanted. "I want to go into legitimate drama," she said, patiently repeating the answer she gave to anyone who asked her. "I may have looks now, but as soon as I start to get a little old they won't want me in musical comedy. I have to do something so that they'll have

Justine ca. 1915, when she worked for Dillingham and Ziegfeld while initiating a strategy for a dramatic career. Courtesy Harry Ransom Center, the University of Texas at Austin.

to *keep* wanting me." When asked why such a beautiful young show girl would be so concerned about growing older, Justine shot back, "You really shouldn't be talking to me. You should be interviewing Mary. She knows more than the rest of us put together." Mary, a former musical theatre performer, was the Ziegfeld girls' dresser.[15]

The *Follies* season ended at the end of the summer and went on tour, but Justine stayed in New York. Charles Dillingham had forgiven her for "spoiling" a performance of *Watch Your Step* and wanted her for his new musical, not in the chorus, but for a speaking role—a small one, but she grabbed it. *Stop! Look! Listen!* was set for Dillingham's flagship theatre, the Globe on West 46th Street (now the Lunt-Fontanne). The show reunited Justine with composer Irving Berlin, whose score in this production included two numbers that would become standards, "I Love a Piano" and "The Girl on the Magazine Cover" (which foreshadowed Berlin's "A Pretty Girl Is Like a Melody" for the 1919 *Follies*). The story concerns a chorus girl trying to get hired as a lead once the star quits. The chorus girl-turned-star was played by French star Gaby Deslys, a ticket-seller known more for her celebrity than her talent. Deslys' personal life had been broadly winked at in *Gaby,* the one-act Justine had appeared in at the Folies-Bergère, which had been written by *Stop! Look! Listen*'s librettist Harry B. Smith.

Justine played the star who quits, a spoiled young comic opera singer named, oddly enough, Mary Singer. Mary throws her latest production into chaos when she decides to desert show business for marriage, backed up by her vociferous manager-mother. Other complications arise when the comic opera's chorus girls threaten to walk because they hate their costumes, only to be persuaded to stay when the manager sings, "leave me my ponies [chorus dancers] and clothes-horses [show girls], and musical comedy will go on,"[16] a nice summation of the genre at the time. All turns out well when chorus girl Deslys goes on and becomes the show's Cinderella-like star. For good measure, a hula dance production number was thrown in as a nod to the country's ongoing Hawaii craze.

The show received so-so reviews, Berlin's music won raves, and Justine got her usual press treatment. "Justine Johnstone, the beautiful" was her *New York Times* mention. "Justine looked cute and acted cute," said *The New York Press*. *Variety* was even more dismissive: "Justine Johnstone is there for, well, looks."[17]

Also there for looks was another beautiful, ambitious young performer who shared a dressing room with Justine. Marion Douras from Brooklyn was the sister of two of Justine's friends, Ethel and Rose, who had been fellow beauty chorines in *Watch Your Step.* The Douras sisters had adopted the more British-sounding surname Davies, and Marion Davies was now doing her third chorus gig for Dillingham. She had much of the posing chores in *Stop!*

4. Ziegfeld's American Beauty

Look! Listen! as Summer, one of the "Magazine Cover" girls, backing up lead singer Joseph Santley.

Marion wanted to be a comic. Justine wanted to be a serious actress. Marion was bubbly, fun-loving and spoke with a slight stammer. Justine was cooler and spoke in low-pitched tones. Marion was not averse to dating wealthy married men. Justine selected her dates carefully and avoided the attached. The two women bonded immediately. Their unlikely friendship became the stuff of Broadway legend, thanks in large part to their friend Anita Loos. According to several sources, Justine and Marion were the inspiration for Loos' comic novel, *Gentlemen Prefer Blondes*—Marion becoming Lorelei Lee, the charming, scatterbrained gold-digger, and Justine Johnstone as Dorothy Shaw, the level-headed friend whom Lorelei would chide for dating non-wealthy men. For good measure, Loos tossed in a character of a newspaper man besotted with Dorothy, as H. L. Mencken was with Justine.

As the story goes—and it almost certainly is just a story, as none of the principals involved apparently ever mentioned it—Justine received a note backstage during a performance of *Stop! Look! Listen!* It was from a very well-known, very wealthy, very married gentleman in the audience, a former politician and friend of Dillingham's, inviting her to dinner after the show. Justine got a lot of these. They both did. She wasn't interested; this guy seemed more of a Marion type. She handed the note to her friend and said, "Why don't you go?"[18] Marion went. And that, as they say, is how 19-year-old Marion Davies met 52-year-old millionaire newspaper kingpin William Randolph Hearst, the father of "yellow journalism," the man who could make headlines out of nothing, and who would make Marion's career.

Justine's best friend Marion Davies ca. 1916, when they both performed in the *Follies*, shortly before Marion began her lifelong relationship with William Randolph Hearst. Bain News Service, Publisher. Marion Davies. [No Date Recorded on Caption Card] Photograph. Retrieved from the Library of Congress, https://www.loc.gov/item/ggb2006002160/. Accessed May 16, 2017.

Justine accepted enough dates to confess that "I had—well, several marriage proposals."[19] She turned them all down, believing that "careers and husbands" didn't "harmonize very well." If she were to get married, she said, she would want a husband in the theatre. The problem was, actors didn't interest her, and she was leery of businessmen. She was seeing "many a case of unhappiness between girls and their businessmen husbands. The girls insisted on remaining on the stage."[20]

So did she. Following *Stop! Look! Listen!*, Justine returned to Ziegfeld for that generous paycheck. Either by coincidence or design, Ziegfeld hired both Justine and Marion for *The Ziegfeld Follies of 1916*. And no doubt by design, Justine had a slightly higher profile in this edition. Her name was mentioned before that of W. C. Fields in press blurbs for the show. Other performers that season included Fanny Brice (in her famous "Dying Swan" ballet), Will Rogers in his *Follies* debut, and Ziegfeld favorite Bert Williams. Marion was a chorus dancer, and her admirer Hearst was an audience regular.

Reports vary as to exactly when the famous "Ziegfeld walk" premiered, but it was created by choreographer Ned Wayburn, who seems to have worked his first *Follies* in 1916. Wayburn, a large, graceful man with pince-nez glasses, had been staging shows at the Winter Garden for the Shuberts and was a master of contemporary theatre dance (particularly "aural" dance, for which he may or may not have coined the term "tap dancing"). For Ziegfeld, Wayburn devised a way for the show girls to best navigate Joseph Urban's staircases, display Lady Duff Gordon's gowns and showcase the body. The basics of the walk seem to be: back straight, boobs out, chin up, shoulders high (no smiling, girls, keep it aloof), arms out, elbows bent, "dancer's hands,"[21] tummy in, butt tucked under so that the pelvis is accentuated, and then (try to) walk in a slow glide, crossing one leg diagonally in front of the other. When you stopped, you posed, weight on one leg, other toe pointed. It seems to have been a standard show girl stance of the day, something Justine would take in a number of her full-body shots.

Justine's assignments for this production were a little wacky. 1916 marked the tercentenary of Shakespeare's death, and the *Follies* saluted him with a number of "travesties" based on Shakespearean plays. Justine was an usually young and beautiful Nurse from *Romeo and Juliet*. *Vanity Fair* ran a photo of her in costume, captioned by critic and humorist P. G. Wodehouse as "an important undergraduate in the Ziegfeld Training School for Nurses."[22] She joined the cast for a screwball segment finale number set to the tune of George M. Cohan's "Give My Regards to Broadway": "Give our regards to Broadway / we're going with old Bill Shakespeare."[23]

Even more bizarre was her return appearance as Columbia, this time in an elaborate wartime-themed sketch. Columbia, again magnificently gowned

4. Ziegfeld's American Beauty 37

in flag and tiara, now wears gold necklaces with the names of the 48 states. She confides to Uncle Sam that she's worried: she's seen strange men lurking about. "Pshaw," says Uncle Sam. "There's no danger, Columbia. Everybody loves you." Then War sneaks up on her and growls, "Gimme them jewels!" as he snatches the gold necklaces from her neck. "O! Who will protect me?" cries Columbia. Enter The Common Man, who thwarts War and saves the day.[24]

A few weeks into the run, Justine quit. According to one newspaper account, Ziegfeld refused to allow her to show a gentleman friend her dressing room, so she reportedly "flared up at such interference with her personal liberty and walked out, leaving the show flat."[25] As was common at the time, the report cited no first-hand sources and included no interviews with either Justine or Ziegfeld. Maybe Ziegfeld did deny her friend's entrance, or maybe the stage doorman did. Perhaps someone said, sure, Ina Claire can have her friends upstairs but you're not a big enough star for that.

Or perhaps Justine was simply tired of being glorified. She made no comment, but her interview with Burns Mantle the previous year had summed up her thoughts about being a professional mannequin.

Ziegfeld took no action except to replace her with another beauty, Allyn King. He would speak highly of Justine in later years. She had been one of his biggest draws, and he never had a problem reminding anyone of that.

5

Oh, Boy!

Justine began seriously appealing to producers for jobs in non-musical productions. In the days when actors regularly did so, she visited managers' offices without appointments and inquired about casting. It was tough going. Ziegfeld and Dillingham had just opened a new glorifying show called *The Century Girl* at the Century Theatre, formerly the New Theatre, where *The Blue Bird* had played in 1910. Justine wasn't even in *The Century Girl* but because she had appeared at the theatre in a small part as an adolescent, she was considered a "Century Girl." A winsome portrait of her by Raphael Kirchner, a pre–Vargas, girl-glorifying artist, was hung in the lobby along with those of other Ziegfeld beauties. It wasn't a great endorsement for someone seeking to change her image. The portrait would remain until the theatre closed in 1936.

Theatrical managers were glad to have Justine stop by their offices but no one was remotely interested in hiring her for a drama. "Everyone was very polite," she said, "indeed, very kind" as they told her no. "I was stamped with an indelible label as a beautiful 'manikin' … I was supposed to be averse to hard work and discipline."[1]

Her reliable friend Dillingham offered her a featured role as Chiquette in a British import called *Betty*, a rags-to-riches musical with a book by Frederick Lonsdale and Gladys Unger. The show starred former *Stop! Look! Listen!* actor Joseph Santley and his future wife, English musical performer Ivy Sawyer.

For Dillingham, Justine was always a ticket-seller, and her having been a Ziegfeld girl was a bonus. Any Ziegfeld girl was a bonus for any producer. Ziegfeld himself once wrote to his press agent: "Ambitions of all producers is to secure a Ziegfeld girl for one of his shows and immediately command increase salaries."[2]

Two Ziegfeld girls were even better—Dillingham hired Marion as well. He gave them a coy little call-and-response trio with Santley, with lyrics like, "I love you both!" ("He loves us both!") "I'll take my oath!" ("He'll take his oath!") "I'm simply mad on all the little girls!"[3] (Structurally, the number could have been a prototype for "The Charlie Kane Song.")

The subhead of the *New York Sun*'s review was "Ivy Sawyer, Justine Johnstone and Marion Davies Among Women in the Cast,"[4] which was something of a boost, except that the review then only mentioned Justine and Marion for their "beauty." Most of the reviews followed suit. A particular gush of effulgence came from *The Syracuse Herald*: "There are the girls! No musical show that has been along recently could boast the sum total of feminine beauty that *Betty* includes. Justine Johnstone, formerly of the 'Follies,' is one of them. Miss Johnstone is so pretty that it almost seems as though the authorities should require her to be equipped with a dimmer when she goes out on the street. Marion Davies is another member of the company who must cause traffic congestion almost everywhere she goes without a veil on."[5]

Marion was not at all displeased with the idea that traffic could only operate efficiently if she wore a veil. She and William Randolph Hearst became lovers. The situation at the time was not unlike Hearst's early relationship with his wife, the much-younger Millicent Veronica Willson, a former chorus girl with whom he had lived for three years before marrying in 1903, possibly because she was pregnant. But unlike his marriage, Hearst's relationship with Marion would last the rest of his life. The reasons why they never married vary: Millicent reportedly told her daughter-in-law that she would give Hearst a divorce, despite her being Catholic, but that he had never asked for one; other sources state that Hearst asked his wife for a divorce by 1920 but was refused. Almost certainly Millicent wanted to ensure the financial futures of her five sons, and no doubt her own. In any event, the arrangement meant that Marion would forever be labeled a "kept woman," a "gold-digger" and worse, although, of course, there was no comparable label for Hearst. Neither seemed terribly concerned by such labels. Nor, apparently, was Marion's family. By 1917 Marion, her mother and sisters were living in an opulent five-story townhouse at 331 Riverside Drive, which Hearst had purchased for them.

Justine adored Marion and was an occasional guest on Riverside Drive. But at least publicly, she led her life as a calculated contradiction of the "kept woman." She lived fairly well, but no townhouse. She moved with her parents into a comfortable apartment on Central Park West. "I have a good home," she said, "and in it is the finest mother a girl ever had."[6] In the summer of 1916, she was doing well enough to lease a home "for the season" on Manhasset, Long Island, opposite the Kensington Waterfront Park, a resort development.

Among her acquaintances—perhaps through Hearst and Marion, the socially well-connected Dillingham, or simply from the stage door—were members of the "400," with names like Peabody, Drexel, Biddle, Chrysler and Stearns. None of the names emerges as a particularly special friend. She was often mentioned in the columns with society friends at sporting events, particularly horse shows, but with wives and daughters of wealthy men, rather than the men themselves.

A 1916 full-page "beauty" article under Justine's byline was syndicated by the Star Company, a Hearst newspaper subsidiary. It was not, however, a typical Hearst story about by a show girl, nor did it contain makeup or hairstyle tips. "I have invented a series of exercises," Justine began, "to keep myself—shall I say beautiful? No.... To keep myself at my best."[7] Declaring that health was far more important than beauty, Justine offered the exercises she had developed by observing monkeys in the zoo: bend over, hands on floor, and walk your feet up to your hands. She also detailed the complexities of digestion, one of her favorite topics. It was no doubt the only article by a Ziegfeld girl that described the workings of the human colon.

Justine distanced herself from show girl labels in numerous interviews. She dismissed the oysters-and-champagne stereotype attached to chorus girls of the time: "I don't care particularly for either item," she told the *Boston Sunday Post*. She talked about working 16 hours a day, "with rehearsals and performances and the private practice in dancing I gave myself," and didn't have time for "chasing the wee, small hours around the clock."[8] Her eyes "twinkled" at the reporter's obligatory question about beauty tips, and said:

> Do you want to know the only really real beauty makers and beauty preservers in the world? They're eight hours' sleep every 24, a good digestion, a good home and a good feeling toward the world. As long as I keep them, I'll keep my youth and whatever beauty I have....
>
> The last ingredient in my beauty recipe—good feeling toward the world—is easy to cultivate if you have the others. I like the world. I like all kinds of people, and when they like me in return, it makes me perfectly happy.[9]

"I have tried to prove that one can be both good and happy at the same time," she said to British reporter J. Herbert Duckworth. "I have found in my work no time for dissipation, even if I were inclined to it. Anyway, the idea that the stage is an occupation for frivolous people, and that life behind the scenes is one big long orgy, is just silly."[10]

For most of the public, that take on show girls just wasn't that interesting. And when things aren't that interesting, people made stuff up. Two such creative storytellers would, for better or worse, seal Justine's and Marion's reputations as Broadway's glamorous, wacky duo.

Betty bombed, and Marion took a small role as a replacement in a show, *Very Good Eddie*, that was winding up a successful run at the Princess Theatre on West 39th Street off Sixth Avenue. The Princess was a jewel-box of a theatre, owned in part by the Shubert brothers and actor-director Holbrook Blinn, and co-managed by producer F. Ray Comstock and theatrical agent Elisabeth Marbury. Comstock and Marbury had developed an idea to create specialty musicals for the relatively small house, rather anti–Ziegfeld pro-

5. Oh, Boy!

ductions with minimal sets and casts, meaning perhaps twelve chorus members instead of fifty. The shows would feature clever, contemporary stories and music, unlike operettas or show girl musicals. *Very Good Eddie* boasted a book by Marbury's literary client, British-American Guy Bolton, and Phillip Bartholomae, author of an earlier play on which *Eddie* was based. Music was by the prolific Jerome Kern, a 30-year-old with almost 50 Broadway shows under his belt (including Justine's 1916 *Follies*). The Princess musicals are today considered watershed moments in musical theatre because, for the first time, the shows actually had coherent plots, and the songs blended into the story. The Princess had cachet.

Marbury and Comstock announced a follow-up to *Eddie* with Kern, Bolton and a third collaborator, P. G. Wodehouse, Justine's tart-tongued admirer and *Vanity Fair* contributor known for his "Wooster and Jeeves" stories. The new show, *Oh, Boy!*, was a mistaken-identity comedy sprinkled with Wodehouse's trademark upper-class characters behaving badly. Young George marries his sweetheart Lou Ellen without the permission of his Quaker aunt, who holds his purse strings, and panics when he receives word that the aunt is on her way. After he sends Lou Ellen to her parents' house on their wedding night, he is suddenly surprised when a spirited girl named Jackie crawls through his window to escape the advances of a lecherous old man. Then his buddy Jack shows up with some college girls. George quickly has Jackie pretend to be his wife Lou Ellen. Then the wife and her parents show up, and Jackie pretends to be the aunt. Then the aunt shows up and—it all turns out in the end.

Justine in *Oh, Boy!*, the Bolton-Wodehouse-Kern musical at the prestigious Princess Theatre, 1917 Courtesy Mr. Justin Wanger.

It's unclear whether both Marion and Justine were approached for the new show, or if Marion alone was asked, having just done a Princess production, and then grabbed the unemployed Justine to join her. In any event, they both signed three-year contracts with Comstock. Unsurprisingly, they weren't offered the lead roles of Jackie or Lou Ellen for *Oh, Boy!* They would be the college girls, as they were still "there for, well, looks." And in that vein, Guy Bolton and P. G. Wodehouse exercised their particular creativity in their entertaining but dubious 1953 joint memoir, *Bring on the Girls!*, in which they recall verbatim a remarkable string of conversations that had taken place over 30 years prior.

Thus we can't really be sure, as much as we might like, that Justine and Marion showed up for a pre-production meeting at the Princess Theatre in two limos, Marion in a Delage and Justine in a Pierce-Arrow with intertwining "JJs" on the hood. Wodehouse and Bolton report that "the girls" wafted into the office in minks, orchids, diamonds on their wrists and "head-spinning perfume, possibly Coty's 'l'Origan' or 'Quelques Fleurs.'" The place was

Justine (right) and Marion in a giggly photo shoot during *Oh, Boy!* previews in Syracuse, 1917. Their friend Anita Loos would base the character of Lorelei on Marion and Dorothy on Justine in her novel *Gentlemen Prefer Blondes*. Key sheet: White Studio (New York, N.Y.) / Courtesy Museum of the City of New York. 50.143.37 © The New York Public Library.

practically a boudoir."[11] One of the men asked how the girls got the minks. "The same way the minks get them," answered another. Rim shot.

Justine, according to the memoir, demanded that they have characters with names, not just First Girl and Second Girl. (She had been playing characters with names for three years, but we just need to accept that she'd have to ask.) "Of course you have names," Bolton replied. "Yours is Polly Andrus." "Is that a play on polyandrous?" Justine asked. Bolton denied it. Nobody else in the room knew what the word meant. Once defined, Marion said to Justine, "You're too well-educated. I just say snuggle-hound. That's what I hear Ray [Comstock] is. I hear he's the worst old snuggle-hound on Broadway."[12] It's an unusual quote from Marion in this book, as it's one of the few where the authors do not replicate her stammering, presumably for what they thought was comic effect. (Wodehouse actually confided to Bolton prior to publication of the memoir that he was concerned Marion might sue.)[13]

"I'm not a patch on Guy," Comstock reportedly responded. "A flick of the finger, a broken heart—that's Guy Bolton." "Really?" "He once kissed a girl on Broadway, and then shot clear up to the top of the Woolworth Building." "You don't say?" "I'm telling you. Just closed her eyes with a little moan and floated up and up and up."[14]

In addition to Bolton's chest-pounding, one of the more amusing stories in the memoir concerns an out-of-town run-through rehearsal in Schenectady. Photographers stopped by to shoot some publicity stills. Marion, stricken with stage fright, downed a few glasses of champagne, which for some reason was readily available backstage. The bubbly made her stammer worse, to the point where she could barely speak. So Marion and Justine came up with a plan. During their scene, Marion simply mouthed her lines as Justine spoke them in a high-pitched voice before swopping down to her natural contralto for her own lines. The effect was bizarre and synchronization hilariously off. The company howled. They stopped laughing when the stage manager asked the photographers who they wanted first, and the response was "We only want Miss Davies and Miss Johnstone."[15] Camera lamps flashed and popped away at the two for twenty minutes. When the stage manager called the cast back on stage to resume rehearsals, he found that most of them had gone. It's a great theatre story but, considering its source, may in fact only be a story.

What can be confirmed is that *Oh, Boy!* was an enormous hit. The sophisticated comedy opened on February 20, 1917, to rapturous reviews for Wodehouse, Bolton and Kern, and to lead actors Tom Powers, Anna Wheaton and Edna May Oliver. Kern and Wodehouse's sweet "Till the Clouds Roll By," sung by George and Jackie to bemoan the trouble they're in, became an American songbook standard (and the title of MGM's 1946 fictionalized biopic of Kern's life).

Justine and Marion got the usual treatment. "Justine Johnstone, as beautiful as ever, makes a hit just standing still letting folks look at her," said the *Brooklyn Daily Eagle*.[16] The *Times* simply said that Justine and Marion were "famed for their beauty from the Battery to Buffalo."[17]

Not mentioned in the reviews, or even in the Wodehouse-Bolton memoir, was the fact that Justine was dating Guy Bolton. This seems to have been the first serious romance for 22-year-old Justine. One can't help but wonder if that description of the girl whom Bolton kissed and then "shot she shot clear up to the top of the Woolworth Building" was a cloaked reference to Justine. The relationship was apparently serious enough for the divorced, debonair, pipe-smoking librettist to have given her expensive gifts such as jewelry (and maybe that Pierce-Arrow). But Bolton was known to be generous with a lot of women. He was, according to a Wodehouse biographer, "sexually confident ... a dapper ladies' man who, having divorced his first wife, became ensnared in a succession of romantic entanglements with chorus girls and singers."[18] Thus the Bolton-Wodehouse memoir description of Bolton, "a flick of the finger, a broken heart," was probably fairly apt. (The phrase actually later found its way into Wodehouse's novel *Ring for Jeeves*.)

A few weeks after the show opened, the theatrical newspaper *The Clipper* reported that Justine and Bolton were engaged. The following week, the newspaper ran Justine's emphatic denial. Soon afterward Bolton married operatic soprano Marguerite Namara, the mother of his baby daughter.

Justine could be pitiless if she wanted to be. When the *New York Herald* ran a story about a jilted woman winning a $225,000 lawsuit against her former lover, a reporter asked Justine what her own broken heart might be worth. "The smallest kind of a little, teeny, tiny dent in my heart," she said, "would cost a cold $1,000,000."[19]

Guy Bolton, British-American co-author of *Oh, Boy!* and general ladies' man who was Justine's first known gentleman caller. Bain News Service, Publisher. Namara and Guy Bolton. [No Date Recorded on Caption Card] Photograph. Retrieved from the Library of Congress, https://www.loc.gov/item/ggb2006009631/. Accessed May 16, 2017.

5. Oh, Boy!

Justine was "willing to be married," said the *Herald*, "but has not announced her decision as to whom."[20] It just wouldn't be Bolton.

Nor would it be Jack Sadowsky, heir to a clothing manufacturing fortune, who apparently thought himself a contender for a while. Jack was a sometime Broadway show investor and general man-about-town. He tried to woo Justine so long that that *Variety* printed a rumor they had secretly wed. The statement was immediately retracted once they heard from Justine's attorney that the couple had never even been engaged. Jack would later marry Spanish dancer Trini Ramos. So it wouldn't be Jack.

And, in spite of his best efforts, it definitely would not be Lee Shubert.

6

The Land of Frocks and Frills

The day before *Oh, Boy!* opened, press agent Walter Kingsley distributed one of his characteristically breathless press releases: "What will undoubtedly be one of the literary sensations of the fall is a biography of Miss Justine Johnstone, to be labeled *Justine Johnstone—Her Book*. Being a young woman of judgment as well as beauty, Miss Johnstone has chosen that connoisseur of beauty and literary light, Walter J. Kingsley, to set down the history of her life." The book promised to include her childhood in Hoboken, "with a flashback to Sweden, the land of her ancestors," and would "trace and the struggles and triumphs of a girl who was a photographer's model seven years ago, then a member of the chorus, and now a star."[1]

Kingsley apparently didn't get far with this effort. Not long after the announcement, Justine dropped him as press agent. One of the co-owners of the Princess Theatre had approached her with an offer that was much more to her liking than a ghost-written autobiography.

Lee (Levi) Shubert and his brother J. J. (Jacob or Jake) were two of the most powerful men on Broadway. Although they claimed to have been born in Syracuse, New York, they were actually born in Europe, possibly Lithuania; the Shuberts were so secretive about their origins that even their exact birth dates, sometime in the 1870s, are uncertain. Their father, an alcoholic peddler named David Schubart, brought the family to Syracuse after fleeing pogroms. He soon pulled his sons out of school for work. The eldest, Sam, peddled newspapers in front of a Syracuse theatre and talked his way into becoming its souvenir seller, eventually progressing to treasurer for a larger house. When he purchased the road rights to a couple of Broadway shows, Lee and J. J. joined him as theatrical managers. The brothers soon began taking over theatres in Syracuse, throughout upstate New York, and finally on Broadway.

Sam Shubert, the most diplomatic and perhaps the most artistically-inclined, was killed in a 1905 train accident. He had been traveling to Pittsburgh to defend a Shubert property against Abe Erlanger and the monopolizing Theatrical Syndicate. Erlanger then told Lee and J. J. that, with Sam's

6. The Land of Frocks and Frills 47

death, they should give up fighting the Syndicate and sell out to him. J. J.'s response was one that wouldn't have made its way into a Hearst newspaper: "*Fuck Erlanger!* Fuck his *sons* to the *last* of their days! Fuck *Klaw* and *Hayman* and *Frohman* the faegele! So they killed Sam! *Did* they? So we take *their theatres* and *their plays* and *we kill them, too!*"[2]

Lee and J. J. expanded their business into an empire, purchasing or leasing much of the theatrical real estate on Broadway and throughout the county. They swept actors out of Syndicate contracts and made them Shubert stars. By the early 1910s, the Shuberts had managed to weaken the Syndicate and assume their own monopoly, utilizing Syndicate-style tactics.

That Ziegfeld did business with Klaw and Erlanger, leasing their New Amsterdam Theatre to him, placed him fairly high on the Shuberts' enemies list. When Ziegfeld backed out of a Shubert contract for Anna Held and refused to refund the advance Lee had provided, Ziggy's name was dirt to the brothers.

The Shuberts regularly beat Ziegfeld at quality, but Ziegfeld still had the corner market on spectacle. They fought each other for stars and moped at defections. Having a Ziegfeld girl as a star in a Shubert show—especially if it were, say, a Ziegfeld type of show—could be calculatingly sweet for Lee and J. J.

Lee, semi-literate, with opaque eyes and dyed, jet-black hair, was dour, ruthless, and miserly. J. J., about four years younger, was plump, volatile, tyrannical, and reportedly a wife-beating bully. Both instilled fear and loathing into their actors. Both had reputations as notorious womanizers and conducted casual affairs with their female performers, usually chorus girls. (The unpublished 1981 memoir of set designer George James Hopkins clamied that Lee was bisexual, and was lovers with costume designer Melville Ellis, but unfortunately this can not be corroborated elsewhere.) In any event, that year, the 46-year-old bachelor Lee became obsessed with 22-year-old Justine.

Lee may or may not have had much contact with Justine when she appeared as a child in their production of *The Blue Bird* several years earlier. Now, he was very aware of her as one of the Princess' main draws. He invited her to dinner and was enchanted by her poise, intelligence, and her sense of decorum (a quality he admired). And, of course, her beauty. He wanted to know if she had any career projections. Did she ever.

Lee offered her a proposal. First, he would heighten her public profile. She would become the professional hostess of a dazzling new cabaret in the basement of his 44th Street Theatre, a few steps from the Shubert offices just off Broadway. Ziegfeld, after all, had a cabaret: his *Midnight Frolic* on the roof of the New Amsterdam. Slightly raunchier than the *Follies*, with booze and nosh and show girls encouraging men to pop their balloon costumes with cigars, *Midnight Frolic* was the go-to after-theatre venue.

But this cabaret, Lee assured Justine, would be strictly class. And unlike Ziegfeld, Lee wouldn't run the show: Justine would. The name of the cabaret would be none other than Justine Johnstone's Little Club.

It seemed promising. A professional nightclub hostess was a chic gig for a woman at the time. It meant commanding a little empire for high rollers, making connections, and being something of a celebrity among celebrities.

Then, Lee said, in the fall, he would star her in a new Broadway show created especially for and around her. She would have top billing, would act, sing and dance, and would have as much creative input into the show as she wished. This show would be no cabaret: no food, drink or smoking allowed. The unofficial Act III of the show would take place downstairs in the club.

And after that, Lee said, he would do everything he could to accommodate her transition into drama.

Justine was wary at first. The contract Lee offered only mentioned the club and the musical show. It was, however, the first time anyone had offered her a lead in anything. Also, she knew that, of the two brothers, Lee was more interested in drama, J. J. in musicals. She decided to take him at his word. In all, it seemed like a better proposition than two more years at the Princess and having to be around her cad of an ex.

To the fury of *Oh, Boy!* producer Ray Comstock, Justine gave notice and ultimately broke her Princess Theatre contract. She then signed for five years with her new best friend. Her salary was $300 a week, to be increased to $400 the following year, plus 50 percent of the club's profits. She negotiated for certain perks, including first-class transportation and a salary for a maid.

The unwritten elements of this agreement are certainly up for grabs. According to at least one source, Lee genuinely loved Justine but never told her so. Other sources assume the two were lovers, which may or may not have happened even if Lee was closeted. But in her letters to him, Justine addresses Lee gratefully, kindly and professionally, not particularly romantically or sexually. This, however, could have been due to the fact that Justine may have heard that Lee could barely read or write, as was rumored; he had letters read to him, and provided dictated responses. She usually began her letters with "Dear Lee" and ended them with "Sincerely, Justine," although at least one is signed "Love."[3] In some of her later letters, Justine reminds Lee that she's still waiting for him to come up with a show for her, and that her financial situation is tenuous. This would indicate that she had no salary except for work, and that—unlike her friend Marion—if she didn't work, she had no other means of support.

Whatever the true nature of the relationship, Lee went to work on his Justine-worshipping strategy immediately. A spinning, circular red light flashing "Justine Johnstone's Little Club" was mounted on top of the 44th Street Theatre. In the basement, the Shubert designers furnished the new club in a

6. The Land of Frocks and Frills   49

A rare photograph of what seems to be the interior of Justine Johnstone's Little Club, with its "hollyhocks" and "country house" décor. Lee booked Shubert acts into the Club. Here, Rolanda's Neo-Classical Modern Dancers perform their gladiator fight dance routine from *Over the Top*. During World War II, the club became the Stage Door Canteen. Courtesy The Shubert Archive.

summery country house style, with hollyhocks winding around the staircase and rose-colored lights adorning blue walls.

Justine's publicity was now being handled by the Shuberts' wily press agent, the aptly-named A. Toxen Worm, a large Dane who gleefully made it his business to plant rumors about Shubert rivals and hint at the immorality of Ziegfeld girls. To distance the Shubert cabaret from Ziegfeld's, Worm decided that the Little Club should be a gathering place for the very wealthy. He had Justine leverage her social connections and set the membership fee at an unheard-of $50.

Newspaper ads, coyly assuming that all the club patrons would obviously have cars, proclaimed, "Don't get 'tied up' in theatre traffic! Dismiss your car and have it wait for you at Justine Johnstone's Little Club." The ads noted that the club was a mere two-minute walk from 27 theatres, each one duly named. Most ads featured an ink illustration of a pert Justine.

The exorbitant membership fee worked according to Worm's plan: the bulk of initial club membership was from the social register. The first to join was Angier Duke, whose wife was a friend of Justine's, followed by Payne Whitney and John Wannamaker.

Marion Davies joked to friends that she, too, would be opening up a club. It would be called Le Petit Souper Club and would be set up in the lobby of the Princess Theatre. Her membership fee, she claimed, would be $100, not a mere $50. Toxen Worm got wind of the joke and exploited it as fact, resulting in rumors that Justine and Marion were cat-fighting. The gossips may have been disappointed when Marion happily showed up to entertain at the club's opening night on April 13, 1917.

It was a huge success. The club became known as the "gem of the galaxy of nightclubs"[4] and the "in" place for the famous or those who aspired to be. Special Broadway (that is, Shubert) entertainment was offered, such as "Maytime Night" with Charles Purcell and the *Maytime* chorus ladies. Jazz bands played sultry tunes. Menu items could include lobster à la Bonnefoy, roasted royal squab au cresson with guava jelly, glace à la Justine, and ten-dollar bottles of Pol Roger champagne.

As the weather warmed, the dance floor was converted into a shallow pool where patrons could wade barefooted (dressing rooms were available for those who wished not to remove their stockings at the table). The bar welcomed single women, unusual for the time. In F. Scott Fitzgerald's 1922 novel, *The Beautiful and the Damned*, Gloria, a beautiful socialite with dreams of becoming an actress, confides to her cousin "a tale of the ends of cigarettes left all over New York in ashtrays marked 'Midnight Frolic' and 'Justine Johnstone's Little Club.'"[5]

New Year's Eve 1917 menu at Justine Johnstone's Little Club, located downstairs from the Shuberts' 44th Street Theatre, 216 West 46th Street; the "in" place for the "400." Courtesy Mr. Justin Wanger.

The unspoken implication of the club's existence was that it was a discreet place for married, monied men to meet actresses. "Not a word in the papers, mind you, about who were here," an unnamed Shubert associate was quoted as whispering to a reporter one night.[6]

6. The Land of Frocks and Frills

Justine proved a gracious and welcoming hostess. She would dash from the Princess to the club every night in a dazzling gown, greeting patrons, table-hopping, introducing the entertainment, conferring with the chef, collecting fees and endorsing checks, as Lee had opened the club's account in her name. She knew where all her regulars liked to sit. She made sure the lighting was right over each table and that the music wasn't too loud. At closing, she'd climb into the back seat of the sedan Lee had ordered for her and fall asleep on her way to her apartment. Invariably, her mother would still be up, waiting for her.

Sophia was a sustaining element in her life. Their relationship, Justine would say, was more important than her success.

Nightclub hostess and musical star: publicity photo promoting Justine as the Shubert's new leading light, ca. 1917. Courtesy The Shubert Archive.

"My mother is a real mother," Justine said. "That's why I could never belong utterly to the Little Club," which probably would have given Toxen Worm the shakes. Justine tempered her comments with "I enjoy entertaining my guests there. But if I gave myself altogether to Broadway I would tire of it and it would tire of me."[7]

Lee saw to it that Broadway wasn't nearly tired of Justine yet. A few weeks after the club opened, he announced that Justine would be starring in their exciting new revue at a specialty venue on top of their 44th Street Theatre. Once a hurricane deck, the space had been converted to a theatre-above-the-theatre by vaudevillian Lew Fields. The Shuberts acquired the building in 1913, and converted the upstairs space into Castles-in-the-Air, a cabaret featuring Vernon and Irene Castle. (Just as Justine's basement club had once been the Castle Club, also named for the couple; no harm in recycling ideas.) Lee now was restoring and refurbishing the deck into a first-class Broadway venue just for Justine. Rumor had it that it would be named the Justine Johnstone Theatre. That may have been a bit much: it simply became the 44th Street Rooftop Theatre. But the revue would be called *Oh, Justine!*

P. G. Wodehouse, never one to pass up a backhanded compliment for Justine, wrote in *Vanity Fair*, "And there is *Oh, Justine!*, the revue in which Justine Johnstone is to star—to be followed, it is hardly possible to doubt, by *Wow, Marion!* (for Marion Davies), and *Golly, Ollie!* in which Olive Thomas is sure to make a hit."[8] The name of the show was changed, first to *The Nine O'clock Revue* and ultimately *Over the Top*. The latter title was in recognition of American's entry into World War I just days before the club opened. "Over the top" was a new slang term referencing a dangerous military maneuver, climbing out of one's trench to combat enemy troupes. To accommodate the show's new title, war-themed numbers and sketches were developed.

Unlike the more highly-developed Princess Theatre musicals, *Over the Top* reverted to a tried-and-true form of a slight story framing vaudeville acts. Justine appeared as a character named, well, Justine, a New Jersey girl who dreams of life and love in the big city, dozes off and dreams up an entire Shubert extravaganza. The dream conceit was reportedly Justine's own, based on *Peter Ibbetson,* which the Shuberts were currently producing at the Theatre Republic (now the New Victory) with John and Lionel Barrymore.

The 44th Street Rooftop Theatre, which Lee Shubert refurbished from a cabaret to a top-notch Broadway venue for Justine in *Over the Top*. Courtesy The Shubert Archive.

Eighteen-year-old Fred Astaire and his 21-year-old sister Adele—like Justine, former students of the Alviene dance school—were yanked from a rapidly-rising vaudeville career for their Broadway debut. Shubert favorites T. Roy Barnes and specialty dancer Mary Eaton were signed. Writer Philip Bartholomae was lured from the Princess for the book. (*The Sun* sniped, "Previously, no one had suspected Mr. Bartholomae of such a thing.")[9] Top Shubert associates were hired, many from their popular Winter Garden revue, *The Passing Show*: composer Sigmund Romberg, director J. C. Huffman, choreographer Allan Foster, and wildly creative costume designer Homer Conant.

An elegant gown design, probably by Homer Conant, for Justine in *Over the Top*, the show Lee Shubert created for her. Courtesy The Shubert Archive.

In a blatant attempt to out-Ziegfeld Ziegfeld, Lee spent $900 on automated aircraft for a scene that echoed a wartime sketch in the previous year's *Follies*. He assembled a chorus and called them "Five Dozen Justine Johnstone Girls," which outmaneuvered Ziegfeld's "Fifty Anna Held Girls." For some of the girls, *Over the Top* was their only Broadway credit; for others, it was their last. A number continued careers with the Shuberts, Ziegfeld and others into the 1920s, including Florence Challenger, the adorably-named Kewpie Collier, Louise Dale, Martha Lorber, Jean Rebera, Flo Summerville, Nina Whitmore, and Hilda Wright.

A dancer-choreographer from Azusa, California named Rosa Rolanda was hired to lead a group called Rolanda's Neo-Classical Modern Dancers and do a girl-on-girl fight number, which echoed Ziegfeld's crowd-pleasing team of female fencers in his 1901 *The Little Duchess*. The talented Rosa (sometimes billed as Rose), born Rosalinda Cowan, became a successful dancer in theatre and film (appearing in the 1918 Famous Players–Lasky production of *The Blue Bird*), married *New Yorker* caricaturist Miguel Covarrubias, and became a well-known artist, photographer and gourmet cook.

There was no chorus of men. The Selective Service Act had been passed in May.

Lee set up Justine with a voice teacher, Thomas Brill, who coached *Maytime* baritone Charles Purcell. He hired Joseph's of Fifth Avenue for some of Justine's costumes. The Norwegian dressmaker's daughter selected her own outfits: a gown of gold sequins, one in black velvet, and another trimmed in sable, which Justine called "toasting hot."[10] One of Joseph's bill for the gowns and a red "paradise" hat racked up $1,940 (over $36,000 in 2017). Lee was happy to fork it over.

Rehearsals began in August 1917, one of the hottest New York Augusts on record. They were disorganized, truncated (as vaudevillians took off for gigs) and unpaid, and lasted a record-breaking 12 weeks. Per Lee's promises, Justine took a hands-on approach, occasionally suggesting costume, song, and set piece changes. Sometimes her requests were accommodated, sometimes not.

After working all day and into the evening, Justine was still required to hostess at the club until 1 a.m. most nights. Toxen Worm sent almost daily notes to Lee with checks endorsed by Justine the evening prior. He decided to drop the $50 membership fee for certain weeknights to keep the club "jammed."[11] The schedule was beginning to take a toll on her. "I must get some rest or I may break down,"[12] Justine pleaded in a note to Worm, which he apparently ignored.

A program was prepared. "Program notes," written no doubt by Worm or one of his associates, included the following overview of Justine's talents: "Miss Johnstone is a beautiful blonde. Her complexion rivals the rarest ivory, and sculptures have declared her form to be perfect. World-famed artists have quarreled over appointments, and her picture has smiled from

Imaginative Shubert costume designer Homer Conant created this chorus dancer costume for the *Over the Top* number "The Justine Johnstone Rag" sung by Justine with Fred and Adele Astaire. Courtesy The Shubert Archive.

6. The Land of Frocks and Frills   55

a dozen different magazines at the same time. Miss Johnstone has a charming contralto voice of rare quality and expression, and her step is as light and fleet as the startled dove."[13]

An out-of-town tryout in New Haven gave rowdy Yale undergrads a chance to hoot and heckle every light-and-fleet step Justine took. It was not encouraging. But it was New Haven. *Over the Top* limped bravely back to New York for its Broadway premiere.

Lee had Worm flood the newspapers with flack items. The critics snapped up Worm's opening night passes. Two days before opening, Worm knew they had a hit. He boasted in a letter to the brothers that although he had handled press for such stars as Bernhardt, Duse, Réjane "and the rest on the list, I am willing to point to yesterday's showing as the world's record for legitimate pictorial publicity for one woman in twenty-four hours."[14]

Opening night: November 28, 1917. Some 800 furred, feathered, perfumed, top-hatted, and eager patrons pour of taxis and trudge in the light snow to the lobby of the 44th Street Theatre. They chatter and wait their turn for the elevator boy to chug them up to the top floor. The place is stunning: no longer a smoke-filled, nosh-serving cabaret, but a beautifully redesigned, ornate, airy, piquant piece of a Broadway theatre.

Curtain up. We see Justine, a simple girl in a simple Homer Conant-designed frock, wistfully singing about adventures she wishes she could have in the big city. Her singing is apparently narcotic, as she stretches, places her hands behind her head and drifts off to sleep. Suddenly she awakens and finds herself transformed magically into a sparkling red and mauve gown. But she's a mannequin. She can't move. Wait; yes, she can. She's a mannequin who comes to life. She's in The Land of Frocks and Frills, a Manhattan dress shop where all the clothes are free and the wares are displayed by dancers with names like Mademoiselle Corset, Mademoiselle Stocking, Mademoiselle Bonneterie and so on. Enter shop patrons Fred and Adele Astaire. Everyone then dances and sings—wait for it—"The Justine Johnstone Rag."

Then she finds herself suddenly swept onto a billboard in Times Square, where she is posing in a green gown with gold streamers and a real parrot on her bodice. Again, she inert, but again miraculously comes to life, and dances with girls dressed as Borax cans, toothbrushes, powder puffs and cream jars.

Scene change, and T. Roy Barnes, as "Mr. Plot," narrates her waking nightmares with sassy one-liners. Whoosh: next scene: she's a sculpture, Galatea, dressed in white gauze girdled with gold, in a Greenwich Village salon. Her sculptor, who happens to be an operatic tenor, sings a song called "Oh, Galatea" to her. And with that, the immobile statue miraculously—you got it.

More scene changes. Mr. Plot tells jokes; mind-readers Harry and Emma Sharrock guess what coins are in audience members' pockets; Mary Eaton pirouettes *en pointe*; the Oakland Sisters, Vivian and Dagmar (stolen from

Ziegfeld), perform a three-way Apache dance with Ted Lorraine; Charles Mack does whatever a blackface comedian does; and Rolanda's Neo-Classical Modern Dancers battle each other in short-skirted gladiator costumes, barefoot and barelegged (Ziggy would have plotzed).

Then everyone is swept into a German aviation camp. The soldiers discuss their fear of an American attack when suddenly a whirring is heard overhead. Thousands of airplanes fill the skies. Lights flash. Shells explode. The bombardment is relentless until finally the orchestra swells and the smoke clears and Justine appears triumphantly "over the top" of the trenches in a shimmering white leather aviation pantsuit and Sam Browne belt waving an American flag. Curtain. End of Act I.

The following morning, *The New York Times* reported what time the show went up (nine o'clock) and when it came down (midnight). Other than that, the review noted that there were "an unusual number of acceptable entertainers" and that "the settings are diverse and highly colored, and they shift with the utmost rapidity."[15]

"No high-brow influence is permitted to mar the entertainment," said *Life* magazine. "New York was starving for another girl-and-music show. Here it is."[16]

The society magazine *Brooklyn Life* called it "a miniature Winter Garden show minus the famous runway and the privilege of smoking" but deemed the show "snappy entertainment." Particularly notable were the "truly marvelous exhibitions by Fred and Adele Astaire," and the fact that one could admire "the beautiful Justine Johnstone in a variety of gorgeous costumes."[17]

Theatre Magazine also gave Justine points for being beautiful. "Winsome Justine sings and dances a little, but it is her good looks and ability to wear magnificent costumes that make her a valued feature of *Over the Top*."[18] On the other hand, Matthew White, Jr., in *Munsey's Magazine* sniped that Justine "would never have had a chance on any stage were she not pretty."[19]

The *New York Sun* was only slightly less harsh, calling Justine, "she of the Charlotte russe color scheme and the open smile, the girlish curves and the frankly amateurish strive to please manner, is the person it is all about." The critic went to some rather florid lengths to say that Justine actually performed better than he had expected and looked great. "She speaks with accent and expression now, and sings with less effort than ever noticeable before. It looks indeed as if J. J. Shubert's plan to develop the fair Scandinavian into a dominating figure of musical farce might be a happy inspiration." (J. J. may have laughed when he read this one. He couldn't have cared less if she developed into a dominating figure of anything, as long as the show made money.) The *Sun* concluded that "the audience had the fullest opportunity to observe every talent that Miss Johnstone possesses in her successive revelations in *Over the Top*. Sometimes these chances left the spectator breathless."[20]

6. The Land of Frocks and Frills

For some critics, her greatest talent was her beauty, and that gave her a pass on everything else. "Her naïve efforts to act," wrote the New York Herald critic, "...were rather interesting and amiably pretty. One always watches such a beauty favorably, whether she be perpetrating parlor elocution on the stage, eating spaghetti or anything."[21]

Music critic Hiram K. Moderwell was considerably more succinct. "Justine Johnstone, who was press-agented out of some chorus or another, rules the roost ... in Delsarte poses copied from Roshanara and Mme. Nazimova."[22] (But then, Moderwell didn't even like the Astaires.)

Variety's "Wynn" topped them all: "With all of its several months of unnecessary rehearsals, its known star and the prominent vaudevillians engaged regardless of expense, *Over the Top* cannot be considered anything but a flop.... Justine Johnstone is the star, pretty, semi-vivacious, gorgeously gowned, etc., but Oh, Justine, who ever told you to 'act'?"[23] The critic pointed out that there were audience walk-outs a half-hour into the show. Some stopped at the elevators long enough to watch the Astaires. Then they left.

It's of course impossible to truly gauge the show's, or Justine's, merits or awfulness. As melodious as her speaking voice was, singing seemed not to be her forte (one critic stated rather tepidly that her singing was "not unpleasant"[24]). She was physically disciplined, her movements were graceful, but by training and inclination, she could not have been considered a dancer.

But the very format that *Over the Top* employed—a cursory book stringing musical numbers and

Newspaper ad for the 1918 post–Broadway tour of *Over the Top*, with comedian Ed Wynn receiving top billing, when the Shubert-Justine honeymoon was nearly over. Courtesy The Shubert Archive.

variety acts together—would be a challenge for most contemporary audiences. The Astaires might hold up, but some of the jokes probably wouldn't. The lady gladiators; who knows. But a female constantly appearing as an inanimate object and then "brought to life" by the magic of pretty clothes or a tenor could potentially harm a theatregoer's brain cells.

It's probably fair to assume that Justine couldn't rise above the material, but maybe nobody could. Even though she was the star attraction, she was given few lines. She may have tried to "act," but there wasn't much to act upon. She had little to do except be a reactive character in a fabulous wardrobe—which basically summed up her career at this point.

For the next few weeks, the Shuberts tried to upgrade the show. Justine's *Follies* friend Ed Wynn, whom the Shuberts had plucked from Ziegfeld for *The Passing Show*, was hired two days into the run as a second comedian. "You have no right to knock this show," Wynn ad-libbed one night. "You got in on passes."[25] The audience loved him. Lead comic T. Roy Barnes did not, and quit. Wynn replaced him as Mr. Plot.

Worm tap-danced a little damage control by setting up press interviews with Justine. A *New York Herald* reporter followed her around backstage one evening and heard her barking orders from a "tube" in the dressing room hall to Shubert business manager Nat Roth in the club downstairs. "How's the soup, Nat? Last night it was too thick. We mustn't let the boarders leave with anything that Mr. Hoover wouldn't [Herbert Hoover was then the head of the FDA]. Now, listen, Nat! The ambassador of something or other is coming tonight. Place him where he can reach the celery and have the salt and pepper caster and the vinegar cruet toward his end. And for heaven's sake, keep that cat out."[26]

When the show came down, she changed into her evening gown and headed to the kitchen. She tossed a blue gingham apron over her couture, tasted the soup, and decorated turkey entrees with little American flags.

Curious about her sudden move from "show girl" to Shubert star, the *Herald* reporter asked her how she had "learned to be an actress since last spring." She bluntly responded, "I know I haven't learned to be an actress in that short a time. But I'm going to." She then threw off the apron and swept into the dining room with a gracious "Good evening, everybody."

The reporter noted that "a young woman doesn't need to worry about rivaling Mme. Bernhardt if she can look—and cook—like this golden beauty."

The next interviewer wasn't allowed in the kitchen. Justine played the party line for the *Sun*, saying that the show was going great. "I love *Over the Top* more than anything else in the world," she said. "There's Craig Campbell, the wonderful singer, and the beautiful Oakland sisters, and just dozens of wonderful things. So much happens up there and so happens fast that it ought to please everybody."[27]

Apparently not everybody. The show closed shortly after the interview appeared with a loss of $17,000.

Even with the failure of *Over the Top,* the Shuberts had no intention of letting Justine go. Aside from having their "famous stage beauty" in their stable, they needed to recoup their losses. In the spring of 1918 they sent *Over the Top* on the road for a six-city tour. With no new Shubert show for her on the horizon, Justine was contractually obligated to go.

For Justine's absence from her club hostessing duties, Lee commissioned a "Justine Johnstone" doll named "Justine, Jr.," made with golden curls, large, heavily-lidded eyes, a pouty mouth and a flouncy French frock. He placed the doll at Justine's table at the entrance to the club with a sign, "I'll Be Back!" In a news shot with the doll, Justine dully gazes at the camera with what may be the most lethargic smile ever photographed.

Toxen Worm sent photos of Justine in elegant costumes to newspapers in every city on the itinerary, and posted ads screaming, "SEE the great airplane invasion, pulsating with patriotism!" "The last word in frills and thrills!" "Cast of 100, including 50 Justine Johnstone Girls!" He may have been a little desperate with "Direct from four months' run in New York!"[28] (At least that was twice as long as the Folies-Bergère show had lasted.)

The show actually fared better with critics out of town than in New York, in that the reviews weren't terrible. One Philadelphia critic fondly remembered Justine as a messenger boy at the Folies-Bergère when she was 16. Another noted wryly that the Neo-Classical Dancers "apparently didn't find anything to suit them in the Land of Frocks and Frills, as they wore neither."[29]

As long as the show sold, the Shuberts were happy. But the star attraction was beginning to get a little tetchy.

7

The Most Awful, Cheap Trash

During *Over the Top*'s Chicago run, Toxen Worm set up an interview with a reporter from Hearst's *Herald and Examiner* in Justine's suite at the Blackstone Hotel. Contrary to what Worm may have expected, the interview proved how frank Justine could be when no press agent was around. The interviewer was Ashton Stevens, known as the dean of American drama critics, a gifted profiler, and the prototype for the character Jed Leland in Orson Welles' *Citizen Kane*. Stevens was clearly taken with Justine (although frankly more besotted with Adele Astaire), and managed to convey her droll humor, perspective and frustration in a way that no reporter had captured before.

Stevens noted with some fascination that Justine didn't look at Nat Roth, the Victor Buono–like company manager, as he admonished her, twice, to "Just be yourself" during the interview before he left. Alone with Justine, a suddenly uncomfortable Stevens said, "I'll take off my overcoat."

"That would be the nice, natural thing to do," Justine said, "I'd be awfully disappointed if you didn't. Do you know Mr. Roth very well?"

"Fairly well," Stevens responded.

"How well?"

"Oh—I gave him a cigar."

"That sounds rather intimate," she said. "I wanted to ask you whether you thought Mr. Roth the right sort of manager for a girl like me."

"But why do you ask me?"

"Oh, he's such a bear at times. He's worse than a conscience. He's worse than the New York Office. If he sees me at supper with a man of less than eighty years he says he's afraid the Shuberts wouldn't approve. Do you know what I wanted to say to him when he spoke to me as he did just now? I wanted to say: 'Mr. Roth, will you please oblige me by sitting on a tack?'"[1]

Charmed, Stevens noted her frankness, her worry about her mother's cough (Sophia was traveling with her), and her unsentimental description of her "more than romantically poor" childhood. "I dote on saving money," she

7. The Most Awful, Cheap Trash   61

said.[2] "This is my first trip [to Chicago]. I'm terribly untraveled. When I was a chorus girl I couldn't afford to leave New York. It would have injured my professional reputation. I had to be a star before I'd consider leaving New York. And then you ought to see my five years' contract—there's everything in it but caviar for the canary. It ought to be a good contract—I copied it from the contract of the most exacting Jewish star that ever played for the Shuberts. But you mustn't tell her name. Of course, nobody can guess it."[3] Stevens didn't guess, at least not publicly, but Justine was probably referring to temperamental Russian actress Alla Nazimova, a friend of a friend.

Flowers, chocolates and a bottle of perfume were delivered during the interview from fans Justine didn't know. Stevens asked if the perfume was named after her. "Not yet," she said. "One usually starts by having cigars named—and then works up to toilet articles. But I dread the cigars. They are usually five-centers, aren't they? I'd hate to have anything bearing my name in the mouth of a man who'd smoke a five-cent cigar."[4]

Stevens appreciated her humor. He suggested that she offer a joke or two for the show.

"What's the use?" she replied. "They'd treat my jokes the way they treat my songs. I go into the Shubert office and suggest a suggestion and they say: 'A very good idea, but let's do it this way. We'll get you a nice new pink dress and let him sing the song to you.' Oh, I say, 'No, it would be cleverer to give him the pink dress and let me sing the song.'"

She actually had given a joke, she said, to Ed Wynn ("'Waiter, my plate's damp.' 'You dern fool, that's your soup'"). She didn't think it was particularly funny, but the audience liked it. Wynn's humor, she said, was "unsubtle."

"I love subtle things," she said. "I love only one thing that isn't subtle."

"What's that?"

"Youth. Youth isn't subtle. I love Stephen Leacock and Gilbert Chesterton and some of Meredith, but I love youth, too. Sometimes I think that someday I'll fall terribly in love with the sheer youth of some lad ... but then, I never could stand a man that liked himself. And all men do—young or old. That's probably why I shall never really love any man."

"Perhaps," Stevens suggested, "an actor—one who could be helpful."

"Love an actor! Haven't I just told you I couldn't even love a man? Actor! No!"[5]

It was an interesting comment, one that could be interpreted any number of ways. It could have come from the exasperation of someone with too many dates from too many unsuitable suitors. "Actor! No!" could also have been a dig: Justine may have been implying that she considered actors less than "real" men. A facile contemporary guess about "I couldn't love a man" might be that it was a comment possibly made by a woman who may have been lesbian or bisexual, whether she was aware of it or not, but any proof of such a theory is lacking. In any event, Justine didn't elaborate on her comment to Stevens—or at least Stevens didn't share it if she did.

She did add, "I don't pretend to be anything that I'm not. I loathe the posing socialist—or any other kind of a poser. I like my own kind of people and only that kind. I'd bore the others, and they me. I wouldn't walk out with a stage-hand because I'm quite sure that neither of us would enjoy it."[6] That probably didn't earn her points with the crew. Interesting that she didn't consider the possibility that a "stage-hand" could be as well read and erudite as, say, a show girl. It was snobbish, but it was honest. She didn't forget where she came from and she also had no plans to return. After all, she "doted" on saving money.

On the other hand, she emphasized that wasn't enamored of status for its own sake. "For that matter," she said, "I've never seen any railroad presidents that are especially delightful company." Or, perhaps, newspaper magnates. She was Dorothy to Marion's Lorelei, the one who didn't date for money.

"Where does your preference lie?" Stevens asked.

"Just people—regular, nice, human people, with, if possible, a sense of humor."[7] Ultimately the human and humor were more important to her than the status or income. She'd met too many people who only were interested in her because she was a star, or beautiful, or both.

Justine recalled her beginnings in the theatre, and her early offer from John Drew, Jr. "And a couple of years have slipped by," she said, "and Mr. John Drew and I are stars playing in the same town—and some nights his receipts at the [Chicago] Princess are $225." Drew was appearing in a well-received revival of an Arthur Wing Pinero play, *The Gay Lord Quex,* and Justine found it abhorrent that her ridiculous show was making more money than Drew's. Very possibly, she herself was making more money than Drew. "And that isn't right," she said. "The public is wrong." She quickly added, "Those receipts are not right, I mean. I'm not saying"—and here Stevens noted that she smiled, perhaps pulling back a bit to tow the company line—"that the public is wrong about me. I'm not that ungrateful."[8]

Stevens noted that she did not speak "maliciously."[9]

She wasn't malicious. She was miserable. And the public probably wasn't wrong about her: they were simply paying money to see the type of show the Shuberts promised them, and she was delivering. She'd reached an enviable position in her career, and was going nowhere.

Her frequent letters to both Lee and J. J. Shubert from the road cover a gamut of complaints, from unprofessional behavior backstage to the sluggish "Justine Johnstone Girls" to the fact that the maid stipulated in her contract hadn't shown up, and her mother Sophia was her volunteer dresser. At the end of one such letter, she added a gentle little hint about what she expected from him based on their pre-contract discussions. "I still feel the same about a career as I did last year," she said. "Trust you will understand the spirit in which this letter was written."[10]

He did. "I talked to J.J.," Lee wrote back, "and he is very anxious to have you go into the next Winter Garden show." It was another revue, but the Winter Garden was Shubert Nirvana, the jewel in their crown. If the book was good, it could be the next step toward a full non-musical play. "The part is a good one," Lee told her. "Let me know if you are satisfied to do this so the part can be written up for you."[11]

Justine was satisfied indeed. She even suggested that her leading man be Bernard Granville, a friend and headliner from her *Follies* days. Lee assured her that J. J. had some great plans in mind.

J. J. Shubert in fact had no interest in what Justine did except to fulfill her contract. He gave her a tepid outline of a tepid show with a tepid part for her, plus a brutal schedule that included her club obligations. Justine was deeply disappointed, but offered a carefully crafted compromise:

Dear J. J.:

Here it is Sunday and I have been thinking of practically nothing else since our talk on Thursday. Since you have expressed your plans to star me in a play for the season 1918–19, and besides to open "the club" again, I really feel I owe it to myself to rest this summer so I am in the best possible mental and physical condition in the fall.

From what I have seen of my proposed part in the revue, it has little to offer me, and the environment and the book is anything but a stepping stone for parts such as Lee discussed for planning my career. So if it is all the same to you, I prefer not to play.

However, I want to do anything I can for both you and Lee, as I fully realize you have been very kind to me, and should you find you must *absolutely* have me for this part, I will do my best, providing you do the following:

The book must be made more attractive to me and to fit my personality. I must have at least three weeks' rest with pay during September before I start rehearsals for the new the play.

Let me hear from you as to just what you want me to do.

Sincerely,
Justine Johnstone[12]

J. J. shot back:

My dear Miss Johnstone:

I have your letter dated June 26. If this were not a Monday, which is usually a blue day, it would give me a huge laugh. Your demands are really unique if nothing else. I do not see anything in your contract wherein you can make any demands whatsoever.

As far as playing the Winter Garden is concerned, you can forget all about it. Perhaps a rest will do you a lot of good. All other matters with reference to your option and in the Little Club, I will advise you to see Mr. Lee Shubert, with whom you have had all arrangements.

Yours very truly,
J. J. Shubert[13]

Not as piquant, perhaps, as when he called Charles Frohman a faegele, but devastating in its effects. Shortly thereafter, Toxen Worm ordered that the flashing, revolving red lettering announcing "Justine Johnstone's Little Club" on top of the 44th Street Theatre be replaced with "Fancy Free at the Astor," the new Shubert musical starring Ed Wynn and Marilyn Miller. The 44th Street Theatre rooftop was renamed for a Cohan star, Nora Bayes. Justine Johnstone's Little Club became simply the Little Club, with dancers Billie Allen (a Ziegfeld "Century Girl") and Helen Maxwell as dual hostesses. It then the Club Alabam, featuring the Fletcher Henderson Orchestra and other black stars for white-only patrons. (Later, during World War II, Lee donated the club space to the American Theatre Wing for the Stage Door Canteen. The entire 44th Street Theatre building was razed in 1945 for expanded *New York Times* facilities.)

The Shuberts kept Justine on the road, tossing her into one of their lesser efforts, *Girl o' Mine*, written by *Over the Top*'s Phillip Bartholomae. It had lasted only a few weeks at the Bijou, and for the road was retitled *Victory Girl* for reasons nobody could understand, except for the ads that called it "the first after-the-war musical comedy." By January 1919, the show's title had changed again, to *Oh, Mama!*, since apparently they couldn't let go of the "Oh" concept. Justine played a young American girl who has moved to Paris to live with her uncle, only to become stranded along with a group of other Americans and ensnared in madcap shenanigans.

The experience was even less palatable for Justine than *Over the Top*. Company manager John Slocum sent Lee a red-flag memo that Justine wasn't getting along well with the second female lead, Helen Shipman. Helen had recently starred in the road company of *Oh, Boy!* and was possibly unhappy with playing second fiddle to a beauty queen. No doubt another distasteful element was lead comic Frank Fay, a vaudevillian who had originated his role in the ill-fated Broadway run. Among his specialties in the show was "a satire on the subject of feminism that is a laugh from start to finish,"[14] according to one review. Frank Fay is perhaps best known today as the grandfather of standup comedy, Barbara Stanwyck's first husband, a notorious anti–Semite and a generally disagreeable human being.

Lee kept trying. In early 1919, he commissioned Bartholomae to write a new musical play for Justine and eagerly had it sent to her. Justine's reaction was not what he might have expected:

My dear Mr. Shubert:

I read it thoroughly and I can't for a moment think that you could have read it. Why, Lee, it is the most awful, cheap trash I've ever read in my life. I'm sure you couldn't have read it and approved it. [Bartholomae] has not one idea in his head. He didn't even have the sense to put your ideas down correctly. He's making the cheapest old wit on the vaudeville stage into a three-dollar show. It simply won't do. People

7. The Most Awful, Cheap Trash

wouldn't stand for it. It's a shame he should have wasted that perfectly good paper to put those words on because it could have been put to so much better use in a lavatory.[156]

It was becoming increasingly obvious that the Shuberts intended to use up Justine's contract with musicals, rather than shifting her to drama, as she expected. The Shuberts had produced more than a dozen non-musical plays since *Over the Top* had premiered. There's no indication that Justine was ever seriously considered for any of them.

One reason could have been that J. J. overruled Lee's ideas about Justine's dramatic abilities. Undaunted, Lee had a new idea. He told Toxen Worm

The habitually humorless Lee Shubert, who developed an obsession for Justine. Courtesy The Shubert Archive.

to announce plans for a Shubert Academy of Dramatic and Musical Art, telling him, rather incredibly, that "if young actresses have nerve and good looks they can be taught to act, even in serious drama."[16] If J. J. thought Justine needed training as a serious actress, Lee would give it to her.

Worm thought the idea was great because it potentially meant additional revenue. He then jumped from Plan B to Plan Z. He came up with a promotional idea for the school that "would generate a great deal of interest." Apparently in earnest, Worm suggested a special matinee at the 44th Street rooftop featuring one act from five Ibsen plays, each performed by actresses not known for "serious drama."

Worm then proposed the following: Alma Tell, a comedic actress, in a scene from *Lady from the Sea*; operetta star Julia Bruns in *Little Eyolf*; Ziegfeld girl Peggy Hopkins Joyce in *The Wild Duck*; Marion Davies in *A Doll's House*; and Justine in the devastating last act of *Hedda Gabler*.

It sounded like a joke. It may have been one. Either way, neither the "special matinee" nor the Shubert Academy ever happened.

Finally, in February of 1919, Justine sent Lee a terse note:

Will you please send me a line confirming our conversation Friday afternoon, as it would be only fair to anyone who would want me to sign up with them.

Please don't delay this as you know better than anyone that I need work as soon as I can get it.

Sincerely,
Justine[17]

There is no known response. Two weeks later, and less than two years into her five-year commitment to the Shuberts, she sent a final note to both Lee and J. J. asking that they cancel her contract "effective immediately."[18]

Lee Shubert was devastated. Almost twenty years later, in an unusually confessional moment, he confided his great heartbreak over Justine to Bert Lahr: "The nights became months. I kept walking, nobody could talk to me, everybody was concerned. I walked the docks. I couldn't eat, I couldn't sleep. Finally, after many months, one morning I woke up and it was gone. The whole weight, that sadness, left had left me like a bad dream. In later years, when I looked back on it—it seemed so silly, so laughable. It was puppy love."[19]

Freed from having to please anyone's press agent, Justine publicly expressed relief. "It was fine for a while," Justine told a reporter. "[But] only a girl without any sense whatsoever would believe she could survive many stage sessions as a mere professional beauty. Perhaps it would have been different if I had been given some stage task, but all I was asked to do was look pretty."[20]

It also may have been different if she had been "born to luxury," she said. "But I wasn't. I come from hard-working, self-respecting Scandinavians, people who have some imagination as well as brains.... But I was ticketed and labeled as a beauty and nobody wanted me to think. In fact, the people with whom I came in contact actually resented it when I thought out loud."[21]

The interview was clipped and saved by someone in the Shubert office, and the last sentence was underlined in pencil.

It wasn't just her cancellation of her contract that caused Lee such pain.

In 1919, Broadway revue composers Bide Dudley and Fredric Watson published a song, "When the War Is Over, I'll Return to You"—"Dedicated to the Famous Stage Beauty MISS JUSTINE JOHNSTONE," with Justine's photo gracing the sheet music cover. The song doesn't actually mention her, and there's no indication that she ever sang it, which may have been a good thing. ("When Sammy comes marching home / Hooray, hooray / Then I'll return to you / There's going to be a happy wedding day / Hooray, for sweetheart I've been true," etc.)

As it happened, Justine actually had a young man in the war, and he was indeed returning to her.

8

Some Change

Born into a wealthy family in San Francisco, 25-year-old Walter Wanger (rhyming with "ranger") was smart, creative, well spoken and well dressed. The family name was originally Feuchtwanger (he was a distant cousin of writer Lion Feuchtwanger) but his mother Stella, in an attempt to socially assimilate and obscure their Jewish-German heritage, changed the name after the death of his father. It was perhaps the first step the creation of Walter F. Wanger, an urban sophisticate with no real middle name. After taking summer courses at Oxford, he perfected his lifelong persona of a suave Anglophile.

Walter was "a dashing figure at first view, but with a naïve side,"[1] according to director Elia Kazan. He was also impulsive and extremely ambitious. Before being kicked out of Dartmouth twice, he produced impressive college dramatic productions. He then fast-tracked from professional theatrical assistant to manager and producer.

Press agent Walter Kingsley, who took credit for almost everything Justine did, claimed that he introduced her to Walter Wanger. However, the couple themselves had a different story in a 1921 interview. In 1916, 22-year-old Walter was associate to Elisabeth Marbury of the Princess Theatre with ambitions to be an independent theatrical producer. Marbury had recently hooked Walter to Alla Nazimova (Justine's presumed inspiration for her demanding contract with the Shuberts), for whom he would mount a lurid melodrama, *'Ception Shoals*, at the Princess.

Walter caught the 1916 *Follies* and, as he often did, found a reason to approach a beautiful show girl afterwards. He introduced himself to Justine and invited her to join his new production. She thought he was hilarious. Of course she wanted to do drama, but she knew all the top producers on Broadway, and this guy was a novice. She brushed him off. "Then," asked the interviewer, "it was not love at first sight? "I should say not," said Justine.[2]

Walter's Nazimova production opened at the Princess in January 1917, and played until Comstock kicked it out for *Oh, Boy!* Walter then moved

'Ception Shoals to Justine's old stomping grounds, the Fulton. During that run, as Justine and Guy Bolton drifted apart, she and Walter drifted together.

Walter enlisted into the army in April 1917, a few days after the United States declared war on Germany. The couple took active roles in the mayor's Committee on National Defense, a wartime propaganda organization. As publicity manager for the Committee's recruitment promotion, Walter engaged Justine's artist friend James Montgomery Flagg to design patriotic posters, such as a recycling of his previously-designed, now-iconic poster "I Want You!" illustration of Uncle Sam. Justine appeared in Committee-sponsored events, including distributing flyers from a parade float down Fifth Avenue, and performing at a Carnegie Hall fundraiser along with Will Rogers, Ethel Barrymore, Laurette Taylor, Nora Bayes and other headliners.

Walter then used family connections and letters of recommendation—including one from Justine's then-employer Lee Shubert—to get into the Army Signal Corps. Justine was spotted visiting him while he was in flyer training at the Massachusetts Institute of Technology, and bidding him farewell as he boarded ship for Europe. Walter kept a photo of Justine in his barracks, which artist-soldiers used as a sketch model.

Stationed in Italy under future New York mayor Fiorello LaGuardia, Walter cracked up five planes in practice maneuvers and won the nickname "the Austrian ace." He had better luck serving as an attaché at the 1918 Paris Peace Conference, learning diplomacy and honing his spin skills.

Walter serving in Italy during World War I. He cracked up several planes in practice maneuvers and earned the nickname "The Austrian Ace." Courtesy Walter F. Wanger Papers, Wisconsin Center for Film and Theater Research.

Justine provided her own comps to servicemen for the *Over the Top*. She performed in a benefit for the Junior Patriots' League, a society women's club that trained young girls in first aid and fundraising for the war effort. She joined the Stage Women's War Relief and pitched its efforts to the press, encouraging women to send clothing to the organization's headquarters at the Fulton Theatre. Gloves, she noted, were particularly valuable, as they could be refashioned as vests for "flying men," not mentioning that she had a special flying man on her mind.

The couple kept in touch throughout the war. "It is quite heart-breaking," Walter wrote from Italy, "not to have been able to be present at the opening of *Over the Top*, but I hope that my seat was kept for the performance, although not occupied."[3] He told her of having his own little *Over the Top* opening night party in honor of her, and begged Justine to think of him. Obviously, she did. She sent him a photo of herself in her Act I finale costume, the white leather aviator garb, and wrote on the back, "From a good-looking aviatrix to a funny-looking aviator—Justine." Walter kept the photo for the rest of his life.

There were more than a few similarities between Justine's *Oh, Boy!* beau Guy Bolton and Walter. Both were considered cultured, urbane, and reasonably well educated; both dressed impeccably and smoked pipes. More important were the similarities between Walter and Justine. Like she, Walter was well read, had multiple interests and was

Justine's Act I finale scene featured her climbing "over the top" of the trenches in a tasteful white leather Conant aviator costume. She sent the photo to her beau Walter Wanger, who kept it for the rest of his life. Courtesy Walter F. Wanger Papers, Wisconsin Center for Film and Theater Research.

curious about the world. He could be as charming, blunt and bull-headedly ambitious as she could be. There were also differences between them. Walter had a habit of paying lip-service to left-wing causes while maintaining a patrician lifestyle (when Justine had told Ashton Stevens that she loathed "the posing socialist," she may have just read a letter from Walter). Other differences between them intrigued her. His background in the burgeoning, experimental "Little Theatre" movement was exciting to her. He'd been to Europe; she longed to go. He was an anomaly, this smart, educated young theatrical producer. Plus, he was Savile Row gorgeous and smelled magnificently of English cologne.

The capper was that this unique specimen actually listened to her. They engaged in conversations on topics that interested them both, other than theatre: art, literature, politics. And he took a genuine interest in her ambitions to become a legitimate actress.

Arguably it would be Justine's contacts that would provide Walter with his own early game-changing career moves. It was reportedly through Justine's friendship with Marion that Walter met William Randolph Hearst. Walter negotiated a contract for Elisabeth Marbury's client, former *Watch Your Step* star Irene Castle, for a 1917 Hearst adventure film serial, *Patria*. Hearst was just one of Justine's friends who would play prominent roles in Walter's professional and social life for years.

But for the moment, Walter was advising Justine. He became her manager. And as per usual with Walter Wanger, his efforts were often hit or miss.

In the spring of 1919, when Walter returned from overseas, Justine made an announcement: she would never again appear in another musical. Going forward, she would appear in straight theatre or nothing. The decision had come to her, she said, after reading a book about self-determination.

A woman exercising self-determination at that time was still something of a novelty. It wouldn't be so for long. By June of 1919, New York women had the right to vote, and national women's suffrage followed the next year. The postwar emergence of the "new woman," prompted by a wartime increase of women in the workforce, was just beginning.

Nevertheless, the press said Justine's announcement "shocked" her friends and the theatre community. Those who actually knew her probably actually weren't, but the "shocking" made for a better press story. A 1940 *Harper's Bazaar* article noted about her decision:

Justine in her Connecticut cottage during her self-imposed exile from Broadway, happily taking minor roles in non-musical productions with the Poli stock company, Waterbury, 1919. Courtesy Mr. Justin Wanger.

"What did they want?" asked the wise guys. "She's a knockout. She's a big hit. They've got her name up in lights. The stage-door Johnnies line up with orchids and champagne. You don't hear Jessie Reed complaining, or Lil Tashman, or Peggy Joyce. What does she want, anyhow?"

Justine Johnstone knew what she wanted.[4]

She had a new plan. For starters, she did something she'd never done before. She auditioned.

Stock theatre throughout the country was considered at the time to be a training ground for burgeoning actors and regular employment for locals. As a member of a set, or "stock," company performing in repertory, an actor could learn the basics of the trade, develop a catalog of diverse roles, and feel free to make mistakes in regions far from the Broadway critics. A known star leaving Broadway to sharpen her skills in stock was not unheard of, but for a "show girl" like Justine, it was unusual.

One of the premier stock managers of the day was Sylvester Z. Poli, who owned a chain of theatres throughout New England. Poli had an agreement with the Shuberts, and often presented the brothers' hits from previous Broadway seasons. Justine was probably aware that, in 1918, actress Evelyn Gosnell—like herself, a Scandinavian beauty—spent the summer season with the Poli theatre in Waterbury, Connecticut, returned to New York and landed a contact with Broadway manager A. H. Woods.

When Justine learned that the Poli company in Waterbury needed for a "general utility woman" for the 1919 summer season, she put on a blue serge dress and sailor hat that, she said, "were sufficiently out of date," brushed her hair back into a severe topknot and walked into the Poli New York offices at 1400 Broadway. She introduced herself to general manager James Thatcher as "J. Johnston" and expressed interest in the "general utility" position. She admitted no theatrical experience. She read some lines. She got the job.

She was so happy that she cried. "You see," she said, "I had arrived at last, not at the end, but at the beginning of a long journey I had dreamed of taking ever since I was a little girl in Hoboken."[5] She rented a small cottage outside Waterbury, cranked up her robin's-egg blue National Motors roadster (no Pierce Arrow) and left Broadway in chugging puffs and backfires.

One of Walter Wanger's talents was promotion. He hired the White Studio to photograph Justine at her Waterbury cottage in a number of poses she'd never done under Kingsley or the Shuberts: watering the lawn of her cottage, washing her car, chopping wood (wearing slacks), and reading, wearing circular black-framed glasses. Some of the more delightful shots are of Justine playing with a neighbor child, a little girl who seemed to have wandered into the shoot.

A few poses were of characters she was portraying: Tessie, a maid serving drinks in *Fair and Warmer*, and Clementina, a scrubwoman in *Mary's Ankle*, washing dishes in a kitchen sink, no makeup, her feet pigeon-toed, her hair pulled back severely, revealing a fierce scowl belied by a half-smile, commenting delightedly on her own unattractiveness.

Justine was more than happy to explain her decision in at least a half-dozen interviews from her tiny dressing room at the Poli company theatre, the Strand on Main Street.

"Some change, isn't it?" she laughed to a *Sun* reporter. She couldn't understand why people thought she was on some sort of "Quixotic adventure."

"I have aspirations to be something more than a show girl, however glorified. I have always wanted to act. I have always believed I could act. And for six weeks I have been acting. If I had the last three or four years to live over again I should begin by going to a good dramatic school. I have, however, absorbed a certain amount of valuable training in such work as I have been doing on the stage. It has not been important, but it has all been necessary, nevertheless. For one thing, I feel at home on the stage. I feel a part and parcel of it. And I have, furthermore, acquired a certain rough technique which I could not otherwise have gained. So the years haven't been entirely wasted."

Justine Johnstone sighed wistfully. Then she lifted a thick saucer and ruefully contemplated an emaciated chocolate eclair reposing thereon. "This," she said, "this is one of those moments when I'd give a whole week's salary for a metropolitan-made ice cream soda."

Above and opposite: **Calculatedly un-glamorous shots during Justine's Poli stock season in Waterbury, Connecticut: as a scrubwoman in the comedy *Mary's Ankle,* reading scripts in her glasses, washing her car. Most newspapers used only glamor shots from this White Studio shoot, with *Vanity Fair* running the scrubwoman photo retouched with lipstick and eye liner. Key sheet: White Studio © Billy Rose Theatre Division, courtesy New York Public Library for the Performing Arts.**

"And how much would that be?" ventured the *Sun* reporter.

"Oh, fifty dollars," was the prompt reply. "Fifty dollars and I'm probably not really worth five, even though I am putting in fourteen hours' work seven days of the week. But what I'm learning! As a matter of fact I often feel that I should be paying the Poli management an honorarium by way of tuition fee."[6]

What she was learning was how to analyze a script, now that she actually had scripts to analyze. She was also experimenting with building a character, "to fill in the skeleton of the character I found in the type-written part."[7] She developed back stories for her characters and tried out bits of "business," activities that would subtly reflect who her characters were and why. It was Acting 101, and it thrilled her.

And she learned to work fast. She rehearsed the role of a society girl in *Eyes of Youth* by day, then returned in the evening to play a gum-chewing maid in *Fair and Warmer*. To address the actors' character-juggling mindset, director William Blair advised the players to arrive at the theatre an hour and a half before curtain "to be fully *en rapport* with the characters we are to play,"[8] Justine said. She arrived two hours prior.

She had nightmares, "terrorized by ghastly dreams in which I mixed two roles and heard myself hissed off the stage."[9] By the third week, she had adjusted into the routine, relishing especially the comedic character roles that were far removed from her public persona. In all, she played thirteen secondary roles in as many weeks, understudying leads in several of the plays. Finally, she said, she felt that her career was headed in the direction she wanted.

One of the most telling insights into Justine's perspective about herself and her career is from an interview with the *New York Tribune*, which touched on a point many press articles failed to note. Justine never expected to become the next Ethel Barrymore or Laurette Taylor. She simply wanted to return to Broadway in the types of small parts she'd been playing in stock, "and with the privilege of understudying several of the more important roles."

"I may not become a very great actress," she said. "There's not a chance in the world I shall be. But I can and will become a good actress."[10]

The Waterbury season was, for Justine's purposes, a complete success. She got exactly what she wanted: the opportunity to learn. And she had played more roles in one summer than she ever had done on Broadway, none in fluffy musicals. Most importantly, she had played roles that had nothing to do with how she looked.

There are no known reviews of that particular Waterbury season, but some of the White photos taken at the cottage did get used. Rather than the wood-chopping or car-washing shots, most newspapers ran photos of her posing prettily in her garden. *Vanity Fair* ran the scrubwoman and maid shots, but retouched them to give her heavier makeup. "Miss Johnstone," ran the caption of the augmented scrubwoman shot, "did her level best to convince the audience that she had crossed the Rubicon and forsaken the old butterfly life forever and ever."[11]

It didn't matter. Her "manikin" days were over. She was now an actress.

As it happened, she returned to New York at the worst possible time to find a job. Actors Equity Association, the actors' union that most producers ignored, declared an unprecedented strike.

In the six years since its founding, Equity had grown from 112 members to over 2,500. In response, in the spring of 1919, theatrical managers formed their own organization. The Producing Managers Association would include the Shuberts, Ziegfeld, Ray Comstock, Morris Gest, George M. Cohan and over twenty others. The PMA vowed never to recognize the actors' union. By that summer, the gloves came off. Actors had endured years of grievances: all-night, unpaid rehearsals, half-pay holiday shows, working up to ten performances a week, filthy and unheated dressing rooms, being stranded after shows closed on the road, supplying costumes with no reimbursement, arbitrary replacement without pay, and other workplace indignities. In addition, Equity's recent recognition by the American Federation of Labor emboldened the actors and strengthened their collective bargaining power.

On August 6, 1919, Equity members voted to strike any PMA member who would not honor the Equity contract. The following evening, twelve Broadway theatres, including the Shubert, the 44th Street and the Princess, went dark due to actor walk-outs. An estimated $25,000 was refunded to patrons that evening's performance. Over the next several days, rehearsals shut down. Playwrights and retired actors replaced cast members onstage. Shows fell in domino fashion. Theatres across the county shuttered. Actors held rallies, parades, and special benefit performances led by star strikers such as Ethel Barrymore, Marie Dressler (who fought for chorus girls, having been one years prior), Ziegfeld comedian Eddie Cantor and Justine's former co-star Ed Wynn.

The strike actually proved a nice bump for Walter. The Theatre Guild, a struggling artistic organization, was not under Equity jurisdiction, as it was considered a "co-operative" venture (the actors were shareholders). The Guild was offering a mediocre play called *John Ferguson*. To the surprise of the Guild board, theatre-starved audiences flocked to it. The Guild was so overwhelmed

8. Some Change 75

with unexpected activity that it needed a business manager, and Walter got the job. As manager of this "co-operative," he was able to share in the profits, and flagrantly promoted the would-be flop as the only game in town.

Variety noted that Justine was seen walking with her manager-friend Walter Wanger "and says she is against the managers."[12] Cute joke, but it didn't happen to be true. Justine was in fact not Equity, and did not support the strike. Many actors did not. Being an Equity strike sympathizer meant alienating managers and thus compromising one's own career. The Shuberts actually sued not only Equity but 300 individual members for half a million dollars, whether or not the members had joined the strike, or were even in town, or, in some cases, were even alive. (They didn't collect.) For an actor trying to build a new career, it was too risky. Justine had much more to lose than Ethel Barrymore.

Not only was Justine non–Equity, she was supporting a rival association that popped up during the strike. The Actors' Fidelity League (derisively called "FIDO" by Equity), led by George M. Cohan, was an odd combination of both actors and managers. FIDO producers promised actors almost everything Equity wanted, such as rehearsal and overtime pay, costumes (yes, costumes, at last), and travel fare home when a show closed out of town. But it did not agree to bargaining power for the actors. That was fine for FIDO actors. Some of them had been negotiating for themselves for years and felt they didn't need a union to arbitrate for them. They, like Justine, counted managers among their friends.

Justine agreed to be a FIDO "advisory member" and appeared at a benefit at the Century Theatre. Her friend, actor and Princess Theatre co-manager Holbrook Blinn, was a FIDO board member. Blinn hosted a party at his Riverdale home for like-minded friends, including Justine and one of her former employers, producer Jesse Lasky.

Soon after the Folies-Bergère fiasco, Lasky had taken the advice about a film studio from his brother-in-law Sam Goldfish. With Sam and writer-director Cecil B. DeMille, Lasky had founded the Jesse L. Lasky Feature Play company. In 1913 DeMille had found a horse barn in an obscure L.A. hamlet called Hollywood and turned it into Lasky's West Coast studio. Lasky ran operations from New York, farming Broadway for talent. He had just joined forces with competitor Adolph Zukor's Famous Players studio to create Famous Players–Lasky, with their films distributed by Paramount Pictures Corp. Lasky and Zukor were now in the process of building what would become the most prestigious film studio in the country.

At Blinn's FIDO party, Justine introduced Lasky her to her gentleman friend Walter. A nice hook was that that Famous Players–Lasky, or FPL, was distributing films for Justine's and Walter's friend, William Randolph Hearst. The media millionaire had created the Marion Davies Film Company in 1918 in a love-blinded effort to promote Marion—the talented, fun-loving comedienne—as a foremost dramatic actress. Now, having inherited an even more colossal fortune after the death of his mother, Hearst was expanding his empire. He re-named his film entity Cosmopolitan Productions for one of his magazines, opened a studio on 126th Street and Second Avenue, and began a subsidiary career as a movie mogul.

Lasky, with a keen eye for both creative and corporate talent, was impressed with Justine's confident, savvy young man from his own hometown of San Francisco. Walter, with a keen eye for opportunity, proceeded to promote himself to Lasky.

A week after the FIDO party, on September 6, 1919, the strike ended. The PMA agreed to recognize Equity and its contracts. Full compliance with the union by managers would take years, but Equity had teeth, and the actors finally had a voice. The union had grown in a matter of weeks from some 2,500 members to nearly 8,000 (as opposed to FIDO's 1,093). Tensions between Equity and FIDO continued for at least a decade until the rival organization was eventually dissolved. Justine never would join Equity.

But her introduction of Walter to Jesse Lasky at the FIDO party would prove a watershed moment in Walter's career. As such, it would also define hers.

9

Real Art

On September 13, 1919, Justine and Walter were married in a civil ceremony at City Hall. It was the go-to wedding venue for a number of theatricals at the time, as it was reasonable and fit easily into show schedules. The brief ceremony was performed by clerk P. J. Scully, a big man with round glasses and a walrus mustache who boasted that he married 15,000 couples a year. Among those in attendance was dear old Ralph Ranlet, Justine's "backer" chum to whom Miss Kellas of the Emma Willard School had written. Also attending was Walter's sister, Beatrice Wanger, a modern dancer who performed under the name Nadja. There's no record of Justine's parents attending, but reportedly Walter's aunts refused to speak with him after he married Justine, for unknown reasons. His mother Stella, however, became close to Justine, and the two occasionally traveled together.

The Wangers had no honeymoon, but settled into their first home at 349 Lexington Avenue, a lavishly-decorated three-story town house Justine had leased from artist and interior designer Paul Chalfin, who had worked Elsie de Wolfe, the life partner of Walter's former boss Elisabeth Marbury.

"Boo-Hoo! Pity the Sad Millionaires" ran one headline about Justine's wedding.[1] The press noted that "all but their nearest friends" were surprised by the wedding, even though the couple had been involved for three years. Actress Ruth Gordon would write years later that when the Wangers married, she'd read in the papers that "he made her give back all her jewelry.... I told that to Guy Bolton, who looked as though she hadn't given him back his. 'She *did?*' was all he said."[2]

Walter, as Justine's manager-husband, announced that she would be starring in his own production of a play called *Profane Love*, "based on a story by Balzac,"[3] in the fall. This, it was noted, was in fact the reason Justine had left musicals for stock. It was a slightly different version of Justine's earlier claims to the press that she'd ventured into stock after reading a self-help book, but it may simply have been Walter's version.

Profane Love wouldn't happen, at least not for Justine. About five months later a play called *Sacred and Profane Love* opened at the Morosco produced by Charles Frohman, Inc., and starring Elsie Ferguson, the Dillingham musical-turned-dramatic actress. The playwright was British Balzac admirer Arnold Bennett, a sometime associate of Walter's first theatrical employer, producer Granville Barker.

Walter wasn't involved in the production. He had started a new venture as manager of the Little Theatre on Delancy Street in Philadelphia, which, he announced, he would rename the Justine Johnstone Theatre. He also stated that she would soon be starring in its plays.

That wouldn't happen, either. Walter and Jesse Lasky had kept in touch since the FIDO party. Lasky was increasing Eastern production and building a new $2.5 million facility in Astoria, Queens (now the Kaufman Astoria Studios) to replace his old studio in Fort Lee. In May of 1920, Walter accepted a position as a manager at Famous Players–Lasky. He would have an office at corporate headquarters, 485 Fifth Avenue, and be involved in hiring, casting and supervising certain productions at the new studio. Thus Walter Wanger began his usually distinguished, often outstanding and sometimes infamous career in the film industry.

One of Walter's major responsibilities was to select plays from in Lasky's amassed collection from Charles Frohman, Inc., the estate of Dillingham's lover who had died in the sinking of the *Lusitania*. One Frohman production that Lasky filmed after Walter joined the studio was *Sacred and Profane Love*, the Balzac-influenced Arnold Bennett play that Walter had originally announced for Justine. Elsie Ferguson repeated her starring Broadway role for the film.

If Walter's career decisions were ever a point of contention in the marriage, there is no record of it. Justine claimed that she had volunteered to put her career on hold and adapt to life as an executive's wife. Her dream, she said, was to have "a country place with a house full of children,"[4] a reflection of the White Studio shots of Justine happily playing with the neighbor child at her Waterbury

Justine and Walter, wedding photo, ca. September 1919. Courtesy Mr. Justin Wanger.

9. Real Art

cottage. A 1920 gossip item reported that "the stork is planning a visit [to the Wangers] in the not-too-distant future,"[5] but there is no indication that she had a child.

There is also no indication that she was working. By all accounts, both she and Walter were enjoying their new lives as a married couple with a steady, healthy income.

They moved to a luxurious apartment at 1 West 70th Street off Central Park West. He built her the country house she wanted, a stone mansion on South Mountain Road in New City, New York, not far, coincidentally or not, from Adolph Zukor's magnificent estate. The Wangers were occasional weekend guests for golf outings on the Zukor's private course. Golf was a social must-have for 1920s professional and business men, and it became a lifetime passion for Justine. Some fifty years later, a longtime New City resident would fondly recall that, as a teenaged caddy for Zukor, he watched Justine play and that she once "lost her underpants when she swung at the golf ball on the eighth tee."[6]

Even though she was not working, Justine was still better connected in the business than Walter. This did not go unnoticed. There was some sniggling that Walter had married so far up he was invisible. A Dartmouth magazine writer pointed out rather snidely that a newspaper recently ran a "photo of Walt Wanger and Mrs. Wanger, or, as the paper put it, Justine Johnson [sic], 'the most beautiful woman.' In Hanover, Walt played the leading role from the Inn steps to Webster Hall, and then some; now he is merely someone's husband!"[7]

She was not only a bigger name, she was a bigger story. Reporters were still more interested in Justine than in Walter. She was asked if giving up her career for marriage was a difficult decision. "I confess I had a few secret pangs," she said, "for

Fashion shoot around the time Walter was preparing to star Justine in a Philadelphia theatre company, a short-lived plan until Lasky called. Courtesy Harry Ransom Center, the University of Texas at Austin.

I dearly loved my stage work. I never got so blasé that I did not feel a real thrill every time I stepped on the stage.... But I put it all aside, relentlessly. Mine was going to be a really successful marriage, I was determined. My husband was going to find me at liberty in all his leisure time."[8]

Part of this assertion came from the generally accepted idea that work and marriage was not possible for women. There was no such thing as work-life balance. For that reason, many women gave up their careers when they married, and would for decades. As Justine had pointed out several years earlier, she had witnessed marriages go bad when "the girls had insisted on remaining on the stage."

It may have been protesting too much, however. Justine may not have been ready to completely give up her career. It didn't take her long to figure out that she could work and still be home in time for Walter to find her "at liberty." Film acting was, after all, a day job.

She had known actor Taylor Holmes since her days at the Folies-Bergère. Now Holmes had his own film company headquartered in Brooklyn with distribution by Metro Pictures Corporation, a five-year-old film company eventually to transform into Metro-Goldwyn-Mayer. Justine signed as Holmes' co-star in a comedy, *Nothing but Lies,* in the spring of 1920.

Film still from the comedy *Nothing but Lies* (1920) with fellow New Jerseyan Taylor Holmes (center) and Canadian actor Rapley Holmes, produced by Taylor Holmes' company in Brooklyn. Courtesy Media History Digital Library.

Adapted from a recent play, the film starred Holmes as a smarmy press agent whose fabrications trap him into tangled webs. It a scenario that Justine may have found deliciously ironic. The film basically came and went, as did so many at the time, but *Variety* noted that Justine, as the agent's lady love, showed "surprising ability."[9]

Not surprisingly, about two months into Walter's tenure at Famous Players–Lasky, Justine signed to star in six films for an FPL subsidiary. Adolph Zukor had established Realart Pictures ostensibly to make fine, literary films and social dramas, but Zukor's main purpose was to lure staff away from his rival, Lewis Selznick, father and boss to budding producer David O.

For a new film star, second-string Realart would have been a better fit than "mainstage" FPL. Realart had a roster of popular Broadway actors such as Bebe Daniels, Alice Brady and Mary Miles Minter. But none had the film marquee value of such FPL megastars as Mary Pickford, whose cloying nickname of "America's Sweetheart" belied her abilities as a shrewd businesswoman (she would leave Zukor and co-found United Artists), or glamorous, couture-draped, sharp-witted Gloria Swanson.

Second-string or no, Realart was under the FPL banner. As such, it had its points. Zukor was big on the star system, and promotion to the grownup's table was certainly possible. Also, it paid well. Money was in fact the only reason most actors even considered working in films. An actor could make twice as much for a film than for a play, and being under contract for a year was far better than a four-week run followed by months of job-hunting. Justine's Realart salary is difficult to determine, although one news article mentioned that it was "many thousands per week."[10] Mary Miles Minter, a Mary Pickford type who had been acting in theatre and films since she was a child in the early teens, reportedly signed a three-year contract for over a million dollars.

The first film announced for Justine was *Moonlight and Honeysuckle,* originally a 1919 romantic farce that had starred Ruth Chatterton on Broadway. It was purchased specifically for Justine, but for reasons never announced, she never did it. She may not have wished to travel to California: the picture was shot at the Los Angeles Realart studio in Westlake, with Mary Miles Minter.

Instead, Justine's first Realart film was a melodrama called *Blackbirds,* based on a 1913 play by that had lasted a whopping 16 performances with Laura Hope Crews (perhaps best known as Aunt Pittypat in *Gone with the Wind*). FPL had already filmed the play in 1915 with Crews, but for some reason thought it worthy of recycling. Justine played Leonie, a member of a band of high-society crooks who falls for an undercover Secret Service agent aiming to nab the gang. In a fairly predictable outcome, she goes "straight" to marry the agent.

Filming seems to have taken place sometime in July and August 1920 in Jacksonville, Central Park (for a car chase scene) and at the FPL studio for interiors. A news article described a day on the set with a group of actresses playing society women at a party. Director Jack Dillon shouted, "Come on, now, give me some action! You women are supposed to be panic-stricken! Turn around, I don't want to see your faces. I want your backs!" A cry of "Oh, my God!" arose from the actresses; they were dressed in fashionable backless gowns and needed to powder their backs for the camera. The story described "a wild scampering of powder puffs" as the women scrambled to make up one other. "For heaven's sake," said one, "don't powder all over this new black dress of mine, even if you are doing me a favor." "Oh, for the life of a movie actress," said the journalist.[11] For the life indeed: they were supplying their own wardrobe and doing their own makeup. Actors Equity had cursory authority over film acting by mid–1920, but the Screen Actors' Guild would not be established until 1933.

Critical response to *Blackbirds* upon its December 1920 release was mixed, but Justine did well. *Variety* noted that she "is given little opportunity, if any at all, to acquaint an audience with her real value, and yet there is every indication of screen intelligence."[12] The *Dramatic Mirror* said, "Miss Johnstone shines out as a new constellation. She gives a splendid interpretation of the part she plays.... She has all the qualifications that go to make up a supremely successful film star."[13] "Justine Johnstone's pensive art and grace in expressing this type of character is distinctly pleasing," wrote a syndicated critic. "Her performance in this production, no doubt, will establish her."[14] Realart was so pleased they took out a half-page ad in *Variety* filled with Justine's glowing reviews.

Realart photograph featuring Justine in a "chrysanthemum" hair style. She worked at the new Astoria film facilities while Walter was managing Lasky's properties and overseeing productions, 1920–1921. Courtesy Billy Rose Theatre Division, New York Public Library for the Performing Arts, Astor, Lenox and Tilden Foundations.

9. Real Art

The studio publicity office, and/or Walter, trumpeted Justine's new film stardom. Much of the press coverage of Justine's Realart affiliation was the usual promo stuff, but some offer more interesting perspectives into her life and work. An article under her byline—but possibly an interview written in the first person—was syndicated internationally. She initially wasn't thrilled with filmmaking, she claimed. "At first, I will confess, I missed the audience.... The strange babel and confusion of the movie studio, the ugliness of the gaunt scaffolding and vast spaces between sets, the apparent slowness of the work—for it takes weeks to make a picture that only runs an hour or two—all these I never thought I'd learn to love. But I have learned to love them."[15]

In particular, she loved the practice of studio musicians playing "mood music" during the shooting of a scene. "Music creates atmosphere," she said. "It buoys up your spirits and helps you live your part,"[16] referencing a technique takeaway from her stock experience.

Interviews with Justine usually meant that she was asked about beauty tips. As always, she championed exercise. "Fresh air, exercise, regular hours, plenty of sleep and a simple diet are all important, but most important of all is absolute cleanliness." She loathed the current trend of heavy makeup. "I think it is the greatest pity that American girls of today use so many cosmetics," she said. "A walk down Fifth Avenue at any hour of the day is a sad commentary on the good taste and the good sense of the young American woman. In the early morning, around nine, you see the business girls going to work, and nine out of ten of them has cheeks rouged as red as flames, noses whitened to resemble marshmallows. Later in the day the shoppers arrive, many from the most exclusive homes in the city, and they are as made up as the business girls."

She hoped the current craze for "stage make-up in private life is only a passing fashion," she said. "Two years from now women may be again whitening themselves to a ghastly pallor, such as was the vogue in Victorian days, when the delicate, not sturdy or athletic type of girlhood was most admired." She herself used "no powder at all, no rouge on either cheeks or lips," except when working.[17] Not even lipstick. Very possibly, Justine was able to live her private life in relative anonymity and take a walk down Fifth Avenue completely devoid of makeup.

In early 1921 Walter accompanied Justine to an interview at the Plaza Hotel with celebrity/sports writer Harriet Underhill for *Picture-Play* magazine. Even before they had ordered lunch, Miss Underhill reported, Walter was yammering away about "pictures and stars and directors," while Justine "just smiled as her husband talked. 'You're not giving me a chance to say a word,' she said at last, 'and I've got a lot of things I want to say, too.'" She mentioned that thus far she had only completed two Realart pictures, which was fine with her. She was "so new at this game" of filmmaking that she

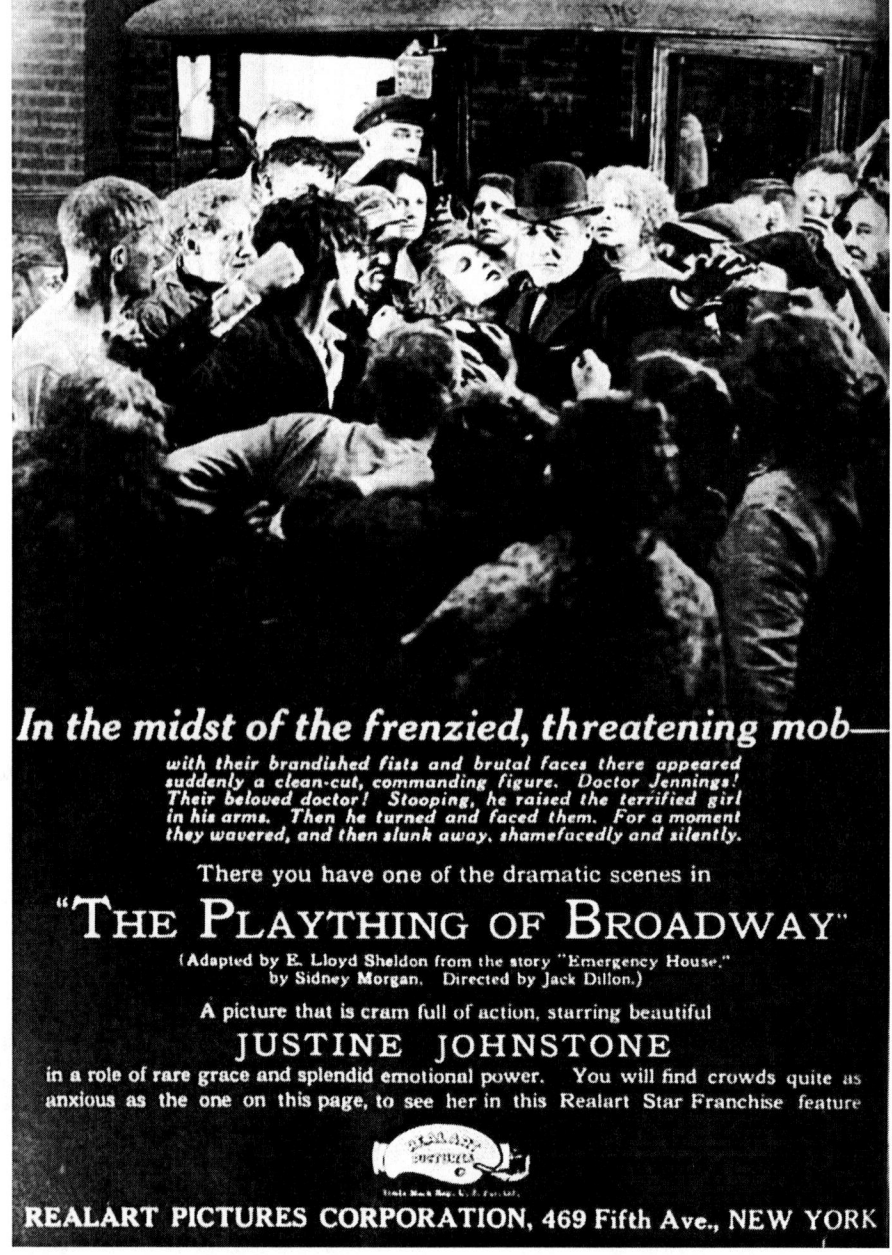

Above and opposite: Full-page trade ads for Realart's *The Plaything of Broadway* (with Crawford Kent), left, and *Sheltered Daughters,* both 1921. Courtesy Media History Digital Library.

wanted to be "eased in" to the public, "and let them get used to me gradually." Miss Underhill told Walter that she was certain Justine would be a success in films because "she is so beautiful." "Oh," said Walter, "it isn't her beauty. Lots of people screen just as well as she does. But she works with her heart and her brain." It might be a given response for some managers, certainly some manager-husbands, but Justine's comment hints that this might not always have been the case.

"Thank you, Walter," she said, "for believing I have both. That is one of the nicest things you've ever said to me."[18]

A big topic reporters would toss to Justine was that of work vs. marriage, as the two were seemingly so incompatible. "What Do Women Want—Husbands or Careers?" asked the Philadelphia *Evening Public Ledger*:

> Justine Johnstone, the charming young Realart star, laughs and asserts that she wants both, that she has both, and that they are on very friendly terms with each other—that husband of hers and her career. Only, she adds, one must select the career as carefully as one selects the husband, for naturally, not all males and not all careers are harmonious....
>
> She says: "It all works out beautifully. We have our home, our work hours, he at his office, I at the studio, and on our evenings and Sundays we are free to enjoy a variety of interests together."[19]

When asked if she cooked his meals or darned his socks, she bluntly answered, "Of course not." (She might have added that if Walter had sock issues he could have just bought new ones.) She didn't want to be characterized as a typical "wife" any more than she had wanted to be thought of a typical show girl.

> Success in marriage, to my way of thinking, doesn't depend on the amount of fussing a woman does over the man of her choice, but upon the number of things both are interested in doing together. My husband and I like to walk and motor and dance and sing and play golf and bridge and tennis together: we like to read and sing and go to the theatre and opera together; we like to argue together, and talk together, and plan my new pictures together.
>
> Perhaps it's because he is an unusual type that I find it way to harmonize my married life with my picture work, but the fact remains that I do, and I'm not ashamed to confess that I'm perfectly crazy about both my husband and my work.

The article noted that Justine had "struck unusual luck."

One aspect of her work that was not so lucky was the quality of her scripts. She seems to have tried to remedy that. "Justine Johnstone, who has been proclaimed the most beautiful woman in America," noted a columnist, again, "is also one of the best-read and cleverest business women in the country. One never sees the Realart star on the set between shots without a book on hands."[20] The reporter quoted Justine relating what she found to be an amusing story: "I went to the library the other day and asked to see some short plays," she told the columnist. "The librarian repaired to the stock room and returned a few minutes later with a book in her hand. 'We don't seem to have very much right now, but here are some miscellaneous plays by George Bernard Shaw.' And then she handed me Shaw's *Misalliance*."[21]

She didn't say why she was looking for "some short plays," but certainly a Shavian one-act could possibly have fit nicely into Realart's professed scheme of "literary films," unlike those she was actually making.

Justine's 1921 films were shot at FPL's new Astoria studio, which officially opened on September 20, 1920. It boasted spacious, sparkling dressing rooms and large commissary, where Justine would meet Walter for lunch. The cavernous sound stage, with its 30-foot ceiling, was variously called "the mad house" or "the boiler factory." Multiple films were shot simultaneously, each with its own crews, lighting, scenery, mood-enhancing musicians and barking directors. It looked like, and was, a factory churning output at a remarkably fast rate. But many actors found it an enjoyable place to work. Gloria Swanson called the Astoria studio "full of free spirits, defectors, refugees, who were all trying to get away from Hollywood and its restrictions. There was a wonderful sense of revolution and innovation in the studio in Queens."[22] That may have been true for top-ranked Swanson, but Realart doesn't seem to have been particularly innovative.

In *The Plaything of Broadway*, Justine was a sassy cabaret girl with a heart of gold who teases a young doctor on a bet, only to fall in love with him in the end. *Life* magazine called it "moderately entertaining" but admired Justine's "skillful portrayal."[23] Her character in *Sheltered Daughter*s was the aptly-named Jenny Dark, a troubled young daughter of a stern policeman, forbidden to go out or even read newspapers. She winds up hallucinating that she's the reincarnation of Joan of Arc and unwittingly gets mixed up with a gangster (Warner Baxter). The film magazine *Wid's Daily* praised the movie as "splendid entertainment with a strong moral," and noted that Justine "plays her part well in her own quiet and very charming way."[24]

For a complete change of pace, in *A Heart to Let* (co-starring the first film actor to use the name of Harrison Ford) she played a wily Southern belle who has to take in a boarder to make ends meet on her estate. To hide her true identity as the estate's owner, she poses as both a maid and an elderly woman. This role seems to have been potentially interesting, as it allowed her to put her shape-shifting stock experience into play. But the premise of the film was rather bizarre: the person for whom she assumes various disguises is blind. Robert E. Sherwood in *Life* magazine praised her work, "but she will have to secure something more tangible in the story line if she is to qualify as a legitimate star."[25]

Unfortunately, none of Justine's Realart films are known to have survived, so a firsthand, contemporary evaluation is impossible at present. Realart may have benefited somewhat from the fact that its chief editor was future Paramount director Dorothy Arzner, now known as a pioneer woman filmmaker, but Arzner worked at the Los Angeles studio, and it's unclear if she had any hand in Justine's films. In addition, it appears that A-list directors didn't do Realart. Swanson was getting Cecil B. DeMille and Sam Wood at FPL. Justine primarily worked with John (Jack) Dillon and his brother Edward, workmanlike directors who split their time between directing and acting. At least

Film stills from Realart's *Sheltered Daughters*, with Justine as a naïve woman who falls in love with a gangster (Warner Baxter) and imagines herself a modern-day Joan of Arc. Courtesy Mr. Justin Wrangler.

according to press reports at the time, some of her films fared better than others, as did she.

All of Justine's films fell into the same general distribution policy of so many at the time: a week's release, shown with a supplementary live performance and/or a second feature, and then forgotten, like a blog post deleted after it receives a few "likes." None of them seemed to challenge her. Interestingly, in all of her interviews at the time, she rarely even mentions her films.

By mid–1921, Justine allowed her Realart contract to drop. She had a better idea. Besides, she was leaving town.

10

Actress-Manager

Walter was being shipped to a new Famous Players–Lasky facility outside London. He'd been contributing considerably to Lasky's portfolio, including the purchase of a story called *The Sheik*, resulting in a monster hit film that made Rudolph Valentino a star. Now salary disputes and policy disagreements were boiling over. Lasky was unhappy with Walter's occasionally volatile management style, and sent him away to cool off. "He has a diabolic knack," Lasky said of Walter, "of fanning the flames."[1]

Before departing, Justine made an intriguing announcement. She would be producing her own films in Europe. Specifically, she would make films that would counter the "false impressions" of women that films created.

"I think pictures today show women in rather a bad light," she said. "They are either pictured as too noble and unworldly for words, or they are made to appear frivolous, selfish creatures given to ridiculous gowns and even more ridiculous manners. I shall try to show women as they are—real people who are doing real work in the world."[2]

Justine would reportedly meet with Swedish feminist Ellen Key for advice, and hoped to recruit Italian writer Gabriele D'Anunzio as a scenarist. Her first film would be called *Fifth Avenue* and would, according to the press, "set forth the development of women in social and civic life during the past quarter of a century, with the growth of New York's famous street as a symbol."[3] Her passport application listed the UK, France, Italy, Germany, Norway, Sweden, Denmark and Belgium as her intended destinations.

Independent film production was a burgeoning business at the time for successful actors, such as Justine's friend Taylor Holmes. The trend notably included by female stars, such as Pickford, Swanson (backed by her lover, Joseph P. Kennedy), Justine's Folies-Bergère friend Olga Petrova, Marie Dressler, Theda Bara, Irene Castle, Mae Marsh, Dorothy Gish and many others. The rationale for the stars was simple: creative and quality control. The trend of female producer-stars would last a few years, then began to fade as the power of major studios increased and filmmaking became exclusively a boys' club.

10. Actress-Manager

Some such independent companies were by financial necessity supported and/or distributed by established studios. The 1921 *Film Daily Year Book of Motion Pictures* reported that Realart "may release" Justine's productions.[4] "She has a tentative releasing agreement with Realart to distribute her pictures," said *Variety*, "contingent upon the future quality of the output."[5] She advertised her film company in trade magazines with the cable address JUSTWANGER LONDON.

The Wangers rented a Mayfair home that Justine had decorated in a mixed modern and traditional English style. They mingled with London society and theatrical friends as Justine networked for film properties. Walter was both admired and chuckled over for his Anglophile pretentions.

The first Continental stop in Justine's search for scenarios was Paris. *The New York Clipper* noted on June 14, 1922, that "American artists are flocking to Paris in greater numbers than ever."[6] Among the current visitors were Irving Berlin, interior and scenic designer Elsie de Wolfe, and Irene Castle, who was performing at a nightclub. Guests at the popular hotel Les Acacias, the article noted, included Marion Davies and Justine Johnstone.

This falls within the time frame of a much-speculated, unproven event in Marion's life of which, if it happened, Justine would have been certainly aware. Sometime in the early 1920s, Marion supposedly gave birth to Hearst's daughter at a Catholic hospital outside of Paris. The child, named Patricia, was raised by Marion's sister and Justine's former *Watch Your Step* friend, Rose Davies. Rose and her husband, George Van Cleve, had recently lost a daughter in childbirth. Soon after the adoption of the child, George suddenly moved from being an Arrow shirt model to head of Cosmopolitan Pictures. Hearst and Marion would be extremely generous and loving toward Patricia throughout her life, including paying for her education and frequently hosting her in their luxurious homes. Rumors about Patricia's "real" parents were whispered or spoken aloud for years, but never printed in either Hearst's or Marion's lifetimes. Shortly before her death in 1993, Patricia Van Cleve Lake, who never knew her exact birthdate, told her son she wished that the truth about her parents be made public. She maintained that Marion had told her after Hearst's death in 1951 that her close, caring and very wealthy "aunt and uncle" were actually her parents.

Whether or not Marion's supposed hospital stay near Paris was a factor, Justine is noted at this time as spending a good amount of her time visiting hospitals and clinics, even observing operations, and was a fundraiser for at least one London hospital. She was still developing for film projects, but she was also beginning to develop a serious interest in medical research.

It was in Paris that Justine made her one known European film. *Survivre*, released in France in 1923, was directed by Edouard Chimot, a surrealist illustrator who made only a handful of films. French cinematographer Maurice

Forster shot the film in black and white with color sequences. Justine starred as a war widow trying to rebuild her life in Indochina with a new beau, and makes the rather startling discovery that her late husband's soul has taken up residence in a young woman. The film was described in a French film magazine as being "extremely curious," as well as a "fascinating psychological drama," and that Justine "is a beautiful woman with beautiful artistic talent."[7] (The last 14 minutes of *Survivre* are maintained in the archives of the Centre National du Cinéma et de l'Image Animée, and its snippets of Justine represent the only known existing footage of her on film.)

The production company for *Survivre* is listed as Maxy's Films, with screenplay by M. Maxy, who may or may not have been Romanian avant-garde artist Max Hermann Maxy. The distributor was Films Artistiques Jupiter. It seems not to have been released anywhere in the States. Unfortunately, there is no information as to whether either Justine or Walter had a hand in its production.

There is also no information as to whether or not Justine made her planned trips to Italy, Scandinavia or elsewhere on her initial itinerary. While scouting actors for Lasky's film version of *Richard III*, Walter received news that Lasky had fired him. The official word was "resignation." "What we are wondering," noted *Photoplay*, "is, how Wanger's resignation will affect the affiliation of his wife, Justine Johnstone."[8]

The answer came quickly. Famous Players–Lasky decided to fold Realart due to postwar recession problems. With no distributor and no backing, Justine's filmmaking plans never got off the ground.

Walter briefly became manager of Covent Garden, dormant since the war, and turned it (temporarily, fortunately) into a lavish movie palace. He then accepted a management position with Provincial Cinema Theatres, got into some nasty arguments with its board members, was again fired, and sued.

Walter was becoming unemployable. Justine was doing print ads for the London jeweler Ciro. In the spring of 1923, she accepted a tour in a musical called *Toni* with popular Scottish song-and-dance man Jack Buchanan, who was an investor in the show. (Buchanan may be best remembered today as Jeffrey Cordova, the pretentious Laurence Olivier–type director in the classic 1953 MGM musical *The Band Wagon* with Fred Astaire.)

Toni was a frothy little piece based on a German operetta. Justine played the flirtatious Princess Stephanie of Mettopolachia, who convinces Toni (Buchanan), the proprietor of a fashionable millinery shop, to command the army of her country. Justine's role as the comic female lead, a sort of young Margaret Dumont type, appealed to her. She seems to have done well enough, in spite of director and co-author Douglas Furber's hiring a dialect coach to tame her American accent. However cultivated her speech, Furber recoiled at its occasional Jersey tinge. "[Justine] insisted on saying 'coy'-nel,'" said actress-coach Flossie Freedman. "It took me hours to teacher her to say 'colonel.'"⁹ On opening night in Edinburgh, the audience was so cool that at intermission a terrified Buchanan hopped on a train to London before remembering he had put his own money into it.

By the end of 1923, Walter managed to land a temporary new job. British revue impresario Andre Charlot needed a publicist for his first New York venture. Charlot's Broadway producer was to be Archie Selwyn, brother of Edgar, who had built the Princess Theatre with the Shuberts. The Selwyns were splitting their time between theatrical and film production, having partnered with Lasky's now-former brother-in-law Sam Goldfish to create Goldwyn Pictures, a mashup of both names that Goldfish would later take as his own.

The Wangers enjoyed Charlot's current hit, *London Calling*, with Gertrude Lawrence and actor/playwright Noël Coward, choreographed by Justine's *Over the Top* buddy Fred Astaire. The new Charlot production, *The Andre Charlot Revue*, would star Lawrence, Beatrice Lillie and Justine's recent co-star Jack Buchanan.

With such an extensive resume in film and theatrical production, being a press agent was something of a downgrade for Walter, but he was in no position to refuse. He jumped into the new project with gusto, creating stunts that he thought would sell tickets to American audiences unfamiliar with the British stars. The husband of the "loveliest woman in America" announced a "loveliest barmaid in Britain" competition for a lucky young woman whose talents as a drink pourer was apparently enough to qualify her to appear in the Charlot show. The winner was a very pretty, unsophisticated young lady named Bobbie Storey whose pub, Rules, just happened to be Charlot's favorite and was located behind his office.

The Andre Charlot Revue opened at the Times Square Theatre in January 1924 to favorable reviews, featuring songs such as Noël Coward's "Poor Little Rich Girl" and "Parisian Pierrot," Eubie Blake and Noble Sissle's "You Were Meant for Me" (not the one in *Singin' in the Rain*), and Philip Braham and Ivor Novello's poignant (as long as you don't sing some of the original lyrics) "Limehouse Blues." The show is primarily notable for introducing American audiences to Lawrence, Lillie and Buchanan, all of whom would enjoy success on both continents.

But Walter's work with Charlot was brief. The Wangers were "drifting apart," according to a friend, lyricist Hilda Brighten. "Their marriage was on the rocks," Hilda wrote in her 1949 memoir, "not for any reason other than compatibility. I fancy both were sorry that that could not get along together, and both realized they had arrived at the parting of the ways. They came to Maddie [Miss Brighten's sister, Madeleine Cohen] separately and together. She did all that was possible to cement their marriage. It was of no avail."¹⁰

Justine returned to New York from London without Walter at least twice, listing her name as "Justine Johnstone, single." It appears that at some point she looked up an old pal.

Guy Bolton was still as dapper, charming, urbane, pipe-smoking and complicated as ever—in other words, still not unlike Walter. He was also still married to opera singer Marguerite Namara but wouldn't be so for much longer, as chorus girl Marion Redford would soon give birth to Guy Bolton, Jr.

What seems to have been of more interest to Justine was that Guy currently had a hit on Broadway. *Polly Preferred*, a non-musical comedy, was being produced by *Oh, Boy!* manager Ray Comstock at the Little Theatre (now the second Helen Hayes Theatre, named after the demolition of the first, the former Fulton/Folies-Bergère).

Polly Preferred revolved around a savvy Brooklyn chorus girl who, through a series of misadventures, becomes a movie star. Sly Bolton may have had someone in mind: it sounds vaguely like the Marion Davies story.

Justine liked the show so much she bought it. She negotiated with Bolton, Comstock and his partner Morris Gest to secure the rights for a London pro-

Above and opposite: London, 1921–1924: Justine toured England in a musical, *Toni*, with Jack Buchanan and purchased the rights to Guy Bolton's *Polly Preferred*, in which she starred. She also found time to relax with a habit she said she picked up from British women. Left to right: Courtesy Mr. Justin Wanger; Harry Ransom Center, the University of Texas at Austin; Media History Digital Library.

10. Actress-Manager

duction. According to the press, the purchase was made "through her husband."[11] As her manager, Walter probably would have had his name on the deal, even if Justine had made it herself. But, perhaps in keeping with the tenor of the time, the wording makes the transaction sound like a concession to the general assumption of a husband's purchasing power over a wife's, even though Justine had been working for years, and Walter was currently unemployed.

Justine was now being referred to as an "actress-manager."[12] What she actually managed was a job for both her husband and herself. In the process, she seems also to have given the marriage a second chance.

In the spring of 1924 the Wangers booked Bolton's *Polly Preferred* at London's Royalton Theatre. They imported the Broadway director, Winchell Smith, and a comic actor, a genial, foul-mouthed newcomer named David Burns who would have a career for the next fifty years.

The play opens as Polly, an out-of-work chorus girl, sits moping at a Broadway Automat. She's just lost her first speaking role to a girlfriend of one of the show's wealthy backers. The caddish backer then enters and tells Polly that she can have her job back, *if*. She angrily brushes him away. In walks Bob, a young salesman who also has just lost his job. Bob and Polly share their sob stories until Bob has an idea: he's such a good salesman that he could pass Polly off as a successful, glamorous actress that somehow nobody has ever heard of, introduce her to society gents, and get them to back her "new film production company." Then she'll become a star and they'll both get rich. Amazingly, the plan works—thus Polly "preferred" becomes a pun on stock shares. She becomes a huge Hollywood star, basking in success, until one of her investors turns out to be the wealthy cad from the Automat. Recognizing Polly, he threatens to ruin everything but, of course, all works out well in the end, and Polly marries Bob.

The show gave Justine a wonderful opportunity to show off her comedy chops, switching from street-smart Polly to the glamorous, sophisticated movie star persona. Walter even managed to produce a "cinematographic interlude" to showcase Justine/Polly in action on screen.

When given the chance, and the material, Justine came through. *Polly Preferred* at last gave her an opportunity to do something, not simply be "there for looks." Bolton's Anglo-American humor translated reasonably well for London audiences, although some found the plot a bit too silly for their taste. But Justine received glowing notices. *The Observer* said, "Miss Justine Johnstone's impersonation of Polly was, to my mind, so life-like that it left me guessing as to whether it was due to art or nature."[13] A visiting *New York Post* critic reported that she was "always fascinating" in the role, and her performance "would be a revelation"[14] to her American fans accustomed to seeing her in musicals.

Variety proclaimed that Justine "totaled a brilliant score" in the title role to which she was "perfectly fitted,"[15] and predicted that she would be the reason the show would succeed. "England applauds her," reported a syndicated review, adding a bit bizarrely that the New Jersey-born actress "has returned to her native county, England, after scoring a success in America with her beauty."[16]

Walter as general manager of Paramount Pictures, 1920s. Courtesy Walter F. Wanger Papers, Wisconsin Center for Film and Theater Research.

After the show's limited run, Justine sailed back to New York to shop for more properties. "Justine Johnstone is seen at all the first nights," wrote theatre columnist S. Jay Kaufman, who called her "the Toast of London … looking lovelier than when she first went abroad as Mrs. Walter Wanger. Justine is filled with the joy of living. She is ever on her tiptoes with exhilaration and radiates vitality. She is looking for plays to take to London for her husband to produce for her."[17]

As it happened, *Polly Preferred* was the first and last show her husband would produce for her. In July 1924, Jesse Lasky paid a call on Walter. Lasky was in town to negotiate screen rights to J. M. Barrie's *Peter Pan*, which had been a Charles Frohman Broadway property. Lasky

10. Actress-Manager

hadn't been happy with Walter's replacements, and came up with a rather spectacular offer: general manager of both the New York and Los Angeles studios. FPL was preparing new production headquarters at 1501 Broadway at Forty-Third Street, a 39-story jewel of a building, soon to be known as The Paramount Building or simply, within the theatrical community, "1501." It would boast spacious offices and a four-thousand-seat, luxurious opera house of a theatre. Walter was promised an office at the new building, frequent travel to the West Coast, and a starting salary of $150,000 a year, double what he'd been making in London. He probably swam to 1501.

11

The Two-a-Day

With the promise of a more financially secure future, the Wangers returned to New York and rented a comfortable apartment on East 55th Street. Justine visited her parents, now living in New Rochelle, where her father had recently become a naturalized American citizen. She also began catching up on the latest theatrical offerings.

She checked out a Connecticut preview performance of a new play called *Dancing Mothers* starring her much-admired acquaintance Helen Hayes and featuring her friend Rae Selwyn, Archie and Edgar's sister. Helen played the flapper-daughter of a concerned mother, who learns that not only is her daughter "stepping out" but so is her husband. The mother threatens to leave the family, but all ends predictably well in the last act.

Justine thought it was terrible. Here was an example of the type of depiction of women she hated, one that presented them as "too noble and unworldly for words." After the performance, she spoke with the writer-producers, Edmund Goulding and Archie Selwyn. Justine "audibly yearned for once in her life to see one of these threatening mothers really walk out," wrote Alexander Woollcott in the *New York Sun*. So she asked Edmund and Archie, why not have the mother run off to Paris with a boyfriend? The producers listened. The last act was rewritten per Justine's suggestion, and the revised play enjoyed a run of nearly a year at the Booth in Shubert Alley. Justine's idea was, Woollcott noted, "not an unintelligent bet."[1]

Walter was embracing his new role at Famous Players–Lasky. The studio had grown to such a degree that Walter no longer was responsible for specific productions; that was now in the hands of studio "heads." He and Lasky were overseeing strategic planning, contracting and budgets. He also announced that he had bought the rights to *Polly Preferred* and would produce a film version starring Justine.

Walter could spot talent, produce eye-catching publicity and envision sometimes spectacular concepts, but when it came to managing the career of his wife, one of the best-known names in entertainment, he seems to have

11. The Two-a-Day

been at a loss. He may not have had time, or may not have wanted to make time. *Polly Preferred* languished at FPL. Ultimately the rights were sold to MGM. Bolton's play was reworked considerably and finally became the 1928 Hearst Cosmopolitan film *Show People* directed by King Vidor. It was a delightful platform for Marion Davies' comedic talent.

As she had in London, Justine took the reins of her own career.

She had been courted by New York vaudeville producers for years but had resisted, preferring to focus on legit drama. But an interesting trend was happening at the moment. Vaudeville producers were on the lookout for big-name legit stage talent to heighten the quality of their variety productions and compete with movies and radio. After enjoying Andre Charlot's revues, Justine decided this might be a route for her. She learned that Genevieve Tobin, who had originated Justine's role in *Polly Preferred* on Broadway, was about to tour in a one-act vaudeville version of the show. Justine found no reason why she couldn't do the same. A thirty-minute sketch in vaudeville could pave the way to a full-length play on Broadway.

She made the rounds with "a rather daring"[2] but unnamed sketch that she had seen Gertrude Lawrence perform in London, and subsequently purchased. Apparently no one was interested in the sketch, but they were interested in her. Max Gordon and Albert Lewis, partner booking agents and future Broadway producers, were delighted to meet with Justine. She could not have done much better: Gordon and Lewis worked for Keith-Albee, the Tiffany circuit of East Coast vaudeville headed by Edward F. Albee (who would become the adoptive grandfather of playwright Edward Albee).

Justine suggested a play she may have had in mind since scouting material for Realart: *How He Lied to Her Husband*, a short, satirical one-act by one of her favorite playwrights, George Bernard Shaw.

Headliner for the Keith-Albee circuit, 1924–1925. The reverse side of the photo is marked "To be returned to Palace Theatre," the vaudeville mecca. Courtesy Billy Rose Theatre Division, New York Public Library for the Performing Arts, Astor, Lenox and Tilden Foundations.

Written in 1905 as a curtain-raiser for Irish-American actor Arnold Daly, *How He Lied to Her Husband* concerns an aristocratic married woman, Aurora, having an affair with a young poet. The woman and her lover are mortified when they learn that his romantic poems to her have been stolen, and suspect that her unpleasant sister-in-law has filched them to show to Aurora's husband. The young poet, Henry, begs Aurora to leave her husband and run away with him immediately. Aurora refuses to be part such of a scandal, and besides, she says, would never leave her husband. Henry, crushed, realizes he is only a dalliance for her. When Aurora's husband Teddy arrives on the scene with the poems, Henry insists that his inspiration was "Aurora," as in the "rose-colored dawn." He angrily claims that he would never write poems for Aurora, as he truly finds her cold and indifferent. Teddy suddenly becomes furious. This, he says, is an insult to his wife, and tells Henry that she has been admired by much better than he. The two men fight, Aurora breaks it up, and the shaken Henry admits that he does indeed love Aurora. Husband Teddy is delighted. He is in fact so gratified that he offers to have the poems published, which thrills both Henry and Aurora. Teddy asks what title they should give the poems: perhaps "To Aurora." "I should call it," says Henry, "'How He Lied to Her Husband.'" (Audience: "Ah!"; curtain.)

The play had the type of wit and sophistication Justine loved. It also was short enough to serve as an introduction of herself as a non-musical actress to American audiences. She knew she could carry it off. Gordon and Lewis agreed. However, Arnold Daly himself, the original Henry from nearly 20 years before, had already approached them with the idea. Daly, a onetime matinee idol now in his forties (and still eager to play an 18-year-old), was suffering a severe career slump. Both Justine and Daly wanted it badly enough, and agreed to collaborate. Morris Stevens, a busy character actor comfortable with both light comedy and Shakespearean tragedy, completed the trio as the husband Teddy.

Daly received top billing with Justine second, but the playlet itself was listed first in advertisements of the bill. In addition to *How He Lied,* the show included coloratura soprano Belle Story; singer-comedian Bert Hanlon; Dollie and Billie, a sister act of wisecracking singer-dancers; acrobatic dancers John Guiran and La Petite Marguerite; and concert pianist Eric Zardo. (For anyone who remembers, or has ever watched videos of, the old *Ed Sullivan Show,* that was vaudeville: eclectic, sometimes anachronistic, but usually something for everyone.)

In August 1924, Justine opened at the Palace, Broadway's vaudeville mecca that Walter Kingsley had determined the ultimate "arrival" venue. It proved a triumph. "Miss Johnstone is one of the rare young women," said the *Philadelphia Inquirer,* "who combine gorgeous beauty with mental brilliancy and exceptional dramatic ability."[3] The bill went on the road, and Justine

11. The Two-a-Day

Broadway at 45th Street, ca. 1921. "The Great White Way" with its animated electrical billboard advertisements. Sign for the Ziegfeld Follies is at center; the Palace, where Justine made her 1924 vaudeville debut, is at right. The Miriam and Ira D. Wallach Division of Art, Prints and Photographs: Photography Collection, The New York Public Library. "Broadway north from 45th St." New York Public Library Digital Collections. Accessed May 19, 2017.

found that she loved it. The Albee circuit at this time boasted luxurious theatres at every stop, with dazzling lobbies and dressing rooms complete with baths and Turkish towels. There was no mannequin posing; all the girlie stuff was done by others. And she was familiarizing herself to American audiences as a non-musical performer. It brought her to an upper rung of the business that, for the first time, had nothing to do with being a "show girl."

One particularly exciting perk of her newly-refurbished career was a visit to the White House. In October 1924, Shubert megastar Al Jolson was recruited by a public relations rep to round up top Broadway players for a publicity event with President Calvin Coolidge. It was no small honor for Justine to be among those invited by Jolson. Others included a number of her friends and acquaintances—Ed Wynn, John Drew, Jr., her fellow Dillingham and Realart star Raymond Hitchcock, dancer-comedienne Charlotte Greenwood, actress (and future American Theatre Wing co-founder) Antoinette Perry, and the notoriously unprofessional but apparently interesting Dolly Sisters.

Justine traveled with the group by midnight train to Washington's Union Station, where they were whisked by limousine to the White House. They breakfasted on pancakes and sausage with President and Mrs. Coolidge in the State Dining Room. The performers then entertained the First Couple on the lawn, with Al Jolson singing with the first jazz band to play the White House. Justine, noted as wearing "a modest brown, topped by a close-fitting felt hat,"[4] sang with a chorus as backup for Jolson. The president's wife Grace, a theatre-lover clearly delighted with the proceedings, also sang along and held an ending high note longer than the pros, to exuberant applause. The president's reaction was, as usual, impossible to gauge. The well-covered event garnered headlines across the country such as "Actor Eats Cake with the Coolidges.... President Nearly Laughs."[5]

"Happy New Year 1925" greeted *New York Telegram and Evening Mail* columnist S. Jay Kaufman in an open letter to a number of New York notables. Included on his list: "To Justine Johnstone, because she gave a splendid performance in Shaw's *How He Lied to Her Husband*."[6]

Also noted was Walter Wanger, "because he is peter-panish." It was both in reference to the recent and charming FPL hit film, and to Walter himself.

Walter's star was rising. He was creating a sophisticated, cosmopolitan style for FPL's East Coast films that would characterize the studio for years. He was also creating a personal style that would characterize him for years. It was by this time, at least, that Walter Wanger began considering infidelity part of his job description.

"A nice enough man under normal circumstances," Ginger Rogers would recall of Walter at the Astoria studio, "but when he arrived on the set for a conference with the director, he always found time to check out the new females. He'd spot a starlet and look her up and down like a horse trader. Most of the crew snickered when they saw him on the prowl."[7]

Some of the women with whom Walter had affairs, if they could be characterized as such, had successful careers, although not necessarily because of him. Louise Brooks was one. A former member of the noted Denishawn modern dance company, Louise was appearing in the 1925 *Follies* when Walter signed the 18-year-old for FPL. They began an affair almost immediately, about the same time Louise had a brief New York fling with Charlie Chaplin and almost certainly while Justine was out of town. (By 1925, Justine was sporting a Louise Brooks shingle bob.) Brooks had some early success at FPL before dumping the studio over a salary dispute. She moved to Europe, and her films for G. W. Pabst would be considered classics of German expressionism.

Another of Walter's (and reportedly Louise's) lovers was Tallulah

11. The Two-a-Day

Bankhead, who also probably didn't need Walter as a career boost but slept with him anyway. Marlene Dietrich accepted an invitation from Walter to join him and Justine for dinner. When he showed up alone and proceeded to "woo Dietrich ardently,"[8] the actress rebuffed him.

Walter's ability to successfully "woo ardently" of course depended on who he was wooing. One of his later lovers, Aileen Mehle, said, "He understood women better than anyone I know. He knew how women thought, how to handle women. He knew women's sensitivities, that they always want to look beautiful and have their best foot forward."[9] In Miss Mehle's world, this was probably true. Otherwise known as Suzy Knickerbocker, Miss Mehle was almost female-impersonator glamorous and a society gossip columnist at a time "when high society still preoccupied mass audiences as passionately as Hollywood stars did."[10]

Most of Walter's shenanigans were with chorus girls. He and other producers would recruit minor female players to participate in studio parties for wealthy investors. Some of the women may have received a line or two in a film for going along with what many women called "business as usual." Of course, sexual harassment would be a more accurate name for it, but at the time, there was no such concept.

Walter seems to think he had no choice in the matter. Speaking of the studio parties, he said, "If you didn't take the young lady on your right upstairs between the soup and the entree, you were considered a homosexual."[11] (Which apparently was worse than taking unfair advantage of another human being, cheating on one's wife, possibly dealing with unplanned fatherhood or having to pay for an illegal abortion, or perhaps getting an incurable disease. But impulse control seems not to have been among Walter's talents.)

Justine, by all indications, looked the other way. It was, after all, business as usual. A lot of studio wives were putting up with husbands' philandering. Some, like Jesse Lasky's wife Bessie Ginsberg, found solace in their own projects and their own lovers. Divorce was humiliating and painful, and among high-profile personalities, also public and expensive. Many studio wives simply stayed with their husbands until they were dumped.

If Justine herself had lovers of her own at this time, no one seems to have written about it. Perhaps her partners were not famous enough for the gossip to have survived. Columnists of the time certainly wouldn't have carried such information; even among the tattlers, such affairs were considered taboo for family newspapers. Justine's affairs, if they existed, were probably extremely discreet, which may have been a good thing considering Walter's reaction to wifely infidelity more than twenty years later.

Beyond that, the dynamics of the Justine-Walter relationship were defined, as in any marriage, by themselves. But it may have been marital issues that led to Justine's decision to spend at least half of 1925 out of town.

During a break from the vaudeville season, she returned to film work. Not for FPL, but for an old friend. William Randolph Hearst had dissolved his distribution partnership with FPL over a disagreement regarding block-booking, the process of packaging chunks of lesser-quality films along with star vehicles to theatres. His films would now be distributed by MGM. Hearst's breakup with Lasky didn't seem to impact his friendship with the Wangers, and Hearst used Justine for a Cosmopolitan film called *Never the Twain Shall Meet*. It was directed by Maurice Tourneur, one of the most celebrated film directors of the time.

Four years off the screen was long enough for Justine not to be considered top box office. The leading roles were played by popular Metro stars Anita Stewart and Bert Lytell, with Justine in a not particularly challenging secondary lead role as a wealthy young society woman. *Never the Twain Shall Meet* was a lavish South Seas romance drama, filmed partially in Tahiti and Moorea and with scenic designs by former Ziegfeld set guru Joseph Urban. Justine's character, Maisie, is the fiancée of wealthy San Franciscan Dan (Lytell) who falls for Tamea, a "half-caste" Polynesian woman (Stewart). Dan runs away with Tamea to her native land, where he finds himself miserable and ashamed. Back in San Francisco, a dismayed but hopeful Maisie convinces Dan's best friend to travel with her to the tropics to haul Dan back. Dan is delighted at their arrival and happily returns home with Maisie, while the now-smitten best friend stays behind with Tamea.

Never the Twain Shall Meet had a splashy New York premiere at the Capitol Theatre in July of 1925. Justine received favorable reviews, as did all the actors (no mention was made of Boris Karloff in a small villainous role). The film was considered visually stunning but overall rather disappointing. Hearst, who took a hands-on approach to his films, was unhappy with the results. He scrapped 140,000 feet of footage, ordered the actors back to the studio for retakes, and fired nearly all his production staff except for Urban.

Interestingly, in Anita Stewart's 1961 *New York Times* obituary, *Never the Twain Shall Meet* was listed first among her "best remembered" picures.[12] It is now considered a "lost" film. It would also be Justine's last.

After shooting, Justine had no problem going back on the road. Vaudeville playlets were being written specifically for her. She considered a piece by Elaine Sterne, a Paramount scenarist, and a comic turn with violinist Edward Stanley de Groot. Prolific vaudeville writer (and soon to be screenwriter) Edwin J. Burke sent her a script for a one-act called *Nora* that he had written with her in mind. She responded with her usual direct tact, elegantly letting him know that she hated it. Burke promptly wrote another, *Judy O'Grady*, about a shop girl who crosses swords with a society woman. Burke based the main character's name on a Kipling verse, "Judy O'Grady and the colonel's lady are sisters under the skin."

Judy the shop girl is approached by a lady novelist who wants to study her as the "average" girl. Judy is insulted, and says that if she had the novelist's clothes, she'd be far from average. Judy challenges the woman to a bet. The woman's fiancé is expected to drop by shortly. Judy contends that the man will pay more attention to Judy than his own fiancée if they were only to switch clothes. The bet is on. The women swap outfits onstage (this being vaudeville), the fiancé arrives, and *boing*—he's blinded from the war. All ends well for Judy as she learns a lesson in the superficialities of appearances and winds up happily ever after with the owner of the shop.

Justine liked it, and loved the idea of playing a shop girl rather than a society woman. Keith-Albee green-lighted it and created a bill around the 18-minute playlet for a Palace opening. *Judy O'Grady* received modest reviews but proved a personal success for Justine. Unlike her stinging *Over the Top* experience, it was noted that she was able to rise above the material. *The New York Times* said that "Justine Johnstone is this week's most interesting headliner at the Palace. Miss Johnstone, by virtue of her beauty and a real dramatic talent, manages to triumph decisively over the poor sketch in which she appears."[13] *Variety* was kinder to her than in the past, but just marginally. "She is a pretty good actress," said *Variety*, "in comparison with the rest of the world's most beautiful women." But the review went on to note that the playlet gave her a good chance "to show her abilities as a comedienne."[14]

The show went on tour, starting at the Orpheum in Los Angeles. Justine received top billing, followed by aquatic star Annette Kellerman, with Jack Benny third. Reviews for the comedian, who would become one of America's best-known and beloved entertainers, were excellent, but there was more ink on Justine for her comic delivery and "versatility of stage gifts."[15] And, of course, her beauty. Ads proclaimed, "Justine Johnstone, the world's most beautiful woman," and in smaller print, "and a great laugh show with Jack Benny."[16]

Justine made good copy in every town she played. She posed with local mayors and sports figures, and was gamely available for interviews that generally asked her the same questions about beauty, makeup, and fashion. A piece in the *Detroit Free Press* proved intriguing. The woman journalist found her backstage at Keith's Temple Theatre working on a dress pattern, "with an ordinary yellow tape-measure hung around her neck, and the tiny black pincushion of a modiste's seamstress" on her wrist. The conversation about dressmaking swerved into "what she believes will be the future of the present-day woman in business and the professions." Justine confessed to being a "feminist," but seemed confused about it.

> "I certainly didn't use to be a feminist," declared this Broadway beauty.... Here was not the Justine Johnstone of sculptured poses in a smart revue, but a more lovely, earnest creature who has begun to think seriously about the problems of her sex.

> "Undoubtedly I shall give my life to the stage, and I shall have to forget all my dreams of children and a home, a country place with dogs and youngsters tumbling about the lawns.
>
> "Lately I've been reading all the books I could get on women, and their place in the world. But the more I read, the more bewildered I get.
>
> "One of my great friends is [Walter's early employer] Elisabeth Marbury. Often we sit and talk of one thing and another, and I think, 'will I, at 62—Miss Marbury's age—want to be going down to an office, or sitting 18 hours a day in a Democratic convention?' Honestly I don't know. Women were put in the world to be mothers of men, and if some of them combine careers and home life, well and good. But for myself, I simply don't know."
>
> Miss Johnstone's husband is Walter Wanger, production manager of Famous Players–Lasky corporation. He is very handsome, says Miss Johnstone, and she is very much in love with him. But the call of the stage will keep her away from New York in the current sketch for many months, and after that, she hopes to star in a new play.[17]

The fact that she "didn't use to be a feminist" is interesting. During the plethora of women's suffrage activities in New York while she was appearing for Dillingham, Ziegfeld and Shubert, there is no evidence that Justine ever made a statement on the issue, but perhaps she wasn't asked. If she had no interest in feminism then, it appears that her now awareness was rising.

First-wave feminism, which grew out of the suffrage movement, was primarily concerned with political equality, with the assumption that social equality would necessarily follow. It didn't necessarily. Many contemporary aspects of feminism, such as equal pay and work-life balance, wouldn't become prominent dialogue for another thirty to forty years. Justine seemed to be struggling particularly with work-life. It wasn't happening for her. Combining husband and career was either-or.

That she "undoubtedly" would commit her life to the stage indicates she was considering the "either." On the other hand, that would mean she'd have to abandon her dreams of a family, and might wind up like Miss Marbury, middle-aged, elderly, working all day and night with no husband or children. (Miss Marbury's longtime companionship with Elsie de Wolfe may not have been recognized by Justine, or the reporter, as a de facto marriage; even if it was, it wouldn't have made the newspaper.) So there was the "or," and it was Walter. And Walter seemed to have no problem at all being married and engaging in extra-curricular activities. That was a conundrum. She had feelings, she had opinions. But her feelings and opinions on this particular matter may have been moot: Walter was the man. Concessions had to be made.

There were other areas in her life where she could break through a mind-numbing pattern of concessions. While playing the Hennepin-Orpheum in Minneapolis in July, Justine was asked to write a "beauty column" for the Minneapolis *Daily Star* every day of her week's engagement. She agreed, and offered up her preference for advice that was far more *Women's Health* than

Glamour. She recommended "walking sharply" for at least an hour a day, "hot or cold, wet or fine, breathing deeply and steadily all the time." Calling on her anatomy studies, she endorsed "nourishing food" and deep breathing to facilitate blood circulation: "For the heart is the pump which sends the blood out to the extremities of our bodies and so keeps all the body cells alive and healthy."[18] If the editor wanted hair and make-up tips for this "beauty column," he didn't get them.

The *Daily Star* was published by a former *New York Times* executive, and Justine's Minneapolis columns may have prompted her next blog. When she returned home in December to play the "Judy O'Grady" bill at the Palace, the *Times* asked her to write a story about her vaudeville experiences. She eagerly penned an elegant and rather giddy love letter, praising producer Edward F. Albee for his fair dealing of his actors (not

Justine in a 1926 photograph addressed to her father, content with her terriers after abandoning her acting career. Courtesy Mr. Justin Wanger.

a sentiment generally shared by most actors about Albee, but Justine may have had an eye on the next season), his magnificent theatres and "a genuine feeling of camaraderie" among her fellow players.

The majority of the piece was a paean to vaudeville life itself. "Instead of missing New York and London," as she assumed she might, "I developed a love for 'the road.'"

> They call it "trouping" in the lexicon of the music hall, but the word has no connection with the old-time "barnstorming." On the contrary, it means a delightful excursion through a wonderful country with amazing cities, whose audiences are eager, alert and cosmopolitan....
>
> I like the actors, expert, sure and finished in their work. I like the audiences, with no time for the poseur, the condescending, or the unready. Vaudeville fans ask for virtuosity and they get it. Again and again I have been staggered by the evidences of hard work done by vaudeville specialists in keeping fit for their turns.

She particularly seemed enamored of the "the argot of the two-a-day": "There are a thousand words and phrases back stage in the music hall that are native to the varieties. To be told by a veteran monologist that 'you had 'em in the aisles, kid,' means more to me than the studied phrase of a critic.... 'Wows,' 'flops,' 'hokum,' 'gravy,' 'squeezing blows,' 'hoofing,' 'ankling,' 'fluffing,' 'topping intermission,' 'next to closing,' 'canceled,' 'moved up on the bill' and a hundred other phrases come to have a deep and vital meaning and withal colorfully expressive. To chatter in the wings with veteran performers is an education in the show business."[19]

Justine felt that she had enough education in "the show business" to now take her next career step—a safe step toward remaking her career as a legitimate Broadway actress. No classics. No *Peer Gynt*. "It was of the highest importance," *The New York Times* would say, "that she would be cast in such a role as would afford her 'adequate possibilities for acting.'"[20]

Not great, of course; adequate. She found one. It turned out to be adequate enough to end her career.

12

A Tissue of Lies

In January of 1926 Variety was announced that a play called *No Questions Asked* had been booked for the 49th Street Theatre, a 750-seat house that Lee and J.J. Shubert had built in 1921. From a production standpoint, things seemed promising enough. Director William B. Friedlander had a good track record with both drama and musicals, as did most of the actors. Frederick Burton, cast in a patriarchal role, had starred in films for Realart, FPL, and Hearst, and had worked for nearly every major producer on Broadway. Future film regulars Cora Witherspoon, Ruth Lee and Kenneth Thomson all had impressive resumes.

One red flag was the producer. Charles K. Gordon was a 20-something Philadelphian and Harvard dropout who had begun his career as a gofer for the Ziegfeld organization, ordering "costumes, sets, and such."[1] He worked his way up to being a regional representative for *Theatre* magazine before deciding to become a producer. He teamed up with fellow Philadelphian Craig Biddle, Jr., of the Drexel-Biddle clan, who had recently abandoned a film acting career. Backed by the oats-sowing young Biddle, Gordon was able to mount a nice flop, *Poor Richard*, in the producers' home town. Biddle then bowed out of the partnership.

Gordon scored three theatrical attempts in 1925: the first was a touring musical, *Brown Derby*, which he co-produced with Fanny Brice and resulted in his being sued in a salary dispute by vaudevillians Bert and Betty Wheeler. The others were Broadway melodramas: *Cape Smoke,* which ran a few weeks, and *Just Beyond*, which ran a few days. His was a negligible resume.

Then there was the playwright. Alfred G. Jackson, a former sports writer for the *Bridgeport Star*, was working as a reader for the Century Play Company, a writers' agency. He had never had a play of his own produced, at least not on Broadway. In September 1925, he read a news story about $750,000 worth of jewels being stolen from heiress Jessie Woolworth Donahue in her suite at the Plaza Hotel. A private detective who returned the jewels and collected the reward was being indicted for the theft.

Jackson, inspired, scribbled a play in a few weeks with the assistance of dramatist Mann Page. They morphed the thief into an innocent victim of blackmail, the heiress into a wealthy judge's niece, and tossed in a romantic subplot between the two characters.

The blackmail victim is a young man who, as a teenager, had been a Wall Street runner framed for theft. Now out of jail, he is engaged to the judge's niece. But a slimy detective steals the woman's diamond necklace and pins the theft on the young man. The hero turns tables on the detective by revealing that the "stolen" necklace is a fake. How he knew enough to replace the genuine necklace, and why nobody noticed the "recovered" jewelry was paste, is not exactly clear. In any event, Jackson's ink was barely dry on *No Questions Asked* before Charles K. Gordon booked it.

The success of crook plays on Broadway was generally unpredictable, but the 1925–26 season had a genuine hit with the comedy-melodrama *The Last of Mrs. Cheyney*, which, coincidentally enough, also involved a stolen necklace. This particular play would have appealed to Justine for a number of reasons: it was produced by Charles Dillingham, written by *Betty* author Frederick Lonsdale and starred her *Follies* friend Ina Claire. It also featured one of Justine's favorite actresses, Helen Hayes (for which the *Mrs. Cheyney* venue, the former Folies-Bergère, would be named for years). *No Questions Asked* seemed like a nice coattail venture.

As Justine's manager, Walter could have booked her into the show between rounds of catch-the-chorus-girl at Astoria, but his Broadway street cred, never tremendous, was now nearly non-existent. More than likely the show came to her, or she went after it.

Part of a "winter regalia" photo shoot for *Theatre* magazine, January 1921, announcing her affiliation with Famous Players-Lasky (Paramount) subsidiary Realart Pictures. The "charming little Colonial frock" was described as black velvet with Mechlin lace sleeves; the hat feathers were bright green. Geisler & Andrews (Frank E. Geisler) photo courtesy David S. Shields Broadway Photographs Collection, University of South Carolina.

12. A Tissue of Lies

Justine signed on as the judge's niece. Her contract guaranteed a salary of $350 per week and a two-week out.

Then, following Jack Buchanan's example with the *Toni* tour, she became a backer for the show. She may have anticipated that the play would be a *Mrs. Cheyney*-type hit, but there were certainly no guarantees of that. It could have signaled that she was intent on learning more about becoming a producer. In any event, she was a silent backer: her $3,750 investment was entered under the name of her cousin, Lester Nielsen from Hoboken. The returns, five percent of the gross, would be directed to her.

Rehearsals began on January 26, 1926, at the 49th Street. They did not go smoothly. An actor was replaced. Scenes were reworked. The title of the play changed from *No Questions Asked* to *Back Fire* and finally to *Hush Money*.

After four weeks of rehearsals, *Hush Money* had a clumsy week-long preview at the Windsor Theatre in The Bronx. It then moved to an official tryout at Poli's New Park Theatre in playwright Jackson's stomping grounds of Bridgeport. An ad in the *Bridgeport Telegram* claimed that the play was both "Al Jackson's Hit" and "Pre-Destined to Be a Great Hit."[2]

It was neither. The reviews, while not particularly embarrassing, were mixed. Justine fared reasonably well, but some critics found the play a disappointing showcase for her, which actually was not the point.

Opinions were fairly summed up by *Variety:* "Miss Johnstone comes through with a vivid portrayal of her character, but were the piece written to feature the heroine more strongly, it would have been a fairer test of Miss Johnstone's ability as a legitimate actress." The play itself was "clever, brilliantly staged and masterfully acted. It is not, however, the play one would expect to be chosen to show off the wares of one so well known as Miss Johnstone."[3] The implication was that a lesser-known actress would not have been expected to "show off" her "wares," but simply be a part of the ensemble of actors. That was potentially problematic for both Justine and the show.

Gordon apparently considered Justine his primary ticket-seller. Although she was in a "leading lady" role, the show was not about her. Nevertheless, Gordon had her name in lights on the 49th Street Theatre marquee. Even Justine didn't feel that gesture was warranted. The script underwent more rewrites, including a completely revised final act. Justine was given more lines, but they basically rehashed her character's previous speeches.

The Broadway opening on March 15 garnered reviews ranging from fair to worse. "Regardless of the fact that it was all old stuff," said the *Brooklyn Daily Star,* "somehow or other it was enjoyable and not a bad piece of workmanship."[4] *Variety* returned to say, "*Hush Money* is interesting and entertaining. It's a question whether this type of play has a chance at this time.... Looks like one of the nearly good stage properties that just miss."[5]

The *New York Times* was particularly viperish, calling the play "of complicated structure and none too well-knit," and the last act "almost incoherent." As for the actors: "For some reason, the beauteous Justine Johnstone finds herself in the centre of all this, and not too hotly involved. Her role calls upon her to announce her sturdy belief in the hero's innocence at frequent intervals, and frequently in ringing phrases. Kenneth Thomson, as the hero, is as lifelike as the situations permit; the others, in the main, are pretty bad."[6] Still, compared to the *Over the Top* reviews, these were raves. A post–Broadway tour was planned. Ads began appearing in Chicago newspapers promising Justine's upcoming appearance in the show.

Then in early April, producer Charles Gordon called Justine into his office. He had a bad-news-good-news-bad-news story. The show was losing money, he said. The initial investment by upscale merchant Arthur Krakauer had run out during previews and Krakauer had refused to cough up more. However, Gordon had a Plan B. Hiram Bloomingdale, department store magnate and sometime Broadway angel, would be happy to provide financial backing.

But there was a catch: Bloomingdale would only hand over the money if a special friend of his took over a role—Justine's. The friend was Denise (Deena Rivka) Moore, a 22-year-old cantor's daughter with no Broadway experience. By remarkable coincidence, Gordon had just fired the actress serving as "general understudy" for the female roles. He replaced her with Denise, just three weeks out of the American Academy of Dramatic Arts.

Justine was no novice. She'd seen married businessmen hook up discreetly with actresses in her club. Her own husband had a string of "special friends." Heck, this scenario was the premise of *Polly Preferred*.

Thus her first reaction was not to directly challenge Gordon's decision. Instead, she asked was whether there was any guarantee Bloomingdale's patronage would benefit the show financially: specifically, would she get a return on her $3,750 investment? "Not necessarily," said Gordon. "In that case," she countered, "I see no reason to leave. It wouldn't be good business."[7] Based on his own reasoning, if Gordon were to replace her, he would want to find a name that belonged on the marquee instead of hers.

Gordon told her it didn't matter what she thought. She was fired.

Unsurprised, Justine asked that he then provide her with two weeks' written notice, "as stipulated in my contract."[8] Gordon told her he didn't have to give her two weeks' notice. He didn't have to honor her contract at all. It was an Equity contract, and Justine was not Equity.

That was a bizarre argument. At the time a producer could hire up to 20 percent non-union actors—known as the "80–20 agreement"—as long as they paid Equity initiation fees and dues for the run of the show. So it was

12. A Tissue of Lies

not unusual to have a non–Equity member working on Broadway. But if Gordon presented her with a contract, and they both signed, neither of them could pretend it didn't exist.

Then Gordon made a move he would later deny: he offered her money. Both Denise Moore and Bloomingdale, he said, would be willing to pitch in.

Justine ignored the bribe and confidently showed up at the theatre for the next performance. Gordon kicked her out. Depending on whether Justine or Gordon was telling the story, she either left quietly, or she didn't. "I simply said, 'hello' to people," she said. "Then I left."[9] And then she sued.

Justine hired prominent entertainment lawyers O'Brien, Malevinsky & Driscoll, attorneys for George M. Cohan, Mary Pickford and her husband Douglas Fairbanks, among others. An injunction suit was filed against Gordon with the New York Supreme Court. In addition to not being given notice, Justine formally claimed that she'd been offered "large sums of money"[10] from Gordon, Bloomingdale and Denise Moore to take a hike.

Gordon submitted an answering affidavit. His reps were the law firm of Heimann and Rubien, who had helped him establish Claire Productions, the producing entity for *Hush Money*. Abner J. Rubien was a star-struck former vaudevillian, wrestler, and race car driver who would be described as "the court of last resort for nine out of ten Broadwayites who get into trouble."[11] He liked to play rough.

According to Gordon's affidavit, he did indeed give her two weeks' notice, and let her go because her performance was "unsatisfactory."[12] Then things spiced things up a bit. Gordon claimed that during an early performance in The Bronx, she was "clearly intoxicated,"[13] stumbled around the stage and forgot her lines.

If Gordon was trying to rattle her, he succeeded. Her next move has all the earmarks of Wanger's habit of, as Lasky said, "fanning the flames." She went to the press.

"Stumble? Forget my lines? Appear under the influence of alcohol? Absurd!" she told an Associated Press reporter. "I take my work very seriously and I've always tried to do my best."[14] To *The New York Times*, she said, "The things in Mr. Gordon said in his affidavit are were horrid," noting that "the entire answering affidavit is a tissue of lies."[15]

She provided minute details of her meeting with Gordon. She also expressed empathy for Denise Moore. "Understand," she said, "I do not blame Miss Moore in the least. She's eager to get ahead, and here was a splendid opportunity to show her unquestionable talent as an actress." That was the extent of her empathy. "That she 'made good,' however, has nothing to do with the rights or wrongs of this case."[16]

Justine publicly challenged Gordon to explain why, if his claim of her intoxication was true, she had not been fired at the time the alleged incident occurred. In fact, she pointed out, it was after her supposedly "intoxicated" performance that Gordon had mounted that "electric sign with my name on it, [even though] I did not think the part justified my being 'starred.'"[17]

As to any returns on her investment, Rubien, Gordon's lawyer, claimed that she hadn't in fact invested in the show at all, since the venture in question had been made in someone else's name. Justine's cousin Lester Nielsen, the name-only "investor," was 17 years old and the son of a coal rigger, so it may have been a bit of a stretch to believe that he had actually put several thousand dollars of his own money into a Broadway show.

Still, reporters were curious about why she had used Lester's name instead of her own. She answered, "because I didn't want my husband to know anything about the transaction. He'd have been very angry if he'd known what I was doing."[18] Possibly. But more likely, she didn't want the theatrical community to know. Either way, it was a clumsy answer. It potentially made her appear girlie-weak when she needed to have the upper hand. Her entire dialogue with the press at this time is odd. For unknown reasons, Justine did not refer such questions to her attorneys.

On tour with the "two-a-day": Demonstrating a high kick to Creighton University footballer (later neurologist) Paul "Red" Fitzgibbon in Omaha, Nebraska. A cropped version of the photo ran with Justine smashing her foot through a *Hush Money* poster after she was fired from the show and sued the producer. Courtesy *The New York Times* / Redux.

The best card she held was her former leading man, Kenneth Thomson, who had already bailed on the show for a film contract with Cecil B. DeMille in Los Angeles. Justine asked Thomson that he, as a witness, issue a statement countering Gordon's claims that she was ever intoxicated at work. Thomson immediately wired a telegram denying Gordon's claim, stating that in fact he, Justine and Gordon had a working meeting following that particular night's Bronx performance. "You certainly were not intoxicated on that evening," Thomson insisted, "nor any other evening during the run."[19]

12. A Tissue of Lies

The telegram wasn't enough. Supreme Court Justice Jeremiah T. Mahoney wanted an affidavit from Thomson. Justine's attorneys asked for an adjournment of two weeks to obtain such a document from California. The judge said no, now.

Justine withdrew her damage suit, "at least for the time being," said her attorneys.[20] They issued a statement: "There has been no adjudication of any kind in this case, and Miss Johnstone is determined to vindicate herself and push the matter to a conclusion which will establish the real facts."[21]

Justine took no further action. "A conclusion" was pushed for her, and from another direction.

The Associated Press ran a full-page extravaganza that was syndicated nationally over the next two months. "A Blonde, a Brunette, an Angel and *Hush Money*" ran the header. Ignoring her points, the article claimed, "They called the play 'Hush Money,' but it just might as well have been titled 'Woman Against Woman.' A radiant blonde found herself aligned against an almost equally beautiful brunette—and then came the explosion!" The story was illustrated with a publicity photo, taken while she was touring in vaudeville, of a smiling Justine demonstrating a high kick to an admiring Omaha college football player. The player was cut out, and grinning Justine's high-kicking, pumped right foot was smashing through a poster for *Hush Money*.

The show dawdled along for another few weeks before closing and going briefly on the road. Denise Moore changed her name to Dennie Moore. She would become a popular character actress on Broadway and in films such as *Sylvia Scarlett* with her friend Katharine Hepburn, and as the gossipy manicurist in George Cukor's *The Women*. What, if anything, became of her relationship with Hiram Bloomingdale is unknown; she apparently never married.

Charles K. Gordon produced three more Broadway shows, one moderate hit (*Jarnegan*, with Dennie Moore in the cast) and two flops, then disappeared from Broadway after 1931. He directed or produced tours of revues and magic shows before landing a job at San Francisco's Treasure Island fairgrounds, where he was arrested on fraud charges in 1939.

Although Justine would occasionally be quoted on various issues in the future, *Hush Money* marked the last time she ever gave a press interview. It was also her last appearance on any stage.

13

The Wife of Justine Johnstone's Husband

Justine could have made any move she wanted at this time and worked with any of the many friends she'd made over the years. She had gone much too far in the business to be undone by the likes of Charles K. Gordon. She knew she wasn't a "great" actress, but was, based on the reports of her work in the final years of her career, a good actress. She wanted to blend seamlessly and successfully into a production with other good actors.

What she hadn't anticipated was how permanent her early, press agent-created public persona would be. Burns Mantle had chuckled at the beautiful 20-year-old Justine's serious ambitions, and the press was still chuckling at the 31-year-old Justine for the same reason.

Management certainly could have been an issue. She had done so much on her own, but any actor's career depends on good representation. Walter had agreed to help, even eagerly so, calling himself her manager. But Walter was a publicity man whose idea of great stunts included "the most beautiful barmaid in Britain" contest. If, as his lover Aileen Mehle said, he knew that women "always wanted to look beautiful," he may not have been the best choice to promote Justine as a legitimate actress. For all his creativity, he seems to have been stumped on this point.

Perhaps any manager would have been. Justin Wanger recalls: "One of my mother's biggest gripes was that when she tried to do serious acting, all anyone could say was, 'There was Justine Johnstone, looking as beautiful as ever.' That was her pet peeve. She wanted to be a legitimate actress, but nobody took her seriously." It seems to have been a no-win situation.

In addition, if Walter advised Justine to do something that he might do, such as her last disastrous rounds of interviews, it was a terrible mistake. After all, Walter was a man. When he stumbled, and he did, he had more opportunities to recover, and did. It didn't work that way for women.

How difficult all this was for Justine personally, how hurtful it may have

13. The Wife of Justine Johnstone's Husband

been, was never discussed publicly. The gossip columnists were either respecting her off-the-record wishes, or simply doing what they usually did: moving on to the next news cycle.

It was rarely, if ever, discussed with members of her family, even years later. Asked if she ever talked about her life in the theatre, Justin Wanger says, "Yes and no. Not to any great extent. I do remember her mentioning Lasky, but not much; just that they were friends." The play *Hush Money* and the name Charles K. Gordon rang no bells for Mr. Wanger. "Theatre was in the past for her," he says.

Justine made a decision. The constant challenges of either-or, husband or career, were over. She now opted for the "or." Justine simply became Mrs. Walter Wanger and re-entered private life for the first time since she was a child. She would voluntarily stay there as well as she could manage it.

She was never reclusive, however. Her name still popped up regularly in the columns. Invariably, her beauty was mentioned. She sometimes got better reviews for how she looked in a theatre audience than what was happening on stage. Wherever she went, most of her activities were linked to Walter's position as a film executive.

The movie industry, and therefore Walter's job, was morphing itself into a new identity. On October 6, 1927, *The Jazz Singer* premiered at Warners' Theatre at 51st and Broadway. The feature-length film was a rather soppy story about a New York cantor's son who wanted to be, well, a jazz singer. It was shot, and performed, as a silent, with the gimmick of sound for the musical numbers to showcase its star, Al Jolson, using the Warner Brothers' Vitaphone soundtrack disc system. It was a fairly new but not unknown technology. The Warners had been releasing Vitaphone sound shorts since 1925, featuring Broadway stars (including Jolson), vaudevillians, opera singers, jazz bands and classical musicians. *The Jazz Singer* was basically a series of sound shorts padded by a feature-length silent story. The film received only so-so reviews, but audiences loved hearing the charismatic Jolson sing.

Certainly Walter, Lasky and other executives were very familiar with Vitaphone, as well as earlier sound-on-film shorts produced by inventor Lee de Forest as early as 1923. But for various reasons, including cost, unpredictable results, and a few patent wars, studio executives did not immediately jump at sound. With the audience reaction to *Jazz Singer*, however, Walter saw the future. He dashed to a phone in the theatre lobby during the premiere intermission and shouted to Lasky in California, "Jesse, this is a revolution!"[1] It was not because he'd just witnessed the most remarkable technical phenomenon of the century, but because the sweetest sound he'd heard all night was applause. He proceeded to push for sound at FPL, now officially known as Paramount, and began hiring or recommending performers who would flourish in the new technology: Maurice Chevalier, Jeannette MacDonald, Ginger Rogers, Claudette Colbert, Miriam Hopkins, Fredric March, Frank Morgan, Ruth Chatterton, and others.

A nice coup for Walter was the Marx Brothers. Justine and the brothers had crossed paths frequently when they played the same towns during both her *Over the Top* and *Judy O'Grady* tours, the latter while the Marxes were being booked through the Shuberts. Harpo became a good friend. Now the brothers were comedy stars on Broadway, and Walter brought them to Paramount for their first film, *The Cocoanuts*, based on their second Broadway show, with catchy tunes by Irving Berlin.

With Walter as production head for both New York and Los Angeles, the Wangers' social industry gatherings included both coasts. Caricaturist Ralph Barton included the Wangers in his now-famous "A Tuesday Night at the Cocoanut Grove," a two-page illustration appearing in the June 1927 issue of *Vanity Fair* depicting top theatre and film names dining at the hot nightclub in LA's Ambassador Hotel. Walter is at table 1 with Hearst and other producers (in not-too-subtle poses depicting the Last Supper, with Louis B. Mayer in the center with a halo). Justine is at table 12, with her short blonde bob haircut, her exaggeratedly large eyes fixed on something Clara Bow is apparently saying, with Anna Q. Nilsson, W. C. Fields and other actors looking on. Barton's caricature became a pattern for flappers' silk party dresses (an example of which is housed at the Smithsonian).

Harpo Marx labeled this photograph "the four imposters": composer Richard Rodgers as Zeppo, Justine as Harpo (in wig and horn borrowed from him), composer George Gershwin as Groucho, and Cartier executive Jules Glaenzer as Chico, at a costume party given by New York society doyenne Elsa Maxwell. Courtesy Performing Arts Reading Room, Library of Congress.

Justine turned heads at one of society matron Elsa Maxwell's splashy New York costume galas, but not for the usual reasons. She joined three friends dressed as the Marx Brothers: Richard Rodgers a Groucho doppelganger, George

Gershwin as Zeppo, and Cartier executive and theatre groupie Jules Glaenzer as Chico. Justine was Harpo, complete with baggy coat, pants, horn and a wig borrowed from Harpo himself. In a photo of the foursome, a delighted-looking Justine mimics Harpo's "gookie" face. "You'd certainly never guess," said Rodgers' wife Dorothy, "that Justine was one of the most beautiful women in the world."[2] Even when she was intentionally unglamorous, she was glamorous.

By design, most of Justine's life was un-newsworthy. She met friends for bridge, golf, auctions or horse shows. As always, she read. A New York reporter ran a piece describing a visit to Justine's London dressing room several years prior. He was astounded that the room did not contain the usual star trappings, but "a high-brow novel and half a dozen serious reviews. I never thought I would find the *Fortnightly Review* in an actress' dressing room in London, but I found it there."[3]

A favorite book of hers at this time was a gift from H. L. Mencken, *The Human Body, a Layperson's Guide to Anatomy* by Trevor Braby Heaton. She and Mencken had remained friends since her chorine days and had kept up lively correspondences. Mencken wrote to his fiancée that Justine was now "a contented housewife, with horn-rimmed spectacles."[4] When Walter didn't respond to Mencken's request for an article for Mencken's magazine, *The American Mercury*, Justine volunteered by submitting her own:

Dear Mr. Mencken:

Before Walter went away, he promised you a contribution but I feel that he is too occupied to fulfill his promise for some time.

So to uphold the honor of the family, I am taking the liberty of sending you an article which is in rather rough form. I am hoping the idea will appeal to you and earn your leniency. You do such marvelous surgery that I am sure you could make it look grand for your swell magazine. It's to be anonymous or, if you like, you may put a trick name onto it. Enclosed is an addressed envelope, which I hope you will not hesitate using if you don't care for the wisdom our anonymous friend deals in.

When you trek up here again why don't you phone me.

Warmest regards,
Justine Wanger[5]

Mencken's response does not survive, but it's intriguing to think that he may have used Justine's anonymous article as a substitute for her husband's. He did call, as she requested, and the three of them dined together, Justine acting as subliminal collaborator as the two men circled each other regarding a potential Lasky deal.

This was a role with which Justine seemed comfortable: general administrator for her husband. She'd long known that concessions had to be made in her marriage. Now she found a niche in which she excelled. After all, Justine's ideas could be, as Alexander Woollcott had noted, "not an unintelligent bet."

Walter welcomed her help. It was Justine who still had the marquee name of the two and, arguably, more social influence within the theatre community at a time when the New York film industry was still farming Broadway talent. There were numerous coincidences (or not) of Walter using people who had either worked with Justine or were her longtime friends. *The Cocoanuts* featured Justine's *Over the Top* dancer-friend Mary Eaton, and was co-directed by her frequent Dillingham castmate Joseph Santley. Walter also arranged for a Paramount screen test for her *Over the Top* friends Fred and Adele Astaire. (Walter liked the results, but the Astaires did not, and took a pass.) It was through Justine's recommendation that he hired her couturier, Travis Barton, for the film *The Dressmaker of Paris*, which launched Barton's long career as a film costume designer.

Walter had been a negligible manager for Justine, but Justine proved an excellent manager for Walter. It was not something either of them ever publicly acknowledged. On the surface, Justine was simply a charismatic, supportive wife, always a plus for an executive. "Walter Wanger is a young man of many accomplishments," wrote columnist O. O. "Odd" McIntyre in 1926, "but is best known as the husband of the beautiful Justine Johnstone, which irks him not one bit."[6] Two years later McIntyre wrote a follow-up story about Walter, noting that even though the young producer was making "twenty round-trips to Hollywood a year" and was "one of the high-salaried men in the film business ... invariably people [still] refer to him as 'Justine Johnstone's husband.'"[7] Even McIntyre's stories promoting Walter were a Justine connection: the columnist had, years earlier, been a publicity man for both Ziegfeld and Dillingham.

The Wanger partnership seems to have been valuable to both of them. In 1928, following the unexpected death of Rudolph Valentino, major film producers began investing in substantial life insurance policies for their stars and themselves. Adolph Zukor and Louis B. Mayer named their companies as beneficiaries. Jesse Lasky named his wife and children. If anything had happened to Walter, one million dollars would be payable to Justine.

Walter may have been personally and professionally careless, but he was not unkind, and in fact could be a generous man. He provided well not only for Justine, but for her parents, Gustav and Sophia, now retired and living in Passaic, New Jersey. Walter continued to provide support for Sophia after her husband died in the 1930s.

Considering her options, Justine certainly could have done worse than living her life as Mrs. Walter Wanger. Not that she cared, but according to the social givens of the day, a former career woman now melding her identity with that of her successful husband was not considered a step back. It was a step up. Marrying well was a goal for many women at a time when job opportunities were often gender-specific and advancement limited. The supportive wife role was an acceptable, even enviable one.

13. The Wife of Justine Johnstone's Husband

Actresses who had left the business with little money, prospects, or reliable husbands were particularly vulnerable. Although Ziegfeld press releases would emphasize the "great wealth" that *Follies* girls married into, few actually did. Mary Eaton married and divorced three times, declined into alcoholism and died at age 47 in 1948. Peggy Hopkins Joyce, Lee Shubert's onetime lover who became a Ziegfeld girl the year after Justine's *Follies* departure, did marry well, again and again (six times). But once her celebrity and youth faded, she too lapsed into depression and alcoholism.

Justine's *Follies* dressing-roommate Kay Laurell died giving birth to her married lover's child. Allyn King, Justine's *Follies* replacement, took her own life, her mental and physical health compromised by starvation diets. Mae Murray, who replaced Irene Castle in *Watch Your Step* and was a fellow 1915 Ziegfeld girl, became an A-list silent film star, but bad management and bad marriages left her impoverished.

Olive Thomas married syphilis-ridden Jack Pickford, Mary's brother. One night in 1920, Olive, reportedly groping her darkened bedroom for a sleep aid, grabbed a bottle of what she thought was a relaxant that actually contained Jack's syphilis sore ointment. She swallowed a few gulps before screaming and died five days later, her death ruled accidental.

Bobbie Storey, the British girl who had won Walter's "most beautiful barmaid in England" contest, was pulled out of the *Andre Charlot Revue* by Ziegfeld for the *Follies*. After a few subsequent short-lived shows, unable to find work, she committed suicide in 1930 by gas poisoning in an architect's apartment.

This roll-call of heartbreak is fortunately balanced by many other former Ziegfeld girls who did have successful, happy lives, most out of the spotlight. A notable example is Mary Eaton's sister, Doris Eaton Travis, a 1918–1920 *Follies* dancer. The youngest and longest-surviving Ziegfeld girl, Doris managed a string of dance studios, enjoyed a 50-year marriage, received a college degree at age 88, wrote an entertaining autobiography (*The Days We Danced*), and appeared in 12 editions of the annual Broadway Cares / Equity Fights AIDS Easter Bonnet Competition fundraiser, the last in 2010, two weeks before her death at age 106.

By whatever combination of temperament, resilience, intelligence, physical and psychological constitution, and sheer luck, Justine was one of the Ziegfeld girls who never became a tragic former anything. The word "former" seemed not to even interest her. Her interests were in the present and future, and what she could do with them.

If anyone had anything to say about Justine having "failed" in the theatre, she had the last laugh. At Elsa Maxwell's 1928 "Come as Your Opposite" party, men dressed as women, women as men, a society lady came as a prostitute, and Fanny Brice was opera singer Mary Garden. Justine arrived dressed as Lenore Ulric, considered one of the finest actresses of the day.

It isn't difficult to imagine that, even if Justine was not Walter's wife, she would have survived. She could have used her intelligence and many connections to leverage a producing or management career of her own, advising others as she was advising Walter. Female producers were rare at the time, but there were notable exceptions, such as Henry Harris' widow Renée, and Edgar Selwyn's wife Ruth, another independent woman often noted for her beauty as well as her smarts.

But being a wife had always been one of Justine's ambitions, and it was one that she was able to fulfill. The fact that she had also married well was a very nice perk indeed.

Actually, she had married so well that her role as Mrs. Walter Wanger was not a full-time job. She was a "housewife," but on Walter's income, that meant someone who oversaw housework, rather than doing much of it herself. She had time on her hands. And, being Justine, her restless curiosity led her to explore her options.

When a peripheral interest led to an opportunity to actually do something that utilized both her abilities and her intellect, Justine plunged into a new commitment to which she would be dedicated for years. The catalyst of the change in Justine's life was no producer, director, manager, or anyone in the entertainment industry. He was, however, a skilled professional who inspired and motivated Justine in a world she found she not only loved, but in which she did very well indeed.

14

Influence of Velocity

Dr. Samuel Hirshfeld had a busy private medical practice with a small office on the Upper East Side. He was far more than just a family doctor. Sam was also staff surgeon at Mount Sinai Hospital, a pharmacology instructor at the Columbia University College of Physicians and Surgeons, and a cancer researcher.

Tall, sturdy, slightly balding, with a gentle face and inquisitive eyes, Sam was, like Justine, born in 1895 and the child of immigrants. He and his younger sister grew up on the Upper East Side, where their Russian-born father Adolph worked as a building contractor. Sam received his MD from Columbia in 1918 and began as an intern at Mount Sinai Hospital the following year. In 1923, Sam's mother Laura, distraught after the death of her husband, committed suicide. The tragedy left Sam devastated and with a deep commitment to understanding the human condition. He developed a lifelong reputation for being an extraordinarily caring doctor and a good listener—so much so that he became not only a valued doctor but a confidant.

Sam lived with his wife Eleanor and son Alan in the Upper West Side university neighborhood. Eleanor was the daughter of attorney and arts patron Elias Rosenthal and sister of Lillian Rosenthal Goodman, who sang in vaudeville as Lillian Rosedale and was a onetime lover of author Theodore Dreiser. The Hirshfelds counted a number of theatre personalities among their patient-friends, including the Wangers.

The most often-repeated story about how Justine became involved in scientific research goes something like this: One evening Sam came to the Wanger home to tend to Walter, suffering from an undisclosed ailment. During the visit, Justine complained to Sam that she didn't know what to do with her life, now that she was no longer in theatre. She was looking for something "real." Sam advised her to try a new field, "like science."[1]

That's at least how the story goes according to a 1941 *Independent Woman* magazine article by Laura Hobson, the only public source for the events leading up to this chapter in Justine's life. "And so," Ms. Hobson wrote, "the strange Justine began to read heavy books filled with complex terminology." This scenario, however, seems a bit suspect. The "strange Justine" had actually been reading such books at least since she was out of high school, and all her friends knew it. Also, Justine was far too savvy about the theatre to consider it anything but "real."

Justine's son, Justin, provides another story: "One of the reasons she got into medical research was her involvement in the anti-vivisectionist movement at the time. She and Walter were at dinner one evening at a friend's house and she began discussing the issue. And a doctor friend said, 'Justine, before you can argue these points, you should know something about it.' The doctors of course felt they had to [practice vivisection] in order to make the advances. But she was going to show these doctors up. So she began taking courses at Columbia."

Columbia University has no record of Justine ever having formally enrolled, and would not have kept records of auditors or lecture attendees. Thus it could be assumed that she attended lectures without officially becoming a student.

There is also no record that Justine obtained a degree at any university, contrary to later reports. There could be any number of reasons for this. One

Columbia University, 1922, a few years before Justine would report daily to the institution's College of Physicians and Surgeons as a research assistant. Courtesy University Archives, Rare Book & Manuscript Library, Columbia University in the City of New York.

could be that having academic letters after her name might have made the twice-expelled Walter look bad. (He'd finally manage an honorary bachelor of arts degree from Dartmouth in 1934.) Another was that subsequent events kept her busy enough.

Whether or not Justine ever changed her mind about the practice of vivisection, she quickly became hooked on medical research. "Medicine," says Mr. Wanger, "was her passion." It also became something of a mission.

In September of 1928 Sam Hirshfeld was exploring the pharmacology and toxicology of melanin (the pigment responsible for skin, hair and eye color). He had noticed that skin cancer was relatively rare among his black patients at Mount Sinai Hospital, and wondered if melanin could be a factor; if so, it might be possible to create a melanin-based drug to inhibit cancer growth.

Sam asked the hospital barber to provide him with black hair cuttings, from which he hoped to create a melanin solution. He contacted Dr. Francis Peyton Rous of the Rockefeller Institute for samples of a "filterable virus"— that is, a viral agent so small it could pass through the bacterial filters used at the time and still remain infectious. (Although controversial at the time, Rous' 1911 determination that cancer could be caused by a virus would earn him the Nobel Prize in 1966. The virus he discovered, named the Rous sarcoma virus, has since been determined a retrovirus, the same virus family as HIV.)

Sam partnered on the melanin project with his loquacious, ambitious colleague, Dr. Harold Thomas Hyman. Harold was another Columbia University pharmacology professor whose private practice counted theatre-industry patients, including producer Arthur Hammerstein, a onetime Justine Johnstone Club regular, and Arthur's nephew and Harold's childhood friend, lyricist Oscar Hammerstein II. (Harold would claim that the 1947 Rodgers and Hammerstein musical *Allegro,* about a doctor's unfortunate marriage to a conniving social climber, was based on his rocky relationship with his first wife. By the early 1930s, Harold was having an affair with his nurse, whom he would later marry.)

Sam and Harold Hyman obtained permission to use the laboratory of their supervisor, Dr. Charles Christian ("C. C.") Lieb, head of pharmacology at Columbia's College of Physicians and Surgeons. But they hit a snag. In order to conduct the work and meet their teaching and patient obligations, they needed help. And funds.

A big problem with funding for cancer research was that it was a hard sell. Until the 1930s, many thought that cancer, any type of cancer, was a form of venereal disease, as symptoms would often be confused. Because of this, and the fact that it was deemed incurable, the word "cancer" was not mentioned in polite society, not spoken on the radio, not listed as a cause of death in obituaries. Donors did not want their names affiliated with cancer.

Enter the Wangers. Sam mentioned his plans to develop a "pure" form of melanin to Justine and Walter, and discussed the problems he and Harold were facing. To his surprise, they were interested. Walter agreed to underwrite the study. Even more surprising, Justine eagerly offered to help in the lab.

Harold Hyman was not especially impressed when Sam told him of the Wangers' offer. The money would be great, but an actress as a lab assistant; seriously?

Fortunately, it wasn't Harold's call. On October 10, 1928, Justine visited Dr. Lieb at the College of Physicians and Surgeons' sprawling, fortress-like new headquarters on West 168th Street. Dr. Lieb, a tall, large, friendly man, was known among his friends for his "civilized" dinner parties, bridge gatherings, and at-home musicales, where he enjoyed nothing more than showing off his stamp collection (he was the proud owner of a rare Inverted Jenny). His wife Henrietta Haaker Lieb, an alumnus of the tony Graham's girls' prep and Hunter College, was on the board of the Third Street Music School Settlement.

Dr. Lieb was pleased to meet with this professional performer. He was also impressed by her scientific knowledge and curiosity. Even more impressive was the talk of money. He discussed her offer with the school's dean, Dr. William Darrach, who seemed to have seen no problem. Dr. Lieb then sent Justine and Walter a proposed budget. The Wangers responded by creating what was known as the Wanger Melanin Fund with an initial donation of $500 toward a total grant of $5,000 to be paid by the end of 1930. Justine, either with Walter or on her own, would periodically make additional donations to the fund ranging from $100 to $700. "I am convinced," wrote Dr. Lieb in a grateful letter to the Wangers, "that a study of the actions of Melanin is distinctly worthwhile, and that your donation will make possible a valuable contribution to general knowledge, even though our hope for finding a cure for cancer may not be realized."[2]

Harold Thomas Hyman, MD, one of Justine's collaborators at the Columbia University College of Physicians and Surgeons, who became a confidant and lifelong friend. Courtesy Mount Sinai Archives.

14. Influence of Velocity

And then Dr. Lieb gave Justine a job. On January 1, 1929, Mrs. Justine Olive Wanger was added to the Columbia University College of Physicians and Surgeons employment roster as a Research Assistant in the Department of Pharmacology. On February 9, she began a trial schedule, renewable on May 6.

It was the beginning of her career that would be variously described pathologist, scientific researcher, even scientist, even though she had no college degree. Interestingly, neither did Thomas Edison or Nikola Tesla, also scientists. Justine may not have possessed inventive genius, but even though she was not a college graduate, she did the work of a medical research scientist, and did it well.

She reported to Dr. Lieb's pharmacology lab, with its tall, broad windows and overhead uncovered light bulbs. One of her first tasks involved phytopharmacology, the study of drugs on plant life. This was no problem: she'd done plant work in the science lab at Emma, "trained to neatness and accuracy,"[3] as the school's catalogue boasted and which she had no doubt retained.

With a full-sized white lab apron slapped over her couture, Justine mapped out a space at a flat, drawered table alongside graduate students. She cultivated a small garden and recorded daily measurements of her plants' response to various chemical solutions. Her lab mates were astonished at how quickly she worked and retained information, a common reaction among people dealing with someone from the theatre for the first time. It's a fair assumption that none of the others in the lab had ever had to pick up a dance routine, perform one role while studying another, or learn an entirely new third act after a show had opened. Still, her methods with the plants were considered "unorthodox"—she was a backyard gardener, after all, not a conventional scientist. But she got results. Dr. Lieb, who had a hands-on approach to his department's lab work, was impressed. When her trial period ended, Justine was approved for permanent employment.

Her salary: zero. This was not unusual. Female research assistants, even those with degrees, were routinely unpaid at the time. Justine, of course, didn't need the money. Besides, she was doing it for the joy of doing it.

She was first assigned to work on "The Pharmacology of Melanin," the name given to the project she and Walter were helping to fund. Harold Hyman's misgivings about Justine as a lab assistant soon evaporated. In his unpublished autobiography, he gushed:

> From the moment she appeared in the laboratory ... she took charge of all the routine work and all its participants. With Al, the peripatetic chauffeur of her Rolls Royce, she left home as soon as she'd taken care of household chores; motored from her home on East 55 St. to P&S on West 168 St.; fed, watered and observed the animals [lab rats] and cleaned their cages; sent Al for sandwiches, soft drinks and sufficient coffee to meet the Professor's [Lieb's] daily needs for a dozen or more cupfuls;

cleaned and sterilized instruments; shaved skin areas where injections were planned; observed and reported results of experiments of previous days; and set Al to 100 St. and Fifth Ave. to get and deliver Sam and/or Rous at the Rockefeller. Later in the afternoon, Al and the Rolls came for me; returned me to the lab, where we observed results of previous experiments, and planned protocols for the next day; and, when work was completed, delivered each of us to our next port of call.

In general, we proceeded as follows: Sam injected Rous virus into the designated areas of the animals' abdominal walls, which Justine marked for identification before returning them to their cages; each morning, Justine carefully palpated injection sites and, if there seemed to be a "take," sough verification by the Professor; if the Professor verified her finding, she called Sam or me and elicited shouts of such joy that any nearby auditor may well have suspected that "unto us" a son had been born.[4]

To the team's delight, they discovered that the cancer tumors induced in the rats were taking up their melanin solution, and that the solution was degenerating the tumors. That was in rats, however. When Sam and Harold tried the experiment on human cancer patients, nothing happened. Sam decided to discontinue the melanin solution experiments, and the Wanger grant for the melanin study was not renewed.

Justine had better luck on a new melanin-based assignment, this time reporting to pharmacology professor Solon Nathaniel Blackberg, known as "Blackie." The eclectic, enthusiastic Blackie had recently taught veterinary medicine at Texas A&M, where his work with ancient animal fossils had led to his becoming the namesake of Miocene Epoch species of horse (*Archaeohippus blackbergi*).

Blackie was curious about the occurrence of melanuria in tests of patients at Presbyterian Hospital, Columbia's affiliated medical institution. Melanuria, characterized by darkened urine, can be a result of faulty melanin production in the body. The problem that Blackie saw was that melanuria was being over-diagnosed in patients who were being treated for diseases unrelated to melanin, and under-diagnosed in those that were. He wondered if the melanuria tests themselves were resulting in pseudoreactions, or false results due to substances used in the test itself.

Dozens of urine samples were gathered from the patients of supportive and heavy-hitting doctor-professors such as Allen Oldfather Whipple, head of the hospital's surgery service and later a pioneer in pancreatic cancer surgery, and Walter Walker Palmer, chair of the Columbia's medical department and director of the hospital's medical service. Justine experimented with various solutions on urine samples, lined up on her lab table in colors ranging from burned orange to "Prussian blue" and everything in between. Some were left standing at room temperature for days to measure chemical reactions. (Science is not for the faint of heart.) Eventually Blackie and Justine created a solution of potassium persulphate and methyl alcohol that rendered reproducible results, providing a stride toward the standardization of the melanuria test.

14. Influence of Velocity   129

Justine and Blackie then embarked on a very different study. This one was financed in part by AT&T, which was looking for improved methods of treating its high-wire technicians for electrical shock. For this study, vivisection seems to have been involved. Blackie was a trained veterinarian; thus, one assumes, his methods were as humane as any animal testing could be at that time. But it should be noted that medical research involving animals prior to the 1966 passage of the Laboratory Animal Welfare Act makes for some uneasy reading, this one included.

Dogs and cats were anesthetized and then administered electric shocks with apparatuses provided by the phone company. Justine and Blackie would then immediately apply artificial respiration to the animal using tracheal tubes. If the animal did not revive, adrenaline was injected into the femoral vein, sometimes more than once. Ultimately Justine and Blackie achieved successful results with combinations of direct heart massage, respiration, and adrenaline timed to split-second precision. "Success" in this case was gruesome: some of their animals were electrocuted and revived a dozen times. The animal-loving Justine must have had tremendous powers of disassociation.

The best-known of Justine's studies was one with Sam Hirshfeld and Harold Hyman. Sam and Harold had for years been studying negative effects of intravenous injections and transfusions, particularly of treatments involving extreme amounts of toxic solutions. Such treatments were critical for those suffering incurable diseases. One such disease was syphilis.

It was the mother of all unspoken horrors. Even more than cancer, syphilis studies were woefully inadequate, often inhibited by wealthy donors' aversion to having their names associated with a venereal disease. That was unfortunate. 1930s estimates of Americans infected with syphilis ranged from one in twenty to one in ten. Treatment was chaotic. Because syphilis announced itself in the form of skin sores, much of syphilis study was done by dermatologists, and topical ointments, such as the one the ill-fated Olive Thomas ingested, were used as palliative care.

Besides the rather negligible skin care treatments, a syphilis patient would be subjected to early chemotherapy techniques, decidedly heavy-metal combinations of arsenic and either bismuth or mercury. The arsenic-based drug Salvarsan, developed by Dr. Paul Ehrlich in Germany, was considered a "magic bullet" for syphilis, and had been in use since 1910. (Penicillin, discovered in 1928, was not made widely available until after World War II.) The problem was that massive doses of the poisonous compounds were required, and because opinions about dosages varied, results could be unreliable. Patients would often suffer, in the quaint parlance of the day, "cardiac embarrassment."

Sam, Harold and Justine considered the possibility that deaths from syphilis treatments ("Ehrlich's various arsenicals,"[5] as Harold called them) were not so much a result of large doses of solution, but the speed with which those dosages were delivered. They called this reaction "speed shock," coining the term. They decided to try a different approach: severely diluting the solutions to allow for small amounts of delivery slowly over an extended period of time.

As this was "pure science" research, Team Justine did not deal with human syphilis patients. Harold rather flamboyantly considered himself and his colleagues "not card-carrying 'scientists,'" but rather "'conquistadors,' or adventurers to use the term Freud applied to himself."[6] Harold wrote: "Once again, we were permitted by the Professor to do our work in his laboratory. Once again, we had Al and the Rolls to solve our transportation problems. And once again we had Justine to 'run the show' that now included care of our menagerie of cats, dogs, rabbit and a monkey, of the smoked paper we needed for kymography [a technique for measuring the movements of organs] and of the more complicated records, illustrating our findings."[7]

Team Justine experimented with various compounds used for various diseases delivered at various slow rates on the animal models. Determining the rate of slowness was one big trick. They began experimenting with 10 ccs of solution per minute. Blood pressure would fall, breathing would become irregular. They lowered the delivery down to 5 ccs per minute; still too fast. How could they slow down even further and keep the solutions flowing steadily for a long time?

Answer: gravity. A bottle, a stand, a rubber syringe and a needle, and voilà: a variation of the Murphy drip, then used primarily for proctology, to deliver drugs directly into the vein. Intravenous drug delivery had been attempted for nearly 20 years, but no one had yet determined a safe rate of delivery speed.

Justine timed the experiments and recorded the animals' blood pressure, heartbeats and breathing. Often she would work alone for hours as the doctors tended to patients and students. Finally, after at least two years' experimentation, the team proved that 2 or 3 cc. per minute (between 60 and 90 drops) was the ideal rate for IV injections and allowed the body to safely adjust to and accept the substances.

Team Justine's mastery of the intravenous system of drug delivery was considered revolutionary. One hundred sets of the intravenous drip apparatuses were in use at Mount Sinai by 1931. IV units and injection timing based on the team's model would become commonplace in hospitals by the 1950s.

(Harold Hyman would be astonished when, in 1943, "the celebrated Creole surgeon" Dr. Rudolph Matas, whose parents were from Catalonia, told him in New Orleans that he, too, had determined that 2 ccs per minute was the best rate for IV injection as far back as 1888. Matas told Harold that his findings had been published in the *New Orleans Medical and Surgical Journal* when he was still a medical student. "His studies, however," Harold qualified, "did not touch on the reactions to rapid injections as described by us decades later."[8])

The main reason that we know about Justine's work in the slow-drip, revivification and melanuria test studies is because she is listed on as a co-author of the published results for each. The thirty-page "Influence of Velocity on the Response to Intravenous Injections" by Samuel Hirshfeld, MD, Harold Thomas Hyman, MD, and Justine J. Wanger appeared in the *Archives of Internal Medicine* in 1931, complete with 16 charts.

Justine then dropped the "J." for Johnstone as a middle name and replaced it with "O." for Olive. "Studies in Revivification—Organization or Resuscitation Measures" by S. N. Blackberg, PhD, and J. O. Wanger was published in the *American Journal of Medical Sciences* in 1932. "Melanuria" by S. N. Blackberg, PhD, DVM, and Justine O. Wanger was printed in the *Journal of the American Medical Association* in 1933. All three papers would be cited in other works, and continue to be available today on medical journal websites.

By and large, the readers of these publications were medical professionals. The mainstream press at the time had nothing about this. It would be years before the general public would know that Justine Johnstone, former *Follies* girl, was the co-author of three scientific papers published in distinguished medical journals.

Not that word hadn't spread about Justine's change of career. In September 1929, Walter Winchell reported in his gossip column for the Hearst's *New York Daily Mirror*, syndicated by King Features: "Playgoers and others probably recall the beautiful Justine Johnstone, who embellished the Ziegfeld corps of good-lookers a decade ago in one of the better 'Follies.' Miss Johnstone, it appears, is a Columbia University student, now taking up the 'finer' things, but she still frequents the 'smarter' first-nights with her husband, Walter Wanger, Paramount movie executive. Much more important, however, is the fact that the Wangers celebrated their tenth wedding anniversary on Friday, the 13th, marking the longest 'Follies' marriage on record!"[9] As was his habit, Winchell was a bit slack on the details. It actually wasn't the longest *Follies* marriage on record: Billie Burke had wed Florenz Ziegfeld in 1914. And Justine was apparently never an official student.

Nevertheless, Winchell's blurb led to some interesting variations. O. O. McIntyre reported in 1931 that Justine was now a "bacteriology student" at Columbia.[10] Other reports claimed that Justine was not only a Columbia student, but had graduated from the institution with an MD. Syndicated columnist Gilbert Swann morphed Justine into an odd combination of Gloria Morgan Vanderbilt and Clara Barton when he wrote, "It has been noted for some time that, although she attends the swankiest and gayest affairs in Manhattan,

Mrs. Wanger usually excuses herself at an early hour and goes home. The answer is that almost every morning she goes up to Columbia where she offers her services to home work among the neediest in the great city. She takes nursing cases and charity work of all sorts."[11]

Justine never attempted to revise or correct any of these items. She was too busy working.

15

Like Paradise

The New York film and theatre industries were in crisis following the stock market crash of October 1929. Comparisons vary, since much of the 1920s boom in Broadway production was due to laundered bootlegging money, but a general estimate is that in 1931 Broadway openings had decreased by 20 percent in just one year.[1] Legit houses became movie theatres, radio studios, cooch joints or were demolished. The Princess on 39th Street, home of the Wodehouse-Bolton hits, ricocheted between being a children's theatre, labor union theatre and cinema for the next twenty years. The *Follies* venue, the New Amsterdam, closed briefly, then re-opened as a second-run movie house. Charles Dillingham lost his beloved Globe Theatre on West 46th; it also became a movie theatre. Ziegfeld died in 1932, Dillingham in 1933, both broken and deeply in debt.

The Shuberts went into receivership. Groucho Marx and Justine's vaudeville director (now producer) Max Gordon were among others in the industry who lost millions. So did Eddie Cantor, a Ziegfeld comedian who had been making "talkie" shorts for Paramount, and famously sued Goldman Sachs. Actors, directors and writers who never dreamed they'd leave New York flocked to Hollywood for work—for cheap, but for work.

Jesse Lasky, wiped out, was fired from the company he co-founded. Paramount closed its beautiful Astoria studios, not even in operation for ten years. Walter, who had been regularly crossing swords with Paramount president Adolph Zukor, was expendable. He was fired from the studio for a second and final time.

Walter considered leasing Hearst's old Cosmopolitan studios in Harlem and producing independently, but he didn't have the cash. He accepted a position as vice president for "poverty row" Columbia Pictures, a considerable step down from top-ranked Paramount. Walter took the job for less money but with the promise of producing the types of films that appealed to him, socially relevant dramas. He was set up at Columbia's corporate headquarters at 729 Seventh Avenue at 49th Street, five blocks up from his more magnificent offices at 1501 Broadway.

But Columbia Pictures had no New York studio, and president Harry Cohn wanted Walter in Los Angeles. After numerous cross-country trips, Walter began talking to Justine about their moving west.

Justine probably would have loved to have stayed on at Columbia University. But the Depression was devastating academia as well: in its 1932 annual report, the university noted a deficit of nearly a million dollars, and scientific research faced severe cuts. Compromising Walter's advancement during difficult economic times would have been unthinkable. Justine agreed to the move, but seemed hesitant to consider it permanent. Her employment record at Columbia University was kept active with the notation that she was "on leave."

A Cuban vacation in early 1932 may have been a consolation gift from Walter for agreeing to relocate. Upon their return, Justine and Walter packed up their belongings from East 55th Street and took the five-day train trip to Los Angeles. One of the first people to welcome them was Justine's longtime friend Marion Davies.

Now an established film star, Marion had permanently moved to California in 1926, the year Hearst and his long-suffering wife Millicent separated

Early 1930s postcard of Marion Davies at her magnificent Santa Monica oceanfront mansion, at the time Justine and Walter moved to California and stayed in one of the "beach house" guest bungalows. Courtesy Werner von Boltenstern Postcard Collection, Department of Archives and Special Collections, William H. Hannon Library, Loyola Marymount University.

15. Like Paradise

for good. Marion and Hearst now openly shared several homes together, including the fabled San Simeon castle in San Luis Obispo County, designed by California's first female licensed architect, Julia Morgan. But Marion's favorite of her homes was another of Miss Morgan's gems: the new beach house Hearst built for her on Ocean Front (also known as Palisades Beach Road, now Pacific Coast Highway) on the Gold Coast of Santa Monica. "Beach house" is a misnomer. It was a sprawling three-story colonial estate with more than 100 bedrooms, 55 bathrooms, three guest cottages and two swimming pools. The Wangers rented one of the cottages while they searched for a home.

Marion was delighted to have Justine in town. She was preparing for her next feature *Good Time Girl* (later retitled *Blondie of the Follies*), a film about two girls and their vastly different ways of getting into show business, co-written by none other than Anita Loos of *Gentlemen Prefer Blondes* fame. Hearst's loyal gossip columnist and general wasp Louella Parsons asked Marion who she thought she play the other girl. "Justine Johnstone!" answered Marion. The role went to another Ziegfeld alumnus, Billie Dove. Parsons noted that Justine "has put the stage behind her."[2]

Justine in fact had other plans. The California Institute of Technology, the prestigious science and engineering university in Pasadena, had recently announced an intriguing study combining physics with medical science. An extraordinary generator, "the world's largest X-ray tube" capable of zapping up to one million volts, was being used as radiation therapy in cancer patients.

The project had been initiated by Dr. Robert Andrews Millikan, a Caltech co-founder, chair of the institute's Executive Council and a 1923 Nobel laureate in physics. Dr. Millikan had read a report from the Radiological Society of New York urging physicists to work with medical doctors on the development of high-tech devices for radiation therapy. X-ray treatments for cancer had been practiced since the early 20th century, but a huge problem: avoiding healthy cells while blasting electrons at high speeds through a human body. Considerable technical upgrades were needed.

Dr. Millikan had just the thing: a whopper of an X-ray mega-tube designed for atomic research designed under his direction by Danish-born physicist Charles C. Lauritsen. Dr. Millikan managed to convince the reluctant Dr. Lauritsen to use the mega-tube for a new cancer study. He recruited radiation specialist Dr. Clyde Emery, founder of a Westlake cancer clinic, to head the medical team. Pasadena cardiologist Seeley G. Mudd was selected to lead the entire project, possibly because Dr. Mudd and his family agreed to put up initial funding. William K. Kellogg, the cereal king, in town to visit his horse ranch in Pomona, agreed to a $150,000 gift provided his name was on the new campus building to house the work—thus Caltech's Kellogg Radiation Laboratory was born. The researchers began experimenting on rodent models, and by 1931 were treating patients from Los Angeles County Hospital, a charity institution affiliated with the University of Southern California.

News of this project almost certainly prompted Justine to drive the 90 minutes from Santa Monica to Pasadena. She entered Throop Hall, the exquisite, mission-style central campus building, and met with Dr. Millikan. In addition to her published papers, her selling points were her contacts within the medical community, including one of Dr. Millikan's own consultants, Dr. Francis Carter Wood, director of Columbia University's Crocker Institute of Cancer Research.

The genial, white-haired Dr. Millikan was a man who readily praised the work of women in science, as long as they weren't physicists. He'd be pleased to have Justine on board, he said, if she could submit letters of recommendation from at least two distinguished researchers. (A cynical assumption would be that there might also have been a donation discussion involved, but evidence is lacking.)

Justine had no problem obtaining assurances from Dr. Lieb at Columbia University, but she hit a snag with others. One was Dr. James Bumgardner Murphy, an associate of "filterable virus" physician Dr. Peyton Rous at The Rockefeller Institute. Dr. Murphy was slow in responding. Undaunted, Justine persisted in reminding the busy specialist that she needed his recommendation, even contacting him during his summer vacation. On July 31, 1932, Justine wrote a gracious but pointed appeal from Marion's cottage, "321 Ocean Front, Santa Monica, Cal.":

> My Dear Dr. Murphy:
>
> I had hoped that I should not need to distract you on your holiday, but in order to get started out here I must have a letter from you saying the usual thing that is said in such letters.
>
> Dr. Millikan at the California Institute of Technology has promised to let me work in their laboratories if I can present a letter from you and one from Dr. Lieb saying the work may have possibilities.
>
> I am so grateful for all your consideration and trust that this further intrusion will not put me in your bad graces.
>
> Most sincerely,
Justine Wanger[3]

She got her recommendation from Dr. Murphy, and the job at Caltech. Barely in California a year, Justine was again in her element. And Caltech was, for anyone new to the area, a glorious place to be, with its Mediterranean arcades, cypress trees and backdrop of the San Gabriel Mountains. "Here in Pasadena, it is like Paradise," wrote Albert Einstein, a Caltech visiting professor at the time. "Always sunshine and clean air, gardens with palms and pepper trees, and friendly people who smile and ask one for autographs."[4] It was a welcome change to be around people more excited by seeing Dr. Einstein than a former *Follies* girl and film star, if they even knew who she was.

Justine was again an unpaid assistant: the institute has no record of her as an employee. There is no precise documentation on her involvement with the tube experiments, other than her working on "cancer studies" at Caltech at this time, so exactly what she did remains unknown. Operation of the mega-tube itself was performed by the physicists and graduate students, but as an assistant, she would have been one of several participants who prepared patients for treatment, measured results, and coordinated follow-up visits.

The patients were brought to the new radiology facility, four stories high, plus a basement level to accommodate the tube. They were laid out four at a time on couches or chairs beneath the behemoth vacuum to receive up to 900,000 volts of newly-produced "artificial radium" for up to twenty minutes. Subsequent treatments were administered within a month to six weeks. Almost all but late-stage patients responded to treatment. The work was almost round-the-clock, with physicists preparing the tube by night for the procedures the following day. The project's participants were an eclectic, social group, particularly the "father" of the tube, Dr. Lauritsen and his accomplished radiologist-wife, Sigrid, who hosted gatherings for the team.

By 1934, results were encouraging enough for Dr. Millikan to detail aspects of the study to the press. He cautioned that no one was claiming that the process was curing cancer, but slowing growth of tumors was in evidence.

Justine made no secret of her new activities among her friends, and as usual such information made its way into the columns without a quote from her. "Justine Johnston [sic], former 'Follies' beauty who had a brief fling at the movies, is doing research work in cancer cures these days at the California Institute of Technology," wrote Hubbard Keavy in 1933. "She's the wife of Walter Wanger, executive."[5]

The wife was content but the executive was as restless and unpredictable as ever. After only a few months in California, Walter realized he wasn't getting what he wanted from Harry Cohn, mainly regarding salary and promotion. But he also realized that opportunity was in California, not New York. He quit Columbia Pictures in late 1932. "Europe is beckoning invitingly to Walter Wanger," wrote Louella Parsons. "There are several reasons why he may not take Justine Johnston [sic], his wife, there." It was characteristic Louella, finding a nice, family-newspaper way of saying that she knew about what a great husband Walter wasn't. She added coyly, "and one is his offer from several film companies to join up as a producer."[6]

Walter didn't go to Europe. He was doing the requisite schmoozy lunches, and ultimately zeroed in on Irving Thalberg, the brilliant but frail "boy wonder" of Metro-Goldwyn-Mayer. "He was an amazingly attractive man," Walter would later write of Thalberg. "He had terrific eyes. You thought you were talking to an Indian savant. He could cast a spell on anybody."[7] The spell was cast, and by 1933 was a producer at MGM.

Unfortunately for Walter, he would not report to Thalberg, but to capricious and manipulative Louis B. Mayer. Walter persuaded Hearst to finance *Gabriel Over the White House,* a bizarre 1933 melodrama that combines fantasy, socialist idealism and fascism, with Walter Huston as a puppet American president who goes gonzo dictator after a visit from the angel Gabriel. It was a Depression-era hit, but Mayer hated it. Again, Walter clashed with his boss. This would usually result in one of two outcomes: he would be fired or would quit. This time he quit—just as MGM was beginning to eclipse Paramount as the gold standard of Hollywood studios.

Walter went rogue, creating the independent Walter Wanger Productions in 1934. Hollywood insiders called him "the lone Wanger." He had Paramount as a distributor before becoming a member of United Artists along with Mary Pickford, Charlie Chaplin, Walt Disney, David O. Selznick, Sam Goldwyn, and his and Justine's old pal Jesse Lasky.

In Walter's office in Universal City, a portrait of Justine was on display. Pictures of wives were *de rigueur* for an executive's office. For a mogul, it could also be a sign to lady friends that he was only available on certain terms. But the fact that it was no mere photograph, but an exquisite oil painting, signaled that Walter was genuinely fond and proud of his wife.

16

Hollywood Snapshots at Random

Many of Walter's contemporaries—Harry Cohn, Sam Goldwyn, Louis B. Mayer, Joseph Schenck, the Warner brothers and others—had grown up battling poverty and anti-Semitism but had reached the pinnacle of the American dream. They weren't willing to give it up. Even deep into the Depression, they found ways to cut costs without sacrificing their personal lifestyles. In 1933, the moguls slashed studio employees' paychecks fifty percent while retaining their own considerable income. (That May, Justine's former *Hush Money* co-star Kenneth Thomson hosted a secret meeting of actors in his living room, which resulted in the formation of the Screen Actors Guild.)

Walter had never been poor, but had been raised by an upper-middleclass mother who went to great lengths to hide the family's Jewishness. As such, he'd had the importance of appearances and a competitive edge imprinted upon him at an early age. He took his cues from his peers.

A primary example of how Walter signaled his status as one of the Hollywood big boys was where he and Justine would live. He needed a home that fit his new mogul profile. Walter may have been a "posing socialist," but he liked to live like an actual capitalist.

Pasadena, San Marino and Glendale were certainly lovely, reasonably close to Universal City, and could have provided a more convenient home for Justine's Caltech commute. But moguls didn't live there.

After their temporary stay at Marion's beach house, the Wangers pretty much started at the top. They leased a magnificent estate in the Benedict Canyon area of Beverly Hills, a grand Tudor mansion on ten acres at the end of narrow, twisty-turny Angelo Drive. "The biggest thrill in Hollywood," wrote Walter Winchell, "is motoring at a fast clip to the home of Walter Wanger and Justine Johnstone, which has a corkscrew approach."[1] The property was, and would be, often used for film exteriors, including Paramount's

1926 *Kid Boots* with Eddie Cantor, Clara Bow, and Billie Dove. The Wangers rented the luxurious abode for $18,000 a year from George Lewis, millionaire owner of the jewelry designers Shreve & Company.

The mansion proved a nightmare to maintain, and Justine and Walter tolerated it for only a year or so. After their departure, the Lewises claimed that they found "cobwebs in the barroom"[2] and the pool full of frogs and dead gophers. So the Lewises sued the Wangers for $4,000 in damages.

Justine "hotly denied"[3] the claims, telling Judge Charles D. Ballard that Walter "went swimming in the pool every day. You don't think my husband would go swimming with frogs, do you?"

She insisted the home was already a mess when they moved in. "The whole interior of the house was frightful," she said. "There was soot on the dining room ceiling and most of the rooms in the lower floors were infested with ants. When we tried to launder the curtains, they fell to pieces."[4]

1935: Mogul's wife, medical researcher, and bespectacled defendant against damage charges brought by the owners of the Wangers' rented Benedict Canyon estate. The owners didn't like finding frogs in the pool; Justine claimed the place was a mess when they moved in (although the frogs may actually have escaped from her basement laboratory). Courtesy USC Libraries Special Collections, University of Southern California.

It wasn't just the interior, she said: the English garden "was an eyesore," the yards were a mess and the entire grounds were in shambles. When Judge Ballard asked her what those gophers were doing in the swimming pool, she said, "I think they just committed suicide."[5]

There's no information on the outcome of the suit, but the story of an $18,000 rental with ants and frogs in a swimming pool was probably wryly amusing for most Depression-era readers. One headline ran, "Swim with Frogs? Not My Husband!"

The Wangers struck gold in Holmby Hills, a lush, secluded Beverly Hills neighborhood just south of Benedict Canyon. A highly exclusive community, then and now, Holmby Hills was fast becoming a magnet for high-end industry professionals, with its palatial homes hidden behind wrought-iron gates, small forests of shrubbery, and English lantern street lamps. Holmby Hills was named by its developer after his family's English estate in Holdenby. Even the streets were named after English locales.

They leased 301 Carolwood Drive (later home to Greta Garbo and, even later, Barbra Streisand), a sprawling three-acre Spanish-style estate with twenty rooms, seven fireplaces made of stone and Spanish tile, and a four-car garage. It had been built in 1927 for Mrs. Queen Walker Boardman, a wealthy horticulturalist from whom the Wangers apparently rented. Finally, in 1936, the Wangers purchased their own home about a block west of Carolwood, a stately Georgian mansion at 351 Delfern Drive, built in 1926 by noted architect John Byers. It was approximately half the size of the Carolwood home, meaning it was only slightly enormous. Still, it had all the amenities: four huge bedrooms, maids' room, a tennis court and, of course, a pool.

According to Walter Winchell, in a story possibly fed to him by Walter himself, Justine hired a young Norwegian maid to assist with housekeeping. Walter, however, found the woman too distractingly attractive to have in his home. He told Justine to fire her. She agreed to let the young woman go only if Walter wrote her a glowing letter of recommendation. As admired as he was for his style and his work, Walter could still be, as screenwriter Frederica Maas called him, a "nincompoop."[6]

Walter began playing the mogul game du jour, polo, a rough, expensive, and decidedly British military shot-an-elephant-in-my pajamas type of sport. Justine's *Follies* friend and expert horseman Will Rogers had learned the game in New Jersey and introduced it to his Hollywood pals in the mid–1920s. Walter kept his own polo ponies and played with buddies Walt Disney and 20th Century–Fox head Darryl Zanuck at the Riviera Country Club in Pacific Palisades. Unlike many of his fellow producers, Walter was actually a decent horseback golfer and played first position. He competed in tournaments with other industry professionals on a team called "Walter Wanger's Hollywood Rangers." After matches, he and his fellow riders would meet up at El Jardin, the restaurant at the Beverly Hills Hotel, so often that hotel owner Hernando Courtwright eventually renamed it the Polo Lounge in their honor.

When she wasn't assisting with radiation treatments, Justine led the rarified life of a mogul's wife. Louella Parsons noted that Justine, Marion and Bebe Daniels were the "best women bridge players in the colony."[7] She was no polo player, but adored horses, especially Anchorage, the race horse Walter purchased for her, which they ran at Riviera's steeplechase course.

Her sport of choice was, as ever, golf. Justine usually played either at Riviera or at Hillcrest Country Club, established by and for Jews in response to exclusion from other such Los Angeles clubs. Cohn, Goldwyn, Mayer, Zukor, the Warners, the Marx Brothers, and anyone who was anyone, devoutly Jewish or not, was a member, so Walter joined. (Justine's membership was almost certainly through her husband: it would be years before the club allowed women as associate members, even longer as regular members). Justine proved so adept that she entered women's amateur golf championship tournaments at Pebble Beach and Desert Springs. She and her Hoboken cousin, Evelyn "Evvie" Nielsen, took golfing trips together. (It may have been through Justine that Evvie met her husband, golf pro Stan Kertes, who coached Babe Didrikson, Bob Hope, the Marx Brothers and other celebrities.)

The Wangers often visited Marion and Hearst at the magnificent, Moorish San Simeon estate. The castle was about 250 miles north of Los Angeles, and guests would either drive up or take Hearst's special train from Pasadena to San Luis Obispo, where they would be met by limousines.

Newspaper clipping of Justine on the links with, from left, Mildred Allenberg, wife of agent Bert and a catalyst in Justine's involvement in social service; and Evelyn Sloto, a recent UCLA grad and department store heiress; preparing for the 1935 Pebble Beach Women's Golf Championship. Courtesy Mr. Justin Wanger.

Or, like Walter and Justine, they could fly in Hearst's eight-passenger Fokker airplane. Canadian actor Raymond Massey, whom the Wangers had met in London, joined them on one such rather rocky flight, and was not a fan. "We flew the two hundred and fifty miles in a single-engined airplane in a few minutes less than it would take by car," Massey wrote in his autobiography. "I was too frightened to appreciate the beauty of San Simeon as we swayed past the house. I heard the pilot's comments after our goony-bird landing. 'There's another San Simeon drop I can walk away from!' I was relieved when Walter promised we would drive back to Los Angeles."[8]

A San Simeon weekend was an event, sometimes lasting up to a week. The dozens of guests could enjoy horseback riding, swimming, tennis, Rembrandts, Raphaels, Rubenses, exotic animals at the world's largest private zoo, picnicking on caviar sandwiches, dining sumptuously in

16. Hollywood Snapshots at Random 143

the Great Hall, movie nights in a palatial screening room, or disappearing at will into their private cabins. The invite list was, of course, always rather exclusive, and could include Calvin Coolidge, Winston Churchill, Amelia Earhart, Howard Hughes, and a host of movie industry names: Mayer, Warner, Garbo, Gable, Harpo, Cary Grant, Gary Cooper, Bette Davis and her not-so-best friend Joan Crawford, and Marion's longtime rumored lover, Charlie Chaplin.

(In 1924, when director Thomas Ince died after a booze cruise on Hearst's yacht, rumors began swirling that Hearst had shot him. Hearst supposedly had mistaken Ince for intended victim Chaplin, whom Hearst had reportedly caught *in flagrante* with Marion. It's an ancient Hollywood legend, but the ulcer-ridden Ince had consumed forbidden drink and food and possibly had a heart attack. And no, Justine was not on the yacht party; that was Julanne Johnston.)

The Wangers were among some 40 San Simeon guests for a special 1933 weekend honoring George Bernard Shaw, a favorite of Justine's, in his first and only visit to the U.S. Shaw declared San Simeon "just as God would have made it, if God had the money."[9] When the playwright noticed Louella Parsons approaching him with notebook and pencil, he grabbed screenwriter Frances Marion and begged, "Don't leave me."[10]

The Shaw weekend included a screening of Walter's *Gabriel Over the White House,* funded by Hearst. But Walter's next film got his San Simeon pass revoked, at least for a while. His 1934 *The President Vanishes*, based on a Rex Stout novel, was a sequel of sorts to *Gabriel,* basically another subtly socialist melodrama about an American president. One character was a slimy millionaire newspaper mogul who, with other disreputable businessmen, persuades the president to enter a war to line their own pockets. This was a noticeable mirror of Hearst and his notorious "creation" of the 1898 Spanish-American War. Hearst was furious. Why Walter thought this was a good idea is unclear, but consequences of his actions seemed not to be a consideration for him at times.

Public insult aside, Hearst's favorite columnist Louella Parsons continued to feature the Wangers regularly in what she called "Hollywood Snapshots at Random," her regular roll-call of star names at places like the Trocadero on Sunset, the modernistic Hi-Hat on Wilshire, and the luxurious Bel-Air Bay Club. Walter and Justine were noted as hob-nobbing with Claudette Colbert, Henry Fonda, Gloria Swanson, Ginger Rogers, Jack and Mary Benny, all of the Marx Brothers, Mary Pickford and her husband Douglas Fairbanks (and later husband Buddy Rogers), George Gershwin, millionaire banker Jimmy Warburg and his composer-wife (and Gershwin's lover) Kay Swift and, of course, the producers: Goldwyn, Selznick, Thalberg and his wife, actress Norma Shearer. There were cocktail parties, dinner parties, yacht parties, costume parties (Marion loved giving those at her "beach house").

The Wangers would occasionally host their own soirees, combining old New York friends with Walter's latest colleagues. By 1933, one particularly special New York friend on their guest list was Justine's Columbia University collaborator, Dr. Sam Hirshfeld.

It was a joy to have Sam in town. San Simeon and that regular roll-call of bold-face names were great. But medicine, as Justine's son would say, was her passion. She and Sam picked up their professional collaboration, and their friendship, where it had left off.

17

Medical Arts

Sam Hirshfeld left Columbia University in the wake of its severe budget cuts early in the Depression. Why he chose relocation to Los Angeles was simple: the recent residency of a growing number of his more successful theatrical patients, such as John Barrymore and Harpo Marx. And the Wangers.

No doubt due to his patient base, Sam's private practice took off immediately, and he soon became the premiere physician to the Los Angeles film community. (He is at least one of the doctors known to have recommended Benzedrine, deemed "safe" in 1937, to David O. Selznick, who famously popped the addictive amphetamine like candy to get through *Gone with the Wind*.) His name began appearing in newspaper articles as attending physician for notables with varying ailments, as well as attendee at social events. He served as his patients' confidant, advisor, and close friend.

Harpo Marx's 1961 autobiography, *Harpo Speaks!*, includes several fond anecdotes about his doctor and friend, who, along with Marion Davies, helped Harpo and his wife Susan Fleming adopt their four children. Harpo wrote, "Sam was our ringleader. Hockey was his special passion among sports. He never missed a match unless had had to be in surgery or with a patient who was confined to bed. Patients who were ambulatory he often brought along with him to the hockey game," including screenwriter Ben Hecht and journalist Gene Fowler. According to Harpo, Sam "would be handy with the hypo"[1] whenever the alcoholic Fowler suffered tremors during a game.

Raymond Massey offered a light story about Sam and Justine in his 1979 autobiography, *A Hundred Different Lives*, describing his experience entering a cocktail party given by the Wangers:

> Before I could speak to anyone a furious fight broke out between two little dogs at my feet. Countess di Frasso [American heiress and Gary Cooper's lover at the time] threw herself at me screaming, "Stop them! Stop them!" I pulled them apart with my hands. I felt a sharp pain. The second finger of my left hand had been bitten off at the base of the nail.

Everybody was commiserating with the Countess who was nursing her little darling. I saw my doctor, Sam Hirshfeld, and hollered, "Sam, do something!" "What a beautiful clean job," he said. "I wish we had the tip. I know just the man to put it back." Gary Cooper found the missing fingertip at once. "Get a cocktail glass and put it in," Sam said. "I've got some alcohol in my bag." Sam did a deft job of cauterizing and fixing me up, assisted by Justine Wanger. "It's a good thing that little beast wasn't hungry," he said. "Now, where's that glass, Coop?" Gary Cooper looked embarrassed. "The bartender says he threw a half-finished Gibson down the drain. That must have been it."[2]

One of Sam's early assignments was as "studio doctor" at RKO, the production company had been formed in 1928 by the merger of the Keith-Albee-Orpheum vaudeville circuit, David Sarnoff's RCA, and the Film Booking Offices of America, owned by Gloria Swanson's lover Joseph P. Kennedy. Selznick was production head, and one of Sam's more challenging patients, John Barrymore, was under contract. (Barrymore at one point unceremoniously dumped Sam when he mistakenly believed the doctor wanted him institutionalized. Barrymore then turned to Sam and Justine's collaborator, Dr. Harold Hyman in New York.)

Barrymore notwithstanding, Sam developed a reputation of going above and beyond in the care for his patients. On her first day at the studio to film *A Bill of Divorcement* with Barrymore and Billie Burke (working to pay off Ziegfeld's debts), Katharine Hepburn was suffering from a minor eye injury, and turned to Sam. When he realized she needed attention requiring instruments he didn't have, he drove her to a specialist, waited while she was treated, and returned her to her hotel.

During one of the Wangers' parties, Justine noticed something familiar about one of the caterers serving hors d'oeuvres. Finally Justine said to the woman, "Has anyone ever told you that you look like that new girl in town, Katharine Hepburn?"[3] It was in fact Hepburn, playing a joke on the partygoers, along with her fellow "servers": her agent and sometime lover, Leland Hayward, and her friend and possibly lover (depending on which Hepburn biographies one reads), American Express heiress Laura Harding. All three were decked out in service uniforms and waiting to see if anyone would notice. Apparently, Justine was the only one who did.

It may have been because they had actually already met. Justine was working for Sam as his assistant "at the Medical Arts Building at Beverly Hills," according to at least one article.[4] The location may have been an assumption. There was no building in Beverly Hills by that name per se. Sam opened his private practice office in the Wilshire Professional Building, 3875 Wilshire Boulevard—at 13 stories, a height-limit skyscraper for Los Angeles at the time—south of Beverly Hills in the area of Central LA now known as Koreatown. The magnificent, zigzagged, Art Deco structure (then simply known as Moderne) had a Sargent's Drug Store with its upscale soda fountain

The Wilshire Professional Building, where Sam Hirshfeld had his offices with Justine as his medical assistant. Up left is the Wilshire Boulevard Temple; to the right is the Wiltern Theatre; across the street is a longtime Los Angeles-area staple, Zinke's Drive-In Shoe Repair. Courtesy USC Digital Libraries.

on the ground floor, next to a fur salon. It was just up the block from the Brown Derby Restaurant, the hat-shaped film colony favorite.

Justine actually had her own research lab. Materials could be difficult to come by during the Depression, so she created a laboratory in the basement of her home and cultivated a colony of mice specifically for cancer research. Perhaps this was the "medical arts building" in Beverly Hills.

Justine and Sam—or "Sammy," as the LA press sometimes called him—apparently spent a great deal of time together. Aside from work, they partnered for golf tournaments at Sunset Fields in Baldwin Hills. And aside from golf, anything more specific is a mere guess. From the late 1920s to at least 1933, Sam's wife Eleanor took several trips abroad without him; still, 1940 census records indicate that Sam and Eleanor were living together along with their son Alan in Beverly Hills. If Sam and Justine were lovers at this time, it may have been one of those situations that used to be called "sophisticated," where spouses were fully aware of the unspoken. Justine had been "sophisticated" about Walter for years.

None of Sam's friends who wrote about him, including Harpo, Massey, Hecht, and Fowler, ever hinted at the precise nature of Sam's and Justine's relationship. If there was anything to talk about, it not only would have been considered bad taste, it would have been a breach of a close friend's trust. Perhaps their friends simply didn't know. The most that can be determined about Justine and Sam socializing at this time was that they went to the same parties and golfing together. But Justine would attend parties with Walter, and she golfed with a lot of people.

Of course it wasn't all parties and golf for either Sam or Justine. As a surgeon, Sam became affiliated with Good Samaritan Hospital in Westlake and Cedars of Lebanon in Beverly Hills, near his Maple Avenue home. He was also continuing his cancer research, both at Cedars and eventually at UCLA. As he would later confirm, Justine was collaborating with him on this work.

Sam launched into a new study that involved melanin, one of his and Justine's favorite topics, in a study funded by Selznick and his wife Irene, the daughter of Louis B. Mayer. (In the late 1920s, the then-unmarried Irene had been a subject of Walter's amorous attentions, but then, who wasn't?) Dr. Gregory Duboff, an associate of Justine's Caltech colleague Dr. Clyde Emery, collaborated on the work.

Drs. Duboff and Hirshfeld found that serum in the blood of cancer patients seemed to slow the activity of tyrosinase, an enzyme which causes or accelerates the production of melanin. Although the doctors didn't find the reason for the slowness (inhibition factor), they declared that the correlation between the enzyme's activity and malignancy was "a new approach to the field of cancer enzymology."[5] Their results were eventually published, but either by choice or circumstance, Justine's name does not appear as co-author.

Much of the details of her work for Sam Hirshfeld and others in Los Angeles is unknown. Projects would have been confidential unless published, and an incalculable percentage of scientific research does not reach the publication stage. Even then, she would only be listed as co-author if she agreed.

She did, however, agree to join a rather prestigious boys' science club. Sam became acquainted with Dr. Leo Tolstoy Samuels, a friendly, witty research biochemist affiliated with UCLA and the White Memorial Hospital in East Los Angeles. Leo, whose lab technician wife Barbara was his uncredited research assistant, initiated an informal monthly gathering of professionals to share ideas and discuss progress in the areas of endocrinology and cancer. Justine was the only woman in the group.

In addition to Sam, Justine, and Leo, the science club members included Dr. Bennet Mills Allen, the gentlemanly head of the zoology department at

17. Medical Arts 149

UCLA, who would become a neuroendocrinology pioneer; Dr. Harry Deuel, a USC biochemistry and nutrition professor, later dean of the graduate school, who had lost a leg to sarcoma; and Dr. Clinton Thienes, head of pharmacology at USC, who soon snatched Leo Samuels from rival UCLA and would later become medical director of Huntington Hospital in Pasadena.

Meetings would rotate at the homes of the eclectic posse, all with similar or overlapping interests and specialties, and committed to disease control and cure. And if they needed mice, Justine, in her now-signature horn-rimmed glasses, made a trip to her basement.

The group collaborated on at least one known study. Leo Samuels was researching the role of hormones in tumor growth. He needed female volunteers "who suffered from menstrual problems."[6] Justine volunteered herself and enlisted at least two friends, both of whom were signed for Walter's first independently-made film, *Private Worlds*: Claudette Colbert and Joan Bennett. All the women volunteers donated $200 each to help fund the study.

Sam Hirshfeld drew blood samples from the women's arms during two menstrual cycles as part of the effort to measure estrogen. Leo then worked on developing a bioassay (a method of measuring the effects of a substance on tissue) for blood hormones. He was unable to develop the bioassay as he wished, but the work helped him toward eventually discovering a chemical method.

Coincidentally or not, Sam was also using blood samples from women with menstrual problems for his own research at this time. It's a fair assumption that many Sam's and Leo Samuels' volunteers were subjects in both studies.

Sam studied 22 women patients for research on what he called "dysovulation," or dysfunction in the ovum release process, a condition can create ovarian cysts, severe pain and emotional disorders. Some of the women in the study were married, some not, some wished to become pregnant, others did not. Five patients had had abortions but Sam found, stunningly, that these women had never actually been pregnant at all ("a subsequent review of their histories revealed that a diagnosis of pregnancy had been completely unsupported").[7] A total of nineteen women had had appendectomies due to misdiagnoses of appendicitis that turned out to be ovarian abnormalities. Sam read his findings before the Southern California Medical Society in April 1934, urging physicians to consider a woman's menstrual history and timing of symptoms before confusing dysovulation with appendicitis.

Of course Sam never mentioned names of patients, but Justine was one of his patients. Another was Margaret Mayer, wife of Louis B. Mayer. Sam had performed a hysterectomy, which was referenced in newspapers merely as a "major operation,"[8] on Margaret in 1933. Her depression that followed led Mayer to inaccurately blame Sam for "bungling the operation"[9] and call for removal of Sam's medical license, only to be dissuaded by Sam's many friends.

"Major operation" was a catch-all phrase used by the press at the time to mean anything the paper wasn't prepared to print, or the subject wasn't prepared to admit. Justine had undergone what Louella Parsons called a "major operation" at Good Samaritan Hospital in December 1932, a month before her 38th birthday.[10] Very possibly the procedure was identical to that of Margaret Mayer's.

The work of the science club continued until at least 1937, when Leo Samuels accepted a position at the University of Minnesota Medical School. He published numerous papers on various topics throughout his long career, including one involving the use of vitamin C components as a cancer treatment (a major cancer-study focus of the 1930s). The December 1940 issue of *The Journal of Pharmacology and Experimental Therapeutics* noted that the study was funded in part by Mrs. Justine Wanger.

Mrs. Wanger probably didn't even notice when, in 1934, another photographer won another prize for a photograph he'd taken of her in New York. That year her Columbia University employment record noted that she was taking an "indefinite leave of absence for research work at the California Institute of Technology."[11]

She had never actually quit Columbia, almost as if she wanted something waiting for her in case Walter's movie-making thing didn't work out. Finally, in 1935, her university record noted that she had officially resigned. It took two volunteer researchers to replace her.

18

The Bliss of Uncertainty

In 1936, Justine and Walter were photographed in New York boarding the *Queen Mary* for England. The photos show a relaxed Justine, always smiling, sometimes directly at her husband. She's in elegant couture with a chic sculptured hat and soft, rather brilliantly blond medium-bob curls. Walter, as in many photos throughout his life, looks like he has heartburn. They were headed to Italy for Walter's head-spinning plans to negotiate a film production alliance with Benito Mussolini, who was building the Cinecittà studios outside of Rome to produce fascist propaganda films. It should be noted in fairness that Walter's supreme naiveté was shared by many Americans at the time who thought (or hoped) that Mussolini could be an ally against Hitler. Walter managed to strike a deal with the dictator, but the project soon collapsed for financial, not political, reasons.

Justine's smiles were a front. Walter's unpredictability and impulsiveness were becoming exasperating. A story syndicated by the Central Press Association (a division of Hearst's King Features) noted that the Wangers were often called "Hollywood's most devoted couple."[1] They were not. Walter Winchell reported that the Wangers were "threeing. She denies it, he admits it."[2] Apparently that meant that Walter was confirming that he and Justine, who was 41 years old, were about to become parents. They did not. After years of both contentment and conflict, the marriage was unraveling for a final time.

Walter was still actively engaged in his professional spinoff pursuits as a philanderer. In 1934, he became smitten with another one of his actresses. A liaison may have seemed unlikely at first: she had just given birth to a daughter, her second child, with her second husband. But an affair began, and it progressed. By 1937, Justine could no longer look the other way. Winchell said that word was going around that Justine had secretly divorced Walter, who denied it. Winchell was so often wrong, but this time he was as close to the truth as he could get.

The actress was Joan Bennett, Justine's fellow blood donor for Leo Samuels' hormone study. Joan was a 26-year-old from an acting family, and her professional and personal life had peripherally brushed against Justine's for years. She had made her Broadway debut in the 1928 melodrama *Jarnegan*, which was Charles K. Gordon's first Broadway production to actually get off the ground after *Hush Money* and featured Dennie Moore. In fact, Joan had starred in the 1931 Fox Film Corporation version of *Hush Money* in a role that was a combination of Justine's and another character's.

Like Justine, Joan was from New Jersey, beautiful, ambitious, could be alternately aloof and warm, and with a mischievous sense of humor. It's impossible to compare acting styles of the two women, but based on Joan's film work, she was perhaps not an outstanding actress but certainly a creditable one, capable of evoking both sweetness and toughness. Initially blonde, Joan had changed to a brunette at Walter's suggestion, establishing a sultry femme fatale look that she kept throughout her career.

Joan and Walter were basically a reboot of the Justine-Walter story. Joan was just as bedazzled by Walter as Justine had been in 1916: his sophistication and intelligence, his suave taste in clothing, his seductive plans for her future. But unlike his early relationship with Justine, Walter was relatively hesitant to commit to anything permanent. He thought Joan too young for him, and wasn't particularly interested in the type of relationship she had in mind. He liked what he had with Justine. But Joan was in love, and she was persistent.

Arriving in New York on the *Queen Mary* following a European trip, 1936, the year Walter's involvement with Joan Bennett became serious. Courtesy USC Libraries Special Collections, University of Southern California.

Walter and Joan were increasingly seen together at social functions. She divorced her husband, producer Gene Markey, in 1937. (Markey would then marry actress-inventor Hedy Lamarr, star of Walter's 1938 film *Algiers*. It gets a little insular after a while.) By January 1938, Walter had moved out of the house on Delfern. After four months of separation, Justine filed for divorce.

18. The Bliss of Uncertainty

In California at that time, she needed specific grounds. Adultery was one, but it would have meant headlines, scandals, and a list going back to at least 1924. Besides, Walter's attorneys could have countered by producing or concocting a list of their own. Justine needed to present as simple but persuasive a case as possible without alienating either Walter or his lawyers: she had been a professional wife for twelve years and had no personal source of income. So she settled on "mental cruelty," a catch-all that covered a sufficient amount of territory.

She told the judge, future California governor Goodwin Jess "Goodie" Knight, that Walter had been "abrupt, surly and discourteous"[3] toward her, a phrase that made the most of the many press stories about the divorce. "When we had dinner engagements, he would purposely be late," she said, "and then he would not join us, just come in, stare at us and go away."[4]

They had been building a home in the luxurious Beverly Hills neighborhood of Bel-Air. When the residence was partially complete, she reported, Walter viewed the site and said, "That's exactly what I don't want."[5] He then abandoned the project, leaving it to her to handle the construction company.

The clincher was her contention that he had been ignoring her for the past three years and told her he no longer loved her, causing her to become "extremely nervous and that her health was impaired as a result."[6]

Judge Knight had seen enough high-profile divorces to know what mental cruelty actually meant. Justine was granted an uncontested interlocutory decree of divorce. Then she took off for South America for a month and left the details to her attorneys.

The divorce became final in June. She got the house on Delfern Drive, the 1937 Buick

Justine ca. 1938, in a photograph used in a story about her divorce from Walter. She apparently wore little makeup: a photo editor enhanced her lipstick, eyebrows and eye liner. Her divorce grounds covered almost everything except infidelity in order to avoid scandal, and her settlement was generous. Courtesy USC Libraries Special Collections, University of Southern California.

sedan, and all the clothing and jewelry Walter had purchased for her. She also got $1,200 a month, a guarantee on a $250,000 life insurance policy, and support for her widowed mother Sophia in Passaic. He got the 1933 Duesenberg, the 1935 Plymouth station wagon, the 1936 Cadillac, and any and all materials relating to his work.

When Justine returned from South America, Louella Parsons asked her about her plans now that she was "free." Was she now going to move professionally into the medical field, or go back to being a movie star?

"I certainly have no intention of taking up medical work," Justine said, "or of returning to the screen. I shall just stick around my Beverly Hills home enjoying the bliss of uncertainty."[7]

Asked and answered. Justine's scientific research was, while a "passion," as her son confirmed, "never a quote-occupation-unquote." She still had no academic degree.

As for the entertainment industry, there was no question. Her friend Claudette Colbert was, in 1938, Hollywood's highest-paid star. Fred Astaire was at the top of his game and would stay there for years. Her long-ago fellow Folies-Bergère performer Archie Leach was now Cary Grant. In New York, Ruth Gordon was establishing herself as a premiere dramatic actress in a revival of *A Doll's House*. The Shuberts had Jack Buchanan at the Imperial and Ed Wynn at the Winter Garden. All of these actor-friends had been working during most of the dozen years since Justine had last set foot on stage. Going back into the business now would have meant starting over. Besides, the very term "going back" was not in Justine's vocabulary.

In December of 1939, Parsons noted coyly in her column that Walter and Justine were seen having dinner together. They were both asked separately if they were getting back together. Both said no.

A month later, on January 12, 1940, Walter married Joan Bennett in Phoenix. The proposal had been impulsive, as was the wedding. The day prior, Walter received a quickly-delivered note from his attorney, Loyd Wright: "Dear Walt: I am enclosing a certified copy of the final decree [of divorce from Justine], and as a matter of precaution I think you should take it with you."[8]

Although Walter had initially told Joan he didn't want children, their 25-year marriage would produce two daughters on whom Walter doted. Like his marriage to Justine, Walter's to Joan would work, except when it didn't.

Justine then embarked on perhaps her most fulfilling and life-changing journey. She herself became a mother. In November 1940, Louella Parsons broke the story that Justine had adopted not one but two infant boys. The babies were born about six weeks apart, although were erroneously referred to as "twins." Justine gave the boys variations of her name. Her son Justin was given the middle name Walter.

18. The Bliss of Uncertainty

At home with her son Justin, ca. 1941. Courtesy of Mr. Justin Wanger.

There was no mention as to when she decided to adopt, or how, or whether Sam or Marion, who had helped the Harpo Marxes with their adoptions, had any hand in the process. As usual, Justine made no public comment. At 45, she now simply focused her life on her children as fondly and diligently as anything she had ever done.

Her son Justin Wanger recalls: "She introduced us to everything. Movies, museums, music, art. I became an art lover because of Mom. My godmother Mildred Allenberg had a box at the Hollywood Bowl, and we'd join her at concerts. I started playing golf when I was about seven at the driving range on Wilshire in Westwood. When the time came, Mom took us to various churches and synagogues and let us decide for ourselves where we wanted to go. My interest in theatre came later, but I know it was because of my mother. She took us everywhere. It was a wonderful upbringing."

Whether or not the plan to adopt had begun while Justine and Walter were still married is uncertain. The history of his adoption seemed not to be a point of great interest to Mr. Wanger. "We didn't know we were adopted until we were eight or nine years old. I vaguely recall Mom telling us. It didn't make a big impact on me.... Years later, when I went to work.... I had to present my adoption papers as part of the security clearance process. Mom gave them to me. While I was waiting in the outer office with the papers, I decided to open them up. I looked at them, went, 'oh,' and closed them up again. It made no difference. Mom was Mom."

19

Her Name Is News

Marion Davies had been in her early thirties when she moved to California, not particularly young by Hollywood standards, and her career in talking pictures had been brief. Hearst's myopic insistence on making her another Norma Shearer had failed. But she had triumphed at her forte, comedy. Marion's best performances had been in just a few films, such as the silents *The Patsy* and *Show People* (the one based on Bolton's *Polly Preferred*), and Walter's musical *Going Hollywood* with Bing Crosby. By the late 1930s, Marion retired from films, and was known primarily as Hearst's companion.

What much of the public didn't know was that Marion was a generous philanthropist. In 1926, the year Hearst bought her the "beach house," she purchased land just east of Santa Monica in the Sawtelle neighborhood of Los Angeles for the purpose of building a children's hospital. A year later, she launched the Marion Davies Children's Clinic with a $250,000 grant. The clinic, now UCLA's Marion Davies Children's Health Center, opened in 1932, and Marion would provide millions of her own money in support of the facility for the rest of her life.

It is unfortunate, then, that Marion should be remembered today as the prototype for a scatterbrained, painfully untalented film character. In Orson Welles' now-classic 1941 *Citizen Kane*, the character of Susan Alexander Kane is considered to be Marion.

Susan becomes the mistress and later wife of Charles Foster Kane, a middle-aged, married, ostentatiously wealthy, megalomaniacal newspaper magnate who creates his own news, dabbles in politics, owns a lavish castle of a home with its own zoo and priceless artwork, and forces Susan into a failed singing career. Susan leaves the stage, plays jigsaw puzzles, and ultimately descends into alcoholism. The character was far from an accurate representation of the savvy, outgoing, talented Marion. But Kane was unmistakably Hearst. Marion was Hearst's mistress, had been promoted by him, had left acting, played jigsaw puzzles, and, as anyone who attended any of her parties was well aware, was a substantial drinker.

Orson Welles had learned about Hearst as a youngster from Ashton Stevens, the Hearst drama critic who had interviewed Justine in Chicago years earlier. (As noted, Welles based Jed Leland, Kane's friend and "dramatic critic," on Stevens.) Welles would maintain, however, that Kane was an amalgam of several industrialists. He insisted that the character of Susan was not Marion, but based on the second wives of Chicago businessmen Harold McCormick and Samuel Insull. Nobody bought that, and the film brought mortifying implications about Marion's talent into harsh focus.

Whether or not Hearst himself ever screened *Kane* is subject to some speculation. Some sources indicate that he did, and admired it, unlike Walter's far less artful *The President Vanishes*. But he was at least aware of the parallels between Susan and Marion, and that infuriated him. His faithful scandalmonger Louella Parsons did see the film, and reportedly made calls to studios threatening to expose considerable dirty laundry—of which she had specific details—if producers didn't publicly denounce *Kane*. (One can only imagine what she might have said to Walter.)

Marion took Hearst's advice and publicly kept quiet. Privately she was extremely hurt. By the 1950s, the name Marion Davies was primarily associated with *Citizen Kane*. Today, to some film historians and Welles aficionados, Marion still haunts the film.

Justine, as with most of Marion's many friends, felt peripheral stings. It was an audacious and humiliating scenario. There were a number of people within Justine's circle directly or indirectly involved, including Welles and his first wife Virginia Nicolson, patients of Sam Hirshfeld.

Justine would have admired Marion's silence. It had long been her own technique, and at the moment, far easier for her than for Marion. Walter was now of the most influential and popular men in the business. He was president of the Academy of Motion Picture Arts and Sciences, sitting on the stage next to emcee Bob Hope during the Oscar ceremonies at the Cocoanut Grove. In perhaps his most blatant Anglophilic gesture, Walter, never seriously observant of his Jewish faith, was attending Episcopalian church services with the new Mrs. Walter Wanger. And it was the new Mrs. Wanger who was starring in Walter's films and hostessing lavish dinner parties for his people.

Mrs. Justine Wanger was de facto non-news. She preferred it that way. But things have a way of happening in the entertainment industry. Around the time that the whispering began about Marion and *Kane*, Justine herself was thrust into an unsolicited spotlight. Unlike the sneers that were following her unfortunate friend, the stories about Justine were decidedly complimentary, flattering, even obsequious. But like the stories about Marion, they were not always true.

On July 2, 1939, *New York Times* science writer Waldemar Kaempffert reported that a "five-day syphilis treatment" was being conducted at Mount Sinai Hospital. The treatment, marking the final phase of clinical testing, was considered "not yet ready for general adoption." But the results were so encouraging that New York City Health Commissioner Dr. John L. Rice said that "it is likely to lead to a radical revision on the management and treatment of early syphilis."[1]

The experimental treatments were being conducted by three doctors. Two were dermatologists and syphilologists on staff at Mount Sinai: the dour, quirky, Russian-born Dr. Louis Chargin, the head of the dermatology unit, and young Dr. William Leifer, who would conduct Army Medical Corps penicillin experiments during the war that led to the use of the drug as an early-stage cure for syphilis.

The third doctor was Team Justine's own Harold Thomas Hyman. Harold was the reason this study made it into the *Times:* he had contacted Kaempffert himself to promote the work.

The three docs had begun their treatments after Justine and Sam had left for California. Beginning in 1933, they hooked up Team Justine's IV apparatus to highly diluted arsenic drugs and, utilizing the "slow-drip" method, treated 376 early-stage syphilis patients at Mount Sinai. Follow-up studies were conducted at New York Hospital and Bellevue Hospital. Not noted in the *Times* article was that some patients proved difficult to locate for the critical follow-up procedures, so Harold had contacted Hearst and asked that ads be placed in his newspapers: "TEN DOLLAR PRIZE: If your name appears on the list below, you may receive ten dollars."[2] The ads then listed the names of the patients Harold was seeking, and a number to call. Harold paid $70 of his own money for each of the ads, and his investment paid off. His team was able to conduct subsequent tests on most, although not all, of their missing patients.

Kaempffert's article acknowledged that Hyman, Chargin and Leifer were using the method of intravenous drug delivery developed eight years earlier by three "physicians and pharmacologists," including "Mrs. Justine J. Wanger."

For most of the press and public, this meant nothing.

Less than a year later, on April 13, 1940, another story appeared in the *Times*, this time announcing that Drs. Hyman, Chargin and Leifer had completed their seven-year research. And it was a game-changer.

The doctors reported that 85 percent of the patients treated exhibited no recurrent signs of syphilis after a single five-day treatment. The remaining percentage of patients showed improvement after a second series three months later. The treatment time, a mere five days, was a considerable upgrade from the previously-required eighteen months. It would cost the patient $90, as opposed to between $200 and $500 for previous methods.

Most incredibly, one week after final treatment, the patients could no

19. Her Name Is News

longer spread the disease. There still was no cure, but the findings of Hyman, Chargin and Leifer confirmed that the disease, for the first time, could be checked.

The *Times* story reiterated that the syphilis research had begun specifically because of the positive results achieved ten years earlier with the slow-drip methods developed by Drs. Hyman, Hirshfeld and Mrs. Justine Wanger.

This time the reporter asked: Mrs. Who?

"Mrs. Wanger," the story confirmed, "before she took up scientific research, in which she gained the respect of medical colleagues, was an actress and Ziegfeld 'Follies' beauty. She is the former wife of the Hollywood producer, Walter Wanger."[3]

From Times Square to Santa Monica, stories whirled in a *Kane*-like spinning newspaper montage.

"Ex-Follies Beauty Heroine of Amazing Medical Cure," ran one headline, followed by:

> Fabulous Broadway awoke yesterday to rub its eyes over a new glory. The avenue of many sinners from whose ranks have emerged few saints, mumbled in awe: "Why, I knew Justine when she was in the Winter Garden chorus"—"I hoofed with her in the Follies"—"Say, when she and Billie Allen were running the Little Club, where Sardi's basement is now, Justine used to serve that stuff right off the boats"—"Remember when she played the Palace?"
>
> They were talking about a scientist, one who may become a world immortal as well as a Broadway legend—Justine Johnstone, heroine of the electrifying scientific development of the five-day syphilis cure.[4]

She'd actually never played the Winter Garden, she'd never been a "hoofer" in the *Follies*, had never worked with Billie Allen (one of her replacements at the Little Club), never served anything "right off the boats" because Prohibition started a year after she left the club, which was in the basement of the 44th Street Theatre, not Sardi's, down the block. And she technically wasn't the heroine of the "five-day syphilis cure" because it wasn't a "cure" and she hadn't participated in the study. But, details.

Jeanette Smits at the Hearst-owned *New Your Journal*, in an article syndicated across the country, wrote that the public was "shocked at the revelation that the celebrated beauty, flinging aside her furs and her jewels, [has] quietly been laboring in medical laboratories."[5] The glowing full-page piece included a photo of Justine, taken after her and Walter's return from their 1936 European trip (Walter was cut out), next to a shot of a winsome Justine from her Realart days. What they couldn't get was a photo of Justine today. So they settled for an artist's rendering: a sketch of Justine at work, with beautifully coiffed (untied) hair, dressed in a white nurse's uniform, cinched belt and shoulder pads worthy of MGM's Adrian, gazing intently and prettily into a test tube.

Some articles noted the fact that she was the ex-wife of the man who had produced such hits *Queen Christina* with Greta Garbo, *Algiers* with Lamarr and Charles Boyer, and *Stagecoach* with John Wayne, an apparent attempt to link Justine directly to big movie names in case all that science stuff was too boring.

Others weren't quite sure who she was. They fondly recalled what a great job she had done in *The Thief of Bagdad* with Douglas Fairbanks (Julanne Johnston again).

"She is Justine Johnstone," proudly announced *The Times* of Troy, New York, home of the Emma Willard School, "and Emma Willard graduate of 26 years ago, ex-Follies headliner, ex-night club proprietor, ex-wife of movie producer Walter Wanger. Still glamorous although she is past 40...."[6]

Much of the focus was on that which had made Justine famous in the first place, her looks. "A beautiful gal who studied chemistry and helped in the discovery of a cure (as important as the one Mme. Curie discovered),"[7] hailed Walter Winchell, apparently too shy to say "syphilis" even though the word had been all over *The New York Times*.

H. L. Mencken wrote to his editor friend St. Clair McKelway of *The New Yorker*: "Have you thought of doing a profile of Justine Johnson [sic]? I suppose you recall her. She was a nightclub star who married Walter Wanger, the movie magnate. I knew her in those days, and like everyone else, I looked upon her as a stupid woman. It turned out, however, that she was greatly interested in medicine.... She has been appearing with increasing regularity of late in the medical journals, and some of her work is extraordinarily original and valuable. I believe that Margaret Harriman could do a good job with her."[8]

Harriman, daughter of the owner of the Algonquin Hotel and a *New Yorker* profile specialist, may have tried. A lot of reporters tried. Justine politely refused them all. "She asks nothing," wrote Robert Barlow of the *Toledo Blade*, "but to be allowed to continue her research work in the Los Angeles hospital with which she is associated."[9]

So the reporters went after Justine's friends. Jeanette Smits of the *Journal* claimed that "a close friend" was "finally persuaded to talk." Miss Smits was an aggressive, thorough reporter, so it's fair to assume that she actually did talk to a "close friend." It may also be fair to assume, given that she was a Hearst reporter, that the friend may have been Marion. Justine, the friend said,

> had confided that the past five years, spent amid microscopes, slides and test tubes, had been the happiest of her life.
>
> Justine, she said, is completely sincere in refusing publicity about her share in the amazing new "magic bullet" discovery. She is continuing her studies in the hospitals of Los Angeles and wants neither fame nor glory from her work.

19. Her Name Is News   161

> She merely desires to keep on being one of the "girls in white"—unsung heroines who labor in grim laboratories, without fanfare or excitement, content in the knowledge that the work they are doing will eventually be of benefit to mankind....
> This is what Justine Johnstone, whom Paul Helleu, the Famous French etcher, called the most beautiful woman in America, sought.
> This is what Justine Johnstone, who was rated as second in popularity to Mary Pickford, sought.
> And this is what Justine Johnstone, whose 18-year marriage [actually almost 20] to Walter Wanger had been heralded as Hollywood's "most perfect"—only to end in divorce—sought.
> But obscurity was denied to her, because—
> Justine Johnstone's name is news.[10]

It was a deliciously perfect Hearstian coda, insisting on making someone news whether they wanted it or not.

Reporters also swarmed over Justine's collaborators, Sam Hirshfeld and Harold Hyman. Both doctors basically reiterated what was already public information, that Justine had been on their team. Neither discussed her current life or speculated on her motives for changing careers. Sam confirmed that Justine was working with him but was "guarded about what they are now experimenting with, except to say that it is in the field of endocrinology and other absorbing problems."[11] From his Park Avenue office, Harold merely said that Justine "is a great and fine woman, one of the most perfectly-adjusted people I know."[12]

Harper's Bazaar managed to run a full-page current photo showing a relaxed Justine in a short-sleeved summer dress, sitting on what may be a stoop outside her home, leaning on a small brass horse and smiling over her shoulder as if to a friend nearby. In the black-and-white shot, her shoulder-length hair appears to be salt-and-pepper and blows freely in the breeze. She is looking, oddly enough for someone who had posed for so much of her life, directly into the sunlight, creating a slight squint in her eyes and crease in her forehead. It's a photo of a healthy, confident, 40-something-year-old woman who couldn't care less about the grey in her hair and creases in her face. But no interviews.

No problem. Columnists found reasons to mention her anyway. The *Los Angeles Times* society reporter noticed her at opening day of the 1941 Pacific Southwest Tennis Championship at the Los Angeles Tennis Club near Hancock Park. "Justine Wanger in sport clothes. Horned-rimmed glasses cannot hide Justine's beauty. She's still quite as lovely as she was in the 1915 Follies."[13]

Louella Parsons started to be on the lookout for any time Justine was seen with a man, as long as he was reasonably famous. "Justine Johnson [sic], formerly Mrs. Walter Wanger, and Gilbert Emery [are] a night club pair at the Grace Hayes Lodge," she wrote in 1940.[14] Justine and writer-actor Emery could have known each other since her vaudeville days, when one of his playlets appeared on the same bill as her Shaw piece. An Australian-American specializing in classy older-gentleman film roles, Emery was also a former Columbia University English professor. He was 20 years her senior, but Justine liked them smart. However serious the relationship was, it unfortunately didn't last much longer, as Emery died five years later.

There was a new gossip-monger in town, and she happened to be an old friend. Elda Furry had graduated from the Folies-Bergère in 1914 to leading woman for the Shuberts and Max Gordon. She played in dozens of films with varying success before a friend persuaded her to write the gossipy stories she was so fond of telling. Elda became Hedda, switched to her married last name, Hopper, and launched "Hedda Hopper's Hollywood" with the Esquire Feature Syndicate in 1937. Her column was soon picked up by the *Los Angeles Times*, a rival to the *Los Angeles Examiner*, the Hearst paper in which Louella's column appeared. Thus Hedda broke Louella's monopoly on dish-hashing.

If Hedda liked someone, she championed them. Justine was one of the people for whom Hedda never had an unkind word or innuendo. They had known each other since they were starting out, and Hedda may have felt in Justine a kindred spirit as an actress who had changed careers.

Hedda actually had the rather hair-brained idea to get the newly-famous Justine back into films. In 1944, Hedda visited the set of MGM's *Ziegfeld Follies*, a colorful extravaganza starring a remarkable lineup of MGM stars: Fred Astaire, Gene Kelly, Judy Garland, Lena Horne, Cyd Charisse, and Lucille Ball, plus Justine's former *Follies* co-star Fanny Brice, and Keenan Wynn, son of Ed. William Powell reprised his 1936 role as Ziegfeld, this time addressing the audience from the beyond.

Hedda cornered producer Arthur Freed, presenting him with a "montage shot showing Justine Johnstone, who's still beautiful, as she goes to work daily in a clinical laboratory where she's made a great discovery for the cure of *that certain disease*."[15] Hedda assured Freed that the film would benefit from having actual former Ziegfeld *Follies* show girl Justine in the cast. Freed told her he'd get back to her on that.

20

The Most Elementary Emotions

In the quiet privacy of her Holmby neighborhood, Justine was caring for her children and her home with her Finnish housekeeper, Jennie Niles, at the start of World War II. The Caltech work was gone: at the onset of World War II, after treating 746 patients without significant breakthroughs, the Caltech cancer radiation studies were suspended. The powerful X-ray machine would be repurposed for nuclear physics studies.

Justine was still assisting a very busy Sam Hirshfeld. Justin Wanger recalls his childhood visits to one of his mother's labs, which he remembers being "either at UCLA or Cedars of Lebanon Hospital," with which Sam Hirshfeld was affiliated. "She did a lot of work down there," Mr. Wanger says, "but she also did a lot of work at home. We had a three-car garage, and over that was a bar and game room. My earliest memory is looking behind the bar and seeing jars of chemicals. That was Mom's lab…. I don't remember animals. But she told me that she'd had them in one of their first homes in Beverly Hills. Apparently, they'd almost been evicted because of the critters." Mr. Wanger doesn't know what types of animals she had used; "maybe rabbits," he says. (Frogs might also come to mind.)

Justine's and Sam's focus continued to be cancer research. Apparently she was preparing a new paper, "correlating [her] notes and observations for presentation," wrote Henrietta Malkiel, "but until they have been accepted and approved, she will not hint as to their possible importance or effect."[1]

Almost certainly she also became involved with war efforts, as she had in 1917. Los Angeles during World War II was a city of blackouts, gas rationing, displaced neighbors, zoot suit riots, false alarms, and frayed nerves. Oceanside residents, anxious about the possibility of a sea strike, relocated or sold their properties. William Randolph Hearst sold Marion's beloved "beach house." Marion had her children's clinic turned into a war hospital and garrison, and it was temporarily renamed the Marion Davies War Work Hospital.

In Beverly Hills, women planted scores of victory gardens, sold war bonds door-to-door, made stretchers and quilts out of scrap work and opened a Russian snack bar and gift shop to benefit Russian war relief efforts. Some of Justine's friends, such as Mildred and Bert Allenberg, lived near anti-aircraft guns camouflaged in the hills from Beverly to Arcadia.

Justine was also attending to a wrenching personal issue. In 1943, she reached a difficult decision to commit her 72-year-old mother Sophia, apparently suffering from a form of dementia, to Greystone Park Hospital in Morris Plains, New Jersey. Sophia lived out her final days at the hospital, a residential facility for patients considered to be mentally ill, as dementia patients often were at the time.

After the war, as if there wasn't enough other news to report, gossip about Justine kicked back up again. In late 1945, Louella panted, "The surprise romance of all time is that of Mrs. Justine Johnston Wanger, ex-wife of Walter Wanger, and Leonard Goldstein, Universal International producer. They are a steady twosome."[2] Why this was a surprise was unexplained, except perhaps that Goldstein was a dedicated bachelor and the producer of low-budget, rather middlebrow films at Universal, later at Fox.

Goldstein was also co-owner of the Ming Room, a popular Cantonese restaurant on La Cienega along Beverly Hills' Restaurant Row. "We used to go there a lot," Justin Wanger recalls. "If we went out to dinner, we went there."

Justine was friends with Goldstein for several years. Mr. Wanger believes that it was through Goldstein that his mother got him and his brother jobs in the early 1950s as child extras in the 20th Century–Fox films *The Robe* with Richard Burton ("we waved palm fronds as Jesus walked by") and *The Scoutmaster*, which Goldstein produced for star Clifton Webb. "That was the extent of my acting career," says Mr. Wanger. "It didn't grab me." More impressive to Mr. Wanger was the day he, his brother and mother were lunching at the Fox commissary, and Marilyn Monroe sat at the table next to them. "You know that white terry-cloth robe she wore in *The Seven-Year Itch*?" he asks. "She was wearing something like that. She smiled and said hello to us, and she and my mother chatted a bit. Very pleasant. I have no idea what they said. I just remember that robe." It's interesting to think of what Justine may have had to say to Marilyn, to whom Lasky would compare her.

Goldstein, Mr. Wanger recalls, "was definitely part of my mother's life, but not in a big way." Gossip pieces about Justine's personal life continued, including one rather bizarre 1946 piece from Hearst columnist Adela Rogers St. John, who had known Justine since at least her Realart days. Adela wrote a story that reads like a *Cosmopolitan* magazine romance. After acknowledging that "even to this day no one has ever had an interview with Justine herself," Adela wrote, "she divorced Walter Wanger, saying that she must devote all her time to her [medical] work," when in fact Justine had said nothing of the kind. Adela did not mention the children, but stated that Justine had been assisting "a young doctor" and that "a little later she and the young doctor were married and vanished forever from the Hollywood scene."[3]

Justine had hardly vanished, and had not in fact remarried. But the tidbit about the doctor, while not precisely accurate, is intriguing.

Mr. Wanger says that other than Leonard Goldstein, he recalls only one other man in mother's life: Sam Hirshfeld. "I have fleeting memories about him. He had dark hair, greying at the temples, and to me at the time seemed like a fatherly figure. He would sit me on his lap in his car and let me pretend to drive. He and my mother saw a lot of each other. I do believe they were in love, and that they were planning on marriage."

If any of their friends knew of that Justine and Sam were hoping to marry, the information has not survived. One thing even Sam's closest friends did not know was that he was suffering from heart disease. During the war, the country had been depleted of civilian doctors, and physicians such as Sam who were too old to enlist became seriously overworked.

On December 12, 1946, Sam Hirshfeld suffered a massive coronary and collapsed. Harold Hyman reported that the bedridden Sam told screenwriter Ben Hecht, "Wouldn't it be wonderful if, in these times, a Jew were to discover a cure for cancer?"[4] The 51-year-old doctor died the next day.

"She called [my brother and me] into the bedroom," says Mr. Wanger, "and told us that Sam had died. That I remember."

Ben Hecht delivered an eloquent, heartfelt eulogy at the Todd & Leslie Chapel in Santa Monica:

> It is a curious thing to stand here praising Sam. It is a curious thing to sit here loving Sam. For that was Sam's job—to praise and to love. For Sam was a man so rich he gave to all. And there lay his one flaw. He gave it all away. All the gaiety and genius and love and wisdom came pouring out of him as if there were no end to what a man could do for others....
>
> The passion to serve mankind that kept Sam from moving without rest from patient to laboratory, that kept him answering calls of friends not half as sick as himself put an end to him. And that was because he loved us more than he loved himself.[5]

Sam's obituary listed his wife Eleanor and son Alan as survivors. Regardless of any plans Sam and Justine may have had, Mrs. Hirshfeld apparently had not divorced her husband. She may have had grounds to take action had she so wished, but perhaps she had not so wished.

Justine was devastated. She wrote a long, rambling, grief-stricken rant to Harold Hyman in New York:

> Harold, if only I felt that I could adequately thank you for all you've meant to Sam and me over the years!... Since Sam's death I've moved about in much the same outward manner I did when he was with me, but reality evades me. Nothing is or seems real. The gestures—the talk—and everything else adds up to nil.

> And Harold, people have been kind—but Christ, for the first time in my egocentric life I've got a real glimpse of what so-called broad-minded people have been thinking and feeling about me. I'm revolted.... Of course, you in your wisdom have always been aware of what motivates most human beings; however, I have never felt as sullied, as cheapened in my life.... What a lack of understanding of the most elementary emotions.... I'm entirely defenseless in this town, and not able to afford feuds, nor to express opinions. It seems I must live on and deny myself the luxury of free expression.... Sam would have been horrified....[6]

She had some choice words for a few non-celebrity acquaintances, stopping herself with "my, don't I sound bitter." She did. She was. Sam had apparently left two widows, and Justine was the illegitimate one.

There may have been an odd kind of jealousy going on among Sam's friends. Everyone felt close to him, and Justine having been closer could have been a source of resentment, as if it infringed on their own personal loss. Many of the "so-called broad-minded people" were certainly not unfamiliar with extra-marital relationships, but Sam was their god. It was a quirky but not unusual hypocrisy that characterized "this town." Nevertheless, Justine indeed could "not afford feuds" in a community that included the likes of Louella and Hedda as its town criers. But her pain was intense. "Christmas and my boys have kept me literally hopping. They're a great joy; also a responsibility, which weighs heavily on my tired back just at the moment. It's hard to figure how they are going to get on from here in; they depended so much on Sam for their fun—he took them wherever they wanted to go. When they wanted to pitch a ball, he was on hand to teach them the right way. He taught them to ride a bicycle—to dine and how to shoot their arrows. He always came with me to call for the boys after school—Sam enjoyed them more than anything and the joy was mutual. It will be hard to fill his place in their hearts."[7]

She was a bit calmer, but still somewhat rambling, in another letter to Harold after receiving a gift from him the following week.

> What a thoroughly charming memento of our very happy association and what healing memories it evokes. Thank you, darling—yours has always been the way of good-will. I've never met anyone to compare with you in understanding and the ability to find a way to contribute to the realization of others' potentialities. Both Sam and I missed the co-operative and congenial work spirit we had found in your company, and as I told you last time we met, we never ceased talking about it.
> Without Sam, I am a very ineffectual do-gooder. Thus far, nothing very concrete has developed towards the Samuel Hirshfeld Memorial Fund. The idea of seeing funds and passing the hat has always been anathema to me. However, as soon as I can get on an even keel again, I propose to work raising the necessary subscriptions to the end that there may be something alive in the world to commemorate that valiant spirit who made life much happier for everyone who circled his orbit.
> Sam's dream as he expressed it to me was very simple. He wanted to see grow up some sort of institution where honest men with ideas and a capacity for work could

20. The Most Elementary Emotions

bring their problems and find encouragement and suspended judgment, and of course financial and spiritual help. You may say, "But, Justine, there are such institutions," and I must reply, "Harold there are such in charter and incorporation papers, but all too few in working spirit." Sam loved experimental investigation, as I need not tell you, and he came up against all the tortuous politics of intolerance and selfishness, and was stymied time and again. He, in the end, was literally crucified by the intrigue necessary to carry on his utterly selfless task.

I only hope in the end someone will discover the validity of his notions so that all his sweat and torture will find justification.

Naming a ward for Sam would hardly reflect his personality, although it is a very nice expression of respect. Don't you think that a research foundation dedicated to perpetuating his memories would be more fitting? Well, at any rate, I am committed to the task of fostering this idea against the inclination of some new friends of Sam's, who feel a hospital ward would be a more concrete monument to his memory.

Please let me have your opinion on this matter. God knows I value it above anyone's.

I am off now to UCLA to see Dr. [David] Appleman, who is carrying on for the time being the research he was doing for Sam. I might tell you that he is getting very little encouragement from these big scientists who were so enthusiastic when Sam was around to do favors for them!

Bless you, my friend, and love to Marion [Mrs. Hyman].

Ever,
Justine[8]

It remains unclear exactly what Sam had had in mind: an institute offering growth potential, financial assistance, and "spiritual" guidance for, perhaps, young doctors, although Justine does not specify the target benefactors. That they may find "suspended judgment" could indicate that Sam wanted this institution to be for members of minority groups, but again, there is no clarification. Nor does she explain what sort of resistance or "intolerance" he met, or why she considered that Sam had been "crucified" as a result of his efforts.

But her own plans of a research foundation named for Sam, even a ward, were very tall orders that she was unable to meet. The only known memorial to Sam was a Samuel Hirshfeld Fund for Surgical Research was established in 1946 at the University of Minnesota, onetime home to the laboratory of Leo Tolstoy Samuels, Justine's and Sam's former science club pal.

Justine's big ideas at this time were trajectories of grief. Taking effective action after a loss can require time. There would be no major monument to Sam, but Justine found focus beyond what she called her "egocentric life." She would also find ways to explore, as Hecht said of Sam, what a person can do for others.

21

Women's Activities

Justine worked with biochemistry professor David Appleman in closing out Sam's lab work at UCLA's Kinsey Hall. Sam and Dr. Appleman had been collaborating with Justine's X-ray project lead doctor, Clyde Emery, and Caltech's Dr. Walter Marx on an examination of enzyme activities and melanin production in cancerous blood cells. Dr. Appleman would continue his affiliation at UCLA for the next forty years, even reporting to his lab after his retirement. But after Sam's death, information about Justine's work in medical research disappears.

She had managed a successful second act in her life. Now she was entering a third.

From the late 1940s until at least the early 1960s, Justine became one of that often-dismissed but vital group of Los Angeles women who existed just prior to second-wave feminism, those who made non-paying careers out of raising awareness and funds for political and social issues. Such women usually had money and knew other people who did as well, which, obviously, they had to. Many of them were either born into wealth or married into it or both. They weren't expected to earn their own living. They were women. They were called "society ladies."

As such, their efforts were often relegated to the "society" sections of newspapers, or, as the *Los Angeles Times* called it, "Women's Activities." The fact was, such women had the smarts, resources and ability to get things done. These weren't the Sondheim-ian ladies who lunch: these were ladies who worked so that somebody else could have lunch.

None of the women who spearheaded projects with which Justine was involved had degrees in non-profit management. There was no such thing as yet. They had advisors (usually husbands, lawyers and financial consultants) but they basically learned how to do what they were doing by doing it. In less than twenty years, LA "society women" would make fundraising big business, their efforts netting $75,000 in 1965 money for worthy causes. As the *Los Angeles Times* reported in 1966, "not a dollar could survive bad management to do a dime's worth of charitable work."[1]

21. Women's Activities

Justine was not among the wealthiest of such women. Even if she enjoyed fundraising, which she didn't—it was, as she had said, "anathema" to her—she certainly did not have, say, Marion's resources. The name "Justine Wanger" was never among the more familiar in the society columns, when it appeared. She was never quoted. What she did would have been more important to her than whether or not the public knew she was doing it.

Mildred Polstein Allenberg seems to have been a catalyst for new directions in Justine's life. Godmother to Justine's sons, golf buddy, and philanthropic leader, Mildred was an NYU graduate and one of the brightest and most beloved "non-professional" women in town. She was also one of the wealthiest and best-connected. Her husband Bert's talent agency had recently merged with William Morris and handled an impressive roster of A-listers, including Judy Garland, Clark Gable, Frank Capra, Robert Mitchum, Edward G. Robinson, Loretta Young, and Frank Sinatra. Many of Bert's clients, including Sinatra, helped Mildred's efforts over the years, as would a number of Justine's friends, such as her former vaudeville pal Jack Benny.

Justin Wanger recalls: "Mildred was very outgoing. She could also be very stern, at least to a kid. You didn't want to get on her bad side. But she could also be warm. We had a love of art in common. And she was very active. There was a whole group of them who gravitated toward those activities: Mildred, Peg Fenwick, [publisher] Helene Boughton. I remember the name Marsha Hunt. All staunch Democrats. From the time I was about seven years old, my mother was always involved with something, usually with Mildred."

One of Mildred's major activities was leading a women's coalition of volunteers at Cedars of Lebanon Hospital, where Justine had been working with Sam. She also an officer of the Beverly Hills Chapter of Hadassah, the women's division of the United Jewish Welfare Fund, and the Beverly Hills chapter of the League of Women Voters.

Justine was still mourning Sam when Mildred pulled her into League meetings. She found that she liked them. One of the League's major activities in the postwar years included efforts to support the United Nations. The UN's commitment to peace, international understanding and assistance to displaced persons was a priority for many during the postwar years.

In 1947, Justine joined the Allenbergs at a star-studded cocktail reception for former Minnesota governor Harold Stassen, a progressive Republican and soon-to-be-perennial presidential candidate. Stassen, seeking film-industry backers for his 1948 presidential run, appealed to liberal voters. Of particular interest was his recent participation in the United Nations formation conference in San Francisco, and that he was an American signer of the UN Charter. Stassen lost the nomination, but Justine's political and social services activities were just beginning.

The League formed a committee focusing on UNESCO, the UN agency dedicated to forwarding international efforts in education, natural sciences, social sciences, culture and communication. Justine joined the committee, which was chaired by another golf buddy, Margaret Fenwick. Known as Peggy or Peg, she had been a reader during the war for the Bureau of Motion Pictures, a branch of the Office of War Information that (much to Walter's and other producer's consternation) reviewed screenplays for elements of wartime patriotism. Peg's play *Meet the World* was selected by the League to serve as a 1950 UN fundraiser in conjunction with the Beverly Hills chapter of the American Association for the United Nations and UCLA's Committee on Theatre Arts Production.

Justine volunteered to produce the play. Her production committee included both Peg and Mildred. She brought in an associate producer, Richard Alan Wilson, a former Orson Welles Mercury Theatre actor, and director Bernard Szold. Program ads were solicited from industry friends. Claudette Colbert bought a full page.

"Justine Johnstone doesn't need help from her ex (Walter Wanger) to produce 'Meet the World,'" Hedda Hopper reported. "Show's tied in with the U. N."[2]

Meet the World, billed as "a living newspaper for our time," was presented on March 30, 1950, at UCLA's Royce Hall, featuring sketches and songs drawing comparisons between current political affairs and the intent and goals of America's founders. The cast of over 100 performers included Jeff Chandler, Margaret Hamilton, Rhys Williams, Marjorie Lord, Irene Tedrow, and Everett Glass. The all-black South Central Civic Adult Chorus performed under the direction of noted composer-conductor Jester Hairston.

In its review, the *Los Angeles Times* declared, "Justine Wanger, with Richard Wilson as associate and Bernard Szold, director, were the primary factors in its success."[3] The performance was filmed, the play was published and made available for production.

It was just as this new phase of her life was taking off that Justine's finances hit a snag. Walter was of course still her only source of income, and he wasn't bringing in the kind of money he had before the war. Her divorce settlement, signed before she had adopted her children, stipulated that revisions to her payments would be required if Walter's income fell below $50,000 a year, and that was happening. Walter Wanger Productions was folded into United Artists in 1941. He was still "semi-independent" but working as a unit producer for major studios.

Then in 1943, Walter's attorneys discovered something that somehow hadn't been communicated properly in the divorce papers. Justine had understood her payments to be a tax-exempt community property settlement—the payments did, after all, come under the header of "Property Settlement

Agreement"—and she had never claimed them as income. Walter, however, was deducting the payments as alimony, resulting in snafus that added to his already burdensome tax problems. Walter's attorneys of course wanted the payments to be considered alimony. They also wanted Justine to accept a $100,000 life insurance policy, reduced from the previously agreed-upon $250,000.

After a three-year legal battle, Walter's attorneys won. Justine paid back taxes she hadn't known that she had owed and took deductions from her settlement allowance, reducing her income by a fourth. Then Walter countered the plan for the insurance policy reduction. He relinquished the entire $250,000 policy (over $3,000,000 in today's currency) over to Justine. She thus ceased receiving regular payments, and began living off of a trust. It was a move that seemed satisfactory to both of them.

UCLA, where Justine assisted Sam Hirshfeld with cancer research. Photograph is of Royce Hall, late 1940s–early 1950s, venue for Justine's production of the 1950 UN benefit, *Meet the World*. Courtesy USC Digital Libraries.

"She never really suffered financially," says Justin Wanger, "but we didn't live high on the hog." Some income-supplementing attempts proved not always to her advantage. "She did make some lousy investments," says Mr. Wanger. "She bought into Douglas Aircraft at 45 and it went to 93. Then her broker sold her out of it at 37."

Justine began adjusting and re-adjusting to a much more moderate income than she'd had in the early days in "paradise." In late 1946, she moved with her children out of the Delfern house, which she and Walter had purchased over a decade earlier. They found a smaller, but nonetheless quite comfortable, home on palm-lined North Hillcrest, just south of Sunset; still in Beverly Hills, but out of exquisite Holmby. After five years, ads began appearing in the *Los Angeles Times* for open-house viewings of the home variously described as "moderne," "a real buy," "bright and cheerful 2- story, perfect condition, 3 family bdrms, 2 bas, paneled study … poudre room, maid's room and bath, children's playroom. Enclosed garden. Priced for quick sales. Bring your checkbook."[4] In September 1951, Justine sold the Hillcrest house to brother and sister Gladys and Harold Rosson for $45,000. Harold was a cinematographer whose many credits included *The Wizard of Oz*. Gladys was Cecil B. DeMille's longtime personal assistant, accountant and mistress.

Justine and the boys moved to a two-story, L-shaped apartment complex about a half-mile south on N. Maple Drive just off Beverly Boulevard, and later to Beverly itself. No maid's rooms, no paneled studies, no "poudre" rooms. It was the first time she lived apartments since she'd left New York. She would never again live in a house.

It was "some change," as she'd once said about her career long ago. But, as usual, Justine evolved with the fluctuating needs of her life. After all, she'd been an Emma girl. Patience rejoices in hardship.

She became vice president of the Beverly Hills League, finance director of the California League, and finance chair of the Women's Democratic Club of Beverly Hills. She organized meetings around UN-related themes, booking conference rooms at the Beverly Hills Hotel, wrangling Girl Scout Troup 838 of Beverly Hills to appear as color guard, and persuading political science professors from USC and Occidental College to address international relations. She and her fellow "society ladies" were, as Justine had said years earlier, "women as they are—real people who are doing real work in the world."

22

Walter, My Dear

Apart from their lawyers' squabbling, Justine and Walter were still occasionally in touch, and still had affection for one another. At least, Justine was moderately affectionate, and certainly civil. In early January 1949, she wrote a post–Christmas thank-you note:

Walter, My Dear:

I am heartily ashamed of this tardiness in wishing you "A Joyous New Year." As always I must crave your indulgence, because you know better than anyone that your happiness and welfare are my sincerest concern. May everything good for you and those you love happen to you and yours this year & ever. The boys have been so busy playing with their laboratory set and trying to master the football game that they haven't yet found time to write and thank you for your gifts. However, I can assure you that they are more than happy with them. As for Justine, she certainly enjoyed her basket and is still at it. The contents are a sweet reminder of a very nice person. As for your check, it has found its way into that all-devouring, never-satisfied household account.

Thanks, Walter, for remembering me so graciously.

Bless you always.

Ever the same,
Justine[1]

"I didn't know him well," says Justin Wanger. "He was not an active participant in our lives. I remember he gave me a cowboy outfit when I was five or six. Mom remained friends with him at least until the end of the '40s."

After the war, Walter Wanger became an emotional and financial wreck. After years of success, his output was becoming negligible. He was borrowing heavily from his brother Henry, a Wall Street financier, and from Joan. Added to his troubles was the heated postwar social climate. Walter, however unwillingly, was one of the architects of the Hollywood blacklist.

The "list" had evolved as a result of the 1947 House Un-American Activities Committee. Writers who had refused to implicate themselves as Communists or name names to HUAC found themselves cited for contempt of Congress. The writers, known as the "Hollywood Ten," also found themselves shunned by their industry by an effective blacklisting process.

For all his New Deal, social equality and perhaps even socialist leanings, Walter felt backed in a corner when it came to postwar fears. But it came down to the bottom line: principles versus profits. Following the HUAC decision, a group of top Hollywood executives, including Walter, Sam Goldwyn, Louis B. Mayer, Jack Warner, Dore Schary (RKO's production chief soon to take over the presidency of MGM from Mayer) and others, met at the Waldorf-Astoria Hotel in New York. After lengthy, heated discussions, the group issued a two-page release, now known as the Waldorf Statement. It said that unless the ten writers purged themselves of their contempt citations and renounced Communism under oath, they would be released from their contracts. The statement further declared that the studios would not "knowingly employ a Communist or a member of any party or group which advocates the overthrow of the government of the United States."

Dore Schary would later acknowledge that the statement was a caving to pressure and fear, and that he felt strong-armed by the conservative Goldwyn. What it came down to was self-preservation: the moguls were terrified of losing their broadest fanbase, middle-American audiences, thus their bankrolls. "To save themselves from the wrath of the anti–Semites," writes film historian Neal Gabler, "this is what they did."[2]

Walter found himself politically tap-dancing among his fellow producers, being called a Communist by the right for his progressive leanings, and a traitor by the left.

Considering his tenuous situation, he made an extremely odd and risky decision—or perhaps not so odd, since it was Walter. He sank what was left of his fortune into his 1948 epic film *Joan of Arc* starring Ingrid Bergman.

He wasn't the only one funding the film. "In exchange for the insurance policy," says Justin Wanger, "Mom invested in *Joan of Arc* as sort of a quid pro quo. Great cast, great flop. I don't think Walter ever fully recovered."

Shortly before the film's release, news broke of the married Bergman's affair with the also-married Italian director Roberto Rossellini. Hedda and Louella engaged in charming rounds of slut-shaming. Walter frantically cabled Bergman, begging her to deny the affair. Bergman refused. The Catholic Church denounced the film, audiences steered away in droves.

Walter was on the verge of bankruptcy. His and Joan's home was in foreclosure. Walter's habitual failure to devise a Plan B was, at long last, becoming a devastating issue.

In another example of old habits dying hard, Walter hadn't been any more faithful to Joan Bennett than he had been to Justine. Only three months after their wedding in 1940, Joan was on the verge of divorcing Walter "for a romantic dereliction," as she said.³ Her mother had talked her out of it. Eventually, Joan developed her own way of dealing with marital problems.

In 1951, Joan told Walter that her agent, MCA's Jennings Lang, had a television series in mind for her, which would be, as much of television still was, shot in New York. Walter was furious. Even though he was nearly bankrupt, he considered Joan working in New York "a challenge to his position as head of the household," Joan later said.⁴ What he actually felt challenged by were his suspicions that Joan and the married Lang were having an affair.

They were, actually. Walter hired a private detective, who confirmed his worst fears. Joan and Lang's "love nest" was an apartment on South Bedford Drive in Beverly Hills leased by one of Lang's assistants, junior agent Jay Kanter. The scenario of the boss getting a special key from a subordinate would become the basis of Billy Wilder's 1960 film *The Apartment*.

There are several reasons why what happened next is even known. One was a much bolder, more aggressive, and more headline-screamingly competitive press than existed, say, when Justine was married to Walter. Another was the legal collapse of the studio system, rendering publicity managers and "fixers" less powerful than they had been in the past. And then there was Walter himself, acting out a script so outrageously noir even he would have rejected it. But it was, at the very least, a pristine example of the societal (certainly Hollywood) double-standard at the time.

On December 13, 1951, Walter drove past the MCA offices and, no doubt suspecting that it was there, spotted Joan's Cadillac convertible parked in the lot. He pulled in and waited. More than two hours later, Lang and Joan arrived, fresh from a tryst at The Apartment. They parked and walked to Joan's car. Joan had just settled into the driver's seat as Walter approached the couple. He leaned on the hood of her car and spoke briefly to Joan. "Leave us alone," she was heard to say. Then Walter turned to Lang. Standing about two feet away from the agent, Walter pulled a .38 out of his coat pocket. "No, no!" Joan screamed. Lang's hands flew into the air like a bad guy in a Western. Walter shot him twice, hitting Lang once in the right thigh and—depending on which sources one wishes to believe—once very close to or actually in Lang's left testicle.

The MCA parking lot happened to be across the street from the Beverly Hills Police Department. Officers were on the scene within moments. Walter was immediately arrested. He not only had the gun, but a large, sheathed hunting knife. "Oh," he reportedly said when asked about the knife. "I use that to open envelopes and sharpen pencils."⁵

Lang survived. But the scenario was Hollywood gossip gold for months. The Los Angeles papers ran bold mega-font front-page headlines and multiple stories covering the shooting, Walter's life, Joan's life, Lang's life, his wife Pam, her friend Jane Wyman (who drove Pam from a dinner party to

Midway Hospital when they received the news), the cops, the doctors, the lawyers and parking lot attendant who heard Joan's screams. Justine was mentioned, with photos from twenty years earlier as "the first wife," but not as often as Joan's previous two husbands.

Walter may have been drunk, or on some sort of medication (or perhaps should have been), but he claimed that he did it because he believed Lang was "breaking up my home."[6] Apparently, he had taken the only possible option under the circumstances. Actually, the circumstances were rather at odds with Walter's interpretation: Lang and Joan had no intention of divorcing their spouses and breaking up their own or each other's homes. They were simply enjoying a casual affair, just like Walter always did.

Walter was charged with assault with a deadly weapon with intent to commit murder. A conviction would mean up to 14 years in prison. His pals Walt Disney, Sam Goldwyn, AMPAS co-founder Joseph Schenck and other producers immediately chipped in for his defense fund. He hired Jerry Giesler, aka "Get-Me-Giesler," a clever attorney known for getting off the most blatantly suspicious high-profile defendants. Giesler persuaded Walter to enter a plea of not guilty by reasons of "temporary insanity," an odd but surprisingly effective defense that implied that the suspect went absolutely bonkers for a minute but of course was just fine now. In a phrase that was much quoted around the country, Giesler claimed that Walter had fired in "a bluish flash through a violent haze,"[7] a nice poetic contrast to Walter's private grilling of his friends for assurance that he'd hit what he was aiming for.

In April 1952, Walter waived a trial in favor of a hearing. Giesler read letters from friends such as Zanuck and Goldwyn telling Judge Harry J. Borde what a great guy Walter was. It worked. The judge sentenced Walter to four months at Wayside Honor Rancho, a low-security farm facility about forty miles north in Castaic.

What it came down to was the "unwritten law," a phrase much in use at the time, meaning that a man could do almost anything with impunity against anyone sleeping with the man's wife. There was, of course, no "unwritten law" for women.

Honor Rancho was primarily known at that time as Robert Mitchum's home-away-from-home after his 1948 pot bust (Giesler had been Mitchum's attorney as well). Mitchum had famously described his experience at the Rancho as "like Palm Springs, but without the riff-raff."[8] Walter had no such perspective. He had expected to be exonerated, and was astounded at the sentencing. He blanched at having to perform such arduous tasks as cataloguing prison library books and seating inmates in the auditorium on movie night. He moped about in his regulation jeans with "Honor Rancho" stenciled on the seat and complained bitterly until his friend and lawyer Mendel Silberberg warned him that his attitude might compromise any chance he might have with a major studio upon his release. So he brightened up, at least superficially, signing letters "Yours from location." Borrowing rather wanly from Mitchum, he called the farm "like Palm Springs without the agents."[9] He was released for good behavior after 102 days. "It was one of the most wonderful experiences of my life," he told the press chipperly as he left.[10]

He rallied fairly well for someone who tried to blast the *cojones* off a guy. It took a couple of years, but Walter managed to crank up his career again. His hundred-odd days as a librarian in a low-security honor farm gave him special insight into the horrors of the American prison system, resulting in such films as *Riot in Cell Block 11* and *I Want to Live!* Even his 1955 *Invasion of the Body Snatchers* (featuring Justine's *Meet the World* actor Everett Glass), now considered a B-movie classic, can be interpreted as a comment on the restrictions of prison life. It can also perhaps be a political allegory. It can also perhaps be just an entertaining sci-fi flick.

As for the other players: Jennings Lang and his key-holding subordinate Jay Kanter received reprimands from MCA but stayed at the agency, where they flourished. Both eventually became A-list film and television producers.

The women, on the other hand, did not fare so well. Pam Lang, wife of Jennings, was not an actress but a stay-at-home mom. Ten months after her shell-shocked face was splattered all over the newspapers after the shooting, Mrs. Lang died of a heart attack. Lang almost immediately began squiring actresses again. Within a few years, he married singer Monica Lewis and, perhaps to Walter's surprise, fathered a child.

Joan Bennett, who never shot anyone, watched her career collapse and never recover.

With her financial dependence on Walter terminated, Justine suffered little except perhaps shock. She was spared the humiliation endured by Pam Lang and Joan Bennett, and had no interest in incorporating herself into the lurid scenario. Pam's and Joan's lives were affected forever because of their husbands' behavior. Women, whether they worked or not, were still defined to a great degree by who their husbands were, and what they did. In this case, the never-remarried Justine had, as a journalist once said about her, "incredible luck."

She may have had concerns that the jokes and nasty little songs about Walter that were quickly spreading might affect her pre-adolescent children, who shared Walter's last name. No doubt Justine was also aware that Joan Bennett had been informed that her and Walter's eight-year-old daughter Stephanie was no longer welcome as a student at the Westlake School for Girls due to the scandal surrounding her parents.

Justine need not have worried. When asked if he recalled the incident, Justin Wanger shrugs, "Oh, sure. But from my standpoint, it had no effect on me. He had no relationship to us at that point. Actually, we used to ride our bikes past the place and laugh. Of all places to do it! We thought, if you were going to do something like this, Mr. Stupid, you don't do it right across the street from the Beverly Hills Police Department!"

Only one columnist obtained a comment about the Walter mess from Justine. She agreed to speak, albeit very briefly, to Hedda Hopper, who had, for better or worse, always supported her. While Walter was singing "The Cell Block Tango," Hedda wrote, "Justine Johnstone Wanger, Walter's former wife and one of the most beautiful Ziegfeld girls, lives quietly in a Beverly Hills apartment taking care of her twin [sic] sons…. Justine became interested in medicine, worked in the laboratory with a famous doctor, and made a discovery which was written up in the leading medical journals some years ago." It was a serene little tidbit amongst the Walter news.

Hedda asked Justine for a comment about her ex. Justine said simply, "Anyone who has had the privilege of knowing Walter will sympathize with him in his present trouble."[11]

Another ex-wife—and ex-investor—might have said just about anything and could have been forgiven. But it was typical Justine: elegant, tasteful, to the point, and somewhat distancing.

And with that, Justine made her last public comment about anything.

23

Producer, Agent, Dramaturg and She Still Looks Lovely

In 1951, the year of Walter's "troubles," Justine enlisted Clore Warne, a politically progressive MCA attorney and Civil Liberties Union board member, to address the Beverly Hills Women's Democratic Club. His subject was the legalities of loyalty oaths.

It was a hot topic. UCLA professors and other academics throughout the state were being fired for refusing to sign such oaths imposed by the UC Board of Regents. Dr. David Appleman, Sam and Justine's UCLA colleague, managed to keep his job, but was subpoenaed before Los Angeles' HUAC-like Tenney Commission for having lectured at the People's Education Center, a labor school with suspected Communists on its staff.

Justine's friend Marsha Hunt, a busy character actress who had worked for Walter, had objected to loyalty oaths recently established by the Screen Actors' Guild. The actress suddenly found herself in the dreaded right-wing name-naming publication, *Red Channels*—and thus instantly unemployable. Cecil B. DeMille followed SAG's lead and demanded a similar requirement for members of the Screen Directors Guild, forerunner of the Directors Guild of America. Nearly every major entertainment union would follow suit. (Among the few unions to ignore blacklisting of suspected Communists was Actors Equity.) Such requirements would remain the books for years, even after the Supreme Court ruled loyalty oaths unconstitutional in 1965.

Justine went to work, literally, to help blacklisted artists. At age 58, she obtained a Social Security card and landed her first paying job in almost 30 years as an assistant agent for the Ingo Preminger Agency. Preminger, an Austrian Jew and the the gentle-natured brother of film director Otto, was one of the few agents at the time representing blacklisted writers.

Ingo Preminger found work for his unemployable clients by using either fake names or "fronts," individuals paid for the use of their names as authors of the blacklisted writers' screenplays. Among his clients while Justine was

The League of Women Voters of Beverly Hills, California

The American Association for the United Nations, Southwest Region

and

The Theatre Production Committee of U. C. L. A.

Present

"MEET THE WORLD"

A DRAMATIZED THEME IN TWO ACTS
By PEG FENWICK

Producer	Justine Wanger
Associate Producer	Richard Wilson
Direction	Bernard Szold
Scene 3 direction	Tom Powers
Scene 6 direction	Howard Banks
Set Design	Arne Nybak
Technical Director	Kate Drain Lawson
Choral Director	Jester Hairston
Casting Director	Mary Louise Elkins
Lighting Director	Richard Wilson

MARCH 30, 1950

ONE PERFORMANCE ONLY

PRESENTED AT ROYCE HALL AUDITORIUM

UNIVERSITY OF CALIFORNIA AT LOS ANGELES

Program for *Meet the World* produced by Justine at UCLA, March 30, 1950. The play by Peg Fenwick was billed as "A Living Newspaper of Our Time," and featured film actors, the all-black South Central Civic Adult Chorus, and a total cast of over 100 performers. Courtesy Mr. Justin Wanger.

working for him were Michael Wilson (whose work included *Friendly Persuasion, The Bridge on the River Kwai* and *Lawrence of Arabia*), Hugo Butler (who, along with "Hollywood Ten" writer and later Preminger client Dalton Trumbo, moved to Mexico and continued to write), and Nedrick Young (using the name Nathan E. Douglas) and Harold Jacob Smith, who won the

Academy Award for their screenplay adaptation of *The Defiant Ones* and were nominated for *Inherit the Wind*.

Working for Preminger was a perfect fit for Justine. She may or may not have needed the money, but Preminger's outlook was consistent with her political ideals. She reported to the Sunset Strip office every morning to exchange ideas with her articulate, down-to-earth boss and his creative clients. Her apartment became stacked with books, manuscripts, and screenplays. It was as close as she ever got to her first childhood ambition, being a librarian. Most importantly, she helped the unemployable get jobs.

Justine acquired at least one client of her own: Peg Fenwick, her fellow League member whose play *Meet the World* Justine had produced. Peg had no screenplays to her credit, and as such, she was not blacklisted, although her political leanings were considerably left. She adapted a novel about Mississippi life, *Blow for a Landing*, by Ben Lucien Burman, a Jewish Southerner once accused of teaching Bolshevism. Justine scored a sale of Peg's adaptation to Universal International. Producer Aaron Rosenberg announced that the film, to be retitled *Mississippi Landing*, would star Audie Murphy, but for unknown reasons, the project never happened. (As late as 1980, novelist Burman complained that "the so-and-so's" at Universal still "have got it on the shelf."[1])

But Justine got Peg "in" at Universal. In 1955, the studio filmed Peg's adaptation of an Edna Lee story that became *All That Heaven Allows*. On the surface, the film, starring Jane Wyman and Rock Hudson, is a colorful soap opera, but it delved into social injustice and class warfare issues. It would be Peg's only film credit before she married noted political scientist Dr. Saul Padover, a professor at the New School for Social Research and biographer of Thomas Jefferson and Karl Marx.

Not all of Justine's projects were political. In 1955, she received a manuscript from her old friend and Team Justine member, Dr. Harold Thomas Hyman in New York. In a scene straight out of *The Man Who Came to Dinner*, Harold, the good doctor, had written a novel. He wanted Justine's feedback and possibly her representation. Apparently, the manuscript was awful.

Justine had no idea what to say. She sent it to Gene Fowler to see if he could help her somehow. Fowler didn't know what to do either. He wrote to Ben Hecht: "Speaking of doctors, I have a problem. Harold Hyman's ms. of his novel is here. Justine sent it to me for comment. I am unable to see the difference between a toy balloon and a cannon-ball. Harold's book seems to lack organization, character, development; is burdened with too many chapter-headings that do not have chapters; and he tells three or four stories in competition with one another. I don't know what to do or say about this, for when it comes to my so-called profession and practice of it, I simply cannot tell a lie. What the hell can I do? Harold is such a wonderful man, and his fiction is not in keeping with his genius."[2]

Someone eventually managed to break it gently to poor Harold. He was fine. In a few years, he had his own popular syndicated newspaper column, "Ask the MD," centering on his area of expertise with a straightforward, chatty writing style.

During Justine's tenure at the Preminger agency, the blacklist began crumbling slowly but exponentially, thanks in large part to such blacklisted writers as Trumbo, who led efforts to highlight the absurdity that curiously unknown writers were no-showing for major awards. After using pseudonyms for years, Trumbo finally began receiving credit for his screenplays of *Spartacus* (assisted by star Kirk Douglas, who became a friend of Justine's) and *Exodus,* directed by Ingo's brother Otto. It was the beginning of the end of the blacklist.

It was around this time that Justine, in her early 60s, discontinued working for Preminger as one son prepared for college, the other for the Army. "She tells me she's retired to devote herself to her two children," Hedda wrote. Just in case anyone was wondering, Hedda added that Justine "still looks lovely."[3]

She was retired from paying work only. In 1955, Justine joined for a cause particularly close to her heart. A new Mount Sinai Hospital was proposed on Beverly Boulevard, with half the over 400 beds offered to low-income patients. Justine joined a committee chaired by Mildred Allenberg and Edie Wasserman, wife of super-agent Lew and philanthropic dynamo (Edie would, among other things, help build the Los Angeles Music Center). They created "Bal de Rose" an invitation-only event at the new Beverly Hilton Hotel. Patrons included the Gregory Pecks, the James Stewarts, the Alfred Hitchcocks, the Jack Warners, the Elizabeth Taylors (Michael Wilding), the Nancy Reagans (Ronnie), and studio executives. The new hospital had its grand opening

Sam Hirshfeld, MD, surgeon, physician, collaborator, friend, and beloved companion, relaxing in Justine's backyard, ca. 1946. Courtesy Mr. Justin Wanger.

23. Producer, Agent, Dramaturg and She still looks lovely 183

within months. In 1961, Mount Sinai merged with Cedars of Lebanon, where Justine had worked with Sam Hirshfeld, and the two hospitals became one facility, Cedars-Sinai Medical Center. Mildred continued to create events for the hospital for years as co-founder and president of the Women's Guild of Cedars-Sinai Medical Center, an organization that continues to thrive.

In the late 1950s, Justine took her last trip to New York. She and her son Justin enjoyed Broadway shows ("We saw *Damn Yankees*," said Mr. Wanger, "which broke my heart. I wanted to see *My Fair Lady*. But it was sold out") and looked up some of her oldest and dearest friends. She lunched with Justin's "New York godmother" Rae Selwyn, an actress from Justine's Broadway days, the sister of the now-departed Edgar and Archie, and recent widow of a stockbroker. In Ellenville, New York, Justine and her son called on one of her favorites, Solon "Blackie" Blackberg, living in retirement with his family—including a daughter named for Justine. The irrepressible Harold Hyman hosted them in Bucks County, PA, where he was semi-retired except for his newspaper column and attending select patients, such as his close friend and neighbor, Oscar Hammerstein.

"Mrs. Darryl Zanuck, the former Justine Johnston [sic], plans to resume her acting career,"[4] Hearst columnist and noted viper Dorothy Kilgallen announced in 1959. Mrs. Zanuck was actually former silent film actress Virginia Fox, estranged from her long-philandering husband and more interested in her grandchildren than getting back into films. And Justine "Johnston" was in fact embarking on a new United Nations project.

Justine was "burning the midnight oil," according to Hedda, for a "UN-ANTA" benefit.[5] The Los Angeles Chapter of the American Association for the United Nations and the American National Theatre Academy (ANTA) were sponsoring a nationwide contest for one-act plays reflecting the ideals of the UN. ANTA, a non-profit theatrical production and training entity established in New York in 1935, had opened a Los Angeles branch in 1957. Among its early members were Charles Laughton, John Forsythe, Groucho Marx, directors, producers, theatre professors—and Walter, who also served on the AAUN board.

The UN-ANTA benefit received some impressive coverage. In her "My Day" column of March 13, 1959, Eleanor Roosevelt wrote:

> The Los Angeles Chapter of the American Association for the United Nations has undertaken a rather exciting new activity. It is sponsoring a nationwide contest for one-act plays, which are to be judged by Robert Anderson, Paddy Chayefsky, William Inge, Emmet Lavery and Dora [sic] Schary.
>
> It is hoped that this project "will inspire the writing of plays which will further the world peace role of the U.N." The one requirement made of contestants is that the dramatic situation be "based on the working out of the ideals and ideas of the United Nations or any of its specialized agencies in terms of human relations and conflicts."[6]

Justine served on the theatre committee as dramaturg, reviewing scripts as she had for Preminger. She scoured 300 manuscripts before making her recommendations to judges Anderson, Chayefsky, Inge, Lavery and Schary, Walter's fellow conflicted co-creator of the Hollywood blacklist. Hedda herself was on the committee that threw a fundraising party at songwriter Johnny Green's home.

The play contest winners were announced in September. First place was a tie: *The Meadow*, Ray Bradbury's adaption of his own short story, and Donald J. Dunlavey's *Border Incident No. 907*, later retitled *The Mercenaries*. Second place went to a comedy, *Leave It to the Little People* by television writer Willard Weiner.

Under the title *Three for Today*, the one-acts were presented on March 30, 1960, at the Huntington Hartford, the former Lux Radio Theatre on Vine in Hollywood. The most popular of the trio was *Leave It to the Little People* with Mary Wickes as a snooping Iowa telephone operator listening as a local farmer calls a Soviet farmer to discuss turkeys, resulting in an international incident. The comedy garnered unexpected laughs when the theatre experienced a technical glitch, and Miss Wickes effortlessly and wittily ad-libbed in a completely darkened theatre.

The UN-ANTA benefit was well represented, on stage and off, by boldface names of the day. Justine may have been out of the business for thirty years professionally, but never socially. Her son recalls:

> Mildred Allenberg would have Christmas parties or swimming parties. Edward G. Robinson would be there; Danny Kaye, Jean Simmons. To me of course, they were just people. Growing up in Beverly Hills, you didn't think too much about their being famous. What you'd do at a party depended on whose house it was. If you went to Pandro Berman's house, you'd watch a movie. If you went to a surgeon's house, you'd watch a medical film he'd made. I remember watching a movie of a gall bladder operation once. It was great....
>
> When I was home on leave from the Army in the late 1950s, Mildred asked me to be her escort to a dinner party at Frank Sinatra's up Coldwater Canyon. It was a small gathering, maybe eight people. Lovely dinner. Sinatra was very charming. After dinner, he asked if we'd like to hear his new album. Well, you're not going to say no. So he premiered "Come Dance with Me" for us.

Among the longtime friends with whom Justine kept in touch were Harpo Marx and Marion Davies. Mr. Wanger remembers playing with Harpo and Susan Marx's daughter Minnie at their Beverly Hills home, and at least one party at Marion's estate on Beverly Drive, just below Coldwater Canyon, when he was a teenager.

"Marion once sent Mom a very strange Christmas present," he said. "It was a Buddha, the ugliest thing I'd ever seen. I really have no idea what it meant. It was some sort of a joke between them." Justine never explained the joke, but it very possibly was a reference to the long-ago past. The first home

23. Producer, Agent, Dramaturg and She still looks lovely

that Hearst had bought for Marion, the beautiful Beaux-Arts townhouse on Riverside Drive in New York, became the New York Buddhist Academy in 1955.

The past must have indeed seemed like an entertaining joke. LA in the 1950s and early '60s was a metropolis of freeways, gas stations, smog, Disneyland, rock and roll, the disc-stacked Capitol Records Building, Googie architecture with spikey antennae on top, baby boomers when they were babies, and nearly six million people throughout the county. Streetcars and trolleys, once a city staple, disappeared. The Lakers migrated to LA from Minneapolis, the Dodgers from Brooklyn. Chavez Ravine was gutted and longtime Mexican-American residents displaced to create Dodger Stadium. The futuristic, space-age Theme Building came to define Los Angeles International Airport. The Jet Propulsion Laboratory, under the auspices of Caltech, was building satellites. The University of Southern California established the first schools in the United States for cinema and television. The first star was placed on the Hollywood Walk of Fame, honoring a woman, the gifted Joanne Woodward. Fundraising efforts were under way for a Los Angeles Music Center and a Los Angeles County Museum of Art.

In the early 1960s, Justine left Beverly Hills for good. Her sons were embarking on their own lives, and she was alone for this first time since her divorce. She relocated to the Hancock Park neighborhood, just south of Beverly Boulevard, and then to Hilgard Avenue in Westwood near UCLA, "across from sorority row," says Mr. Wanger. She found contentment in the collegiate neighborhood, with its quaint, prewar Spanish-style architecture, walking distance to the university's arts complex and new medical center.

And yet dear old Hedda Hopper was still trying to get Justine back into the movies somehow. In 1959, she eagerly asked Walter if his proposed new epic film, *Justine*, was based on his ex-wife. "No," he replied, quickly explaining that the story was one of four books by British author Lawrence Durell, "about love and sex in Alexandria."[7]

The project would go through several incarnations before eventually morphing into 1962's *Cleopatra* with Elizabeth Taylor and Richard Burton. The notoriously troubled production went $42 million over budget and nearly bankrupted 20th Century–Fox, which fired Walter. He gained back a little cash with a rather self-serving tell-all book, *My Life with Cleopatra*, focusing largely on his fascination with the then-married-to-others Taylor-Burton romance, a tabloid hit of the day. *Cleopatra* bombed exquisitely but won four technical Academy Awards. Walter was even nominated as the film garnered (but lost) a Best Picture nod.

It is not known how Justine voted. In 1960, she became a voting member of the Academy, Actors Branch. Her recommendation for membership almost certainly came from someone very well connected, such as, perhaps, a former

Academy president who never forgot that it was his ex-wife's introductions to her friends and acquaintances that started him in the film industry.

Late that year, a small newspaper in Bath, Maine reported, "The feature picture at the Opera House tonight is *Blackbirds* starring the beautiful screen artist Justine Johnstone."[8] After forty years, after talkies, a Depression, a Second World War, penicillin, television, blacklists and space exploration, somewhere in a small town in the upper Eastern United States, an audience was enjoying Justine Johnstone's first film for Realart, a studio that no one had even heard of any more.

24

Her Own Woman

"Mother was a bit of a character," said Justin Wanger. "When she first moved to California, she'd do something like jump in the car with her cousin Evvie and golf from Mexico up the coast of California. But she was disciplined. I don't recall her ever drinking at home. I don't think she ever smoked. She had instilled these characteristics in herself long before."

That lifelong discipline may explain why Justine remained healthy and vital into the 1960s and beyond. She also retained her sense of decorum. Mr. Wanger recalls an event sponsored by the League of Women Voters featuring 1962 gubernatorial candidate and former Vice President Richard M. Nixon. "Mom was to escort Nixon up to the dais," says Mr. Wanger, "and oh, she said she was never so insulted in her life. She held out her arm for him to take, and he brushed it off. He refused to take her arm! 'That rude, rude man!' she said. I don't think she ever forgave him."

Justine combined humanitarian aid with classical music for the 1963 "Twilight Garden Concert," a benefit for the UN's Freedom from Hunger Campaign spearheaded by formerly-blacklisted actress Marsha Hunt, now dedicating her life to UN work. Justine became chair of the arrangements committee. She, Marsha and Helene Boughton persuaded Sirpuhe Philibosian, philanthropist and co-founder of the Los Angeles Music Center, to host the event at her Holmby Hills estate. Entertainment was provided by the Los Angeles Chamber Orchestra conducted by Henry Lewis and featuring mezzo-soprano Marilyn Horne, Lewis' wife at the time.

The following year, Justine joined Marsha on the host committee for a reception honoring UN activist Jane Shields Freeman at the home of Dr. and Mrs. Omar Freed, a Beverly Hills internist who had worked with Dr. Albert Schweitzer. The guest list was an interesting mix of the entertainment, medical and philanthropic communities: the John Forsythes, the Jim Backuses, actress-activist Whitney Blake, tennis player Lady Mary Hardwicke, James Roosevelt, Dr. Gladys Emerson of the UCLA School of Public Health, and Carmen Warschaw, the spirited Democratic party activist and fundraiser.

Justin Wanger recalls assisting as a sort of stagehand on such projects; "I was the brawn," he laughs.

As Justine entered her seventies, her work with the League decreased, but she kept in touch with her fellow members. Her activities centered on her bridge club, her family and her friends. "A girlfriend I dated in those days was just in awe of her," says her son. "She said, 'She is a LADY!' They were shopping at Robinson's Westwood once and a saleslady was rude to them. My girlfriend said Mom turned to the woman and said, '*Really*, my dear. There is *no* call. For *that*.' Just frosted her! My mother had such a wonderful way about her."

Through her bridge club she met London-born Frances Dorothy Zucco, a former stage actress known as Stella. Justine and Stella discovered they'd been on stage in London at the same time 50 years earlier, but had never met. Stella had recently lost her husband, British character actor George Zucco. The two friends decided they no longer wished to live alone, and Stella became Justine's apartment mate.

"Stella could be reserved," says Mr. Wanger, "but then, my mother could be reserved. They got along very well. I remember how Stella enjoyed her evening sherry. Even now, when I have a sherry, I think, 'Where's Stella?'"

Justine in her early 50s with son Justin in the backyard of their Beverly Hills home, ca. 1946. Courtesy Mr. Justin Wanger.

Stella proved a pleasant and like-minded new companion. But many of Justine's inner circle from the early days were beginning to disappear.

Marion had become seriously ill by the early 1960s, wracked by cancer and alcoholism. She and Hearst had last stayed at San Simeon in 1947, after which Marion brought her ailing lover to her Beverly Hills estate, where he died in 1951. Marion then married an old friend, Horace Brown, continued to give fabulous parties and devote herself to her charities until her health declined. Hospitalized at Cedars in 1961, she learned that Marilyn Monroe was

24. Her Own Woman

recovering from gynecological surgery in the same wing, and told Louella Parsons, "We blondes seem to be falling apart."[1] Marion died at the hospital on September 22, 1961, age 64. At her death, her estate was worth an estimated $20 million.

Harpo Marx died almost exactly three years later, on his and wife Susan's 28th wedding anniversary, at Mount Sinai following heart surgery. The beloved comedian had only recently announced his retirement: at 75, he had still been doing television and personal appearances, even though he was a wealthy man. Groucho's son reported that Harpo's funeral was the only time he had seen his father cry.

Jesse Lasky died broke in New York in 1958. His widow Bessie appealed to the Motion Picture Relief Fund for assistance. The application, submitted anonymously, was initially rejected, but immediately approved once Fund co-founder Mary Pickford learned who the applicant was.

Even the gossip columnists who found excuses to talk about Justine were gone or fading. Hedda Hopper may have never succeeded in getting Justine back into the business, but she did manage a number of television and film guest spots herself, such as *Sunset Boulevard* with Gloria Swanson. She continued her column almost daily until she died at age 80 in 1966 at Cedars. By that time, ailing Louella Parsons' columns were being written by others and eventually discontinued before her death in 1972. Walter Winchell died just a few months after Louella. He had retired to the Ambassador Hotel, where he would type his columns and hand them out to strangers on street corners.

In 1965, Joan Bennett finally divorced Walter Wanger after years of estrangement. Joan was appearing in the gothic soap *Dark Shadows,* broadcast in a late afternoon post-school time slot to reach a dedicated audience of children and teens. In 1978, she married film critic David Wilde who, as "Gail" Wilde, maintained a salon for his fellow transvestites. The "Gail" persona would be suspended during the marriage per Joan's preference and re-emerge the day after Joan's death in 1990.

After Joan, Walter had a few crushes on much younger women, but he never remarried. His fortune had long been compromised and he, like Justine, was obligated to give up a few luxuries. He moved back to New York and found an apartment—not exactly in Hell's Kitchen, this being Walter after all, but in the Stanhope Hotel on Fifth Avenue and 81st Street. On November 18, 1968, at age 74, ill and exhausted, Walter suffered a heart attack in his sleep and died alone. The bulk of what was left of his estate, about $18,000, went to his and Joan's unmarried daughter Shelley.

Walter's obituaries invariably included mention of Justine having been "the world's most beautiful woman," "America's most beautiful showgirl," and all the other labels that had first been applied to the now 73-year-old woman when she was fifteen years old.

Justine made no public comment about Walter's death. It's possible no one asked her for one, and unlikely she would have obliged if they had.

"She could be a stubborn lady," says Mr. Wanger. "Yes, I would call her a feminist, but not in a go-man-the-towers kind of way. Just a very strong-willed person who wouldn't back down at slights. She was her own woman."

Justine, who once had such trouble defining feminism for herself, lived to see what would become known as the second wave emerge in the early 1970s. She and other women of her time had to work from within a static male-centered social system; women's voices were usually silenced or ignored. Now feminist leaders such as Betty Friedan, Gloria Steinem, and Bella Abzug were setting up the mics. Women were being approved for their own credit cards, getting no-fault divorces, entering male-only Ivy League schools, competing in sports, and gaining legal control over their own bodies. Work-life balance, one of Justine's concerns, was finally on the table, as would be legal definitions of sexual harassment. Many of the challenges would continue into the 21st century. But in the 1970s, womanhood was being redefined, and not exclusively by men. A woman was no Ziegfeldian mannequin. She was a person.

It was something that, of course, Justine had always known. For someone who had buffeted against gender stereotypes all her life, the contemporary feminist movement was an inevitability. Justine's focus was always on the present and future. The past was so remote and unimportant to her that, according to her son, she never even spoke of her parents or of her childhood.

There is, however, evidence that Justine cherished certain moments. Through all her moves to various homes over the decades, she kept a collection of some of her early modeling photos and clippings, photos of herself and Walter, a small snapshot of what seems to be a party at San Simeon, photos of Sam, of course many photos of her children. She apparently kept no photos or clippings regarding her Ziegfeld performances. But she did retain something that was no doubt a prized possession: her graduation certificate from Emma Willard.

Her last home was a condo in Santa Monica near Pacific Palisades, to which she and Stella relocated after a few years in Westwood. It was not far from her first California home, Marian's "beach house," by now consisting only of abandoned servants' quarters, tennis court and pool. (Restored in the 1990s, the property is now called the Annenberg Community Beach House.)

Justine was delighted when, in the 1970s, her son Justin named his daughter for her. She was a doting grandmother. "I remember everything my grandma gave me," says Justine Wanger Nutter. "Always very high-end jewelry: a necklace, a bracelet. I would get those gifts from her for years. She was so elegant. She awed me with her speech. She spoke beautifully. She dressed beautifully. Never jeans or sweats. Always tailored suits."[2]

Justine was particularly close to Ms. Nutter's mother. "My grandmother would take my mother to various gatherings at stars' homes," says Ms. Nutter, "such as Frank Sinatra or Kirk Douglas. Apparently I was brought to a party at Kirk Douglas' house when I was a baby. Mom tells me that Michael Douglas bounced me on his knee."

Like her father, Ms. Nutter was given little information about her grandmother's life in theatre or film. "I never recall her talking about the past," she says. "I knew that she had been a *Follies* girl. Apparently, each of the girls were known for something: their legs, their hands. She was known for her back and her neck. But that's all I knew. I didn't know anything about her film career until about ten years ago when I looked her up on the Internet and came across information about her movies. It definitely surprised me."

Justine may not have discussed her career, but she never lost her entertainment business savvy. The former photographer's model decided that her baby granddaughter was quite photogenic. Justine connected Ms. Nutter's mother with Nina Blanchard, soon to be one of Los Angeles' powerhouse modeling agents. Fifty years after Justine Johnstone became a professional child model, her granddaughter was doing the same. Ms. Nutter appeared in national commercials and print advertisements from babyhood to approximately age five. She is as blasé about her modeling career as her grandmother had been. "My mother tells me I was the original Pampers baby," she says, "but I don't know if that's true."

More interesting to Ms. Nutter is another aspect of following in her grandmother's footsteps, albeit unknowingly. Now a professional nurse, Ms. Nutter says, "I had no idea that my grandmother had such a background in medicine until much later. When I was in nursing school, they never mentioned that she helped develop the IV drip. That was a little disheartening. Can you imagine? I could have boasted that she was my grandmother!"

Family Christmas luncheons were festive occasions, Ms. Nutter recalls fondly, "always at a hotel in Beverly Hills." One such spot was the Beverly Hills Hotel, Justine's venue of choice years earlier for her League meetings. The iconic, Art Deco, pink and green hotel was still very much an "in" place in the 1970s, a curious blend of old Hollywood and new pop culture, catering to anyone from Charlie Chaplin (in his return to the States to receive his 1972 honorary Oscar) to John Lennon and Yoko Ono. The Eagles used a sunset photo of the hotel for the cover of their 1976 album "Hotel California." The Polo Lounge, named for Walter and his fellow polo players decades earlier, was still there. In the restaurant, deals were still being scribbled on napkins, pages still roamed the premises alerting celebrities to telephone calls, and Justine Johnstone Wanger was still a patron.

One wonders if anyone in the restaurant ever took notice of the refined, tailored, beautifully-spoken, elderly lady at the festive family table. More than likely an actress, someone may have thought. There were many elderly women in and around Beverly Hills who had been silent-film actresses. But if anyone had been told her name, it probably would have meant nothing.

As it happened, there were those who still remembered.

In the early 1960s, theatre critic Henry W. Clune saw the name "Justine Johnston" on a cast list outside a Rochester summer theatre, and stopped in his tracks. "I thought surely that must be the Justine Johnston [sic] who opened in Rochester many years ago in a musical called *Betty*," he wrote. "Miss Johnston and Miss Marion Davies were in the chorus, but they were not ordinary chorus girls. They were the two most famous show girls in America. After excited inquiries of the management, I found that no one had ever heard of the 'old' Justine Johnson; that the one playing that night was a relatively young woman. The information was disappointing."[3] The actress was, of course, not Justine Johnstone Wanger, but Justine Johnston (1921–2006), a popular character actress, singer, and 39-year member of the Actors Equity Council.

In a 1973 review of the *Irene*, a musical revival trying out in Washington, D.C., Levin Houston wrote, "Although I thoroughly enjoyed both Miss [Patsy] Kelly and Miss [Ruth] Warrick, when I saw that Justine Johnston (formerly there was a final 'e' on her name) was the stand-in for both of them, I was hoping that one or the other might have a crippling but short-lived indisposition so that I might see again the most beautiful woman who ever appeared in the Ziegfeld *Follies*, the one who has been my secret love all of these years."[4]

Again, wrong Justine. Mr. Houston apparently missed columnist Leonard Lyons' 1971 column where he tried to set the record straight. Lyons, father of future film critic Leonard Lyons, said no, the Justine Johnston signed for a new Hal Prince-Stephen Sondheim musical was *not* the Justine Johnstone "who once married Walter Wanger and won fame as a medical researcher."[5]

Lyons overlooked the coincidence of the title of the new Sondheim show in which Ms. Johnston was appearing: *Follies*.

Former *Follies* girls remembered. In 1936, Gladys Feldman Braham, a Follies performer from 1914 to 1918, founded the Follies Club. It wasn't strictly a social club: the forward-thinking Miss Braham created it as a charitable organization that assisted retired Ziegfeld girls down on their luck, and the group became affiliated with the New York Federation of Women's Clubs and the Actors Fund. As late as the 1960s, Mrs. Braham was happy to mention the Follies girls who had done well. For years, any time anyone asked her, she would mention Justine, "who was one of our renowned beauties, is in California and is engaged in medical research."[6]

"Dr. Justine Johnson [sic] got a medical degree and became a medical pathologist," noted a 1975 *New York Times* feature article about the Follies Club. The facts, let alone the spelling of her name, may not have been strictly

24. Her Own Woman

spot on. But it was the 1970s, and remarkably, the story of the Follies girl who entered the medical field was still being shared.

In 1983, Bolton and Wodehouse's *Oh, Boy!* was revived at the Goodspeed Opera House in Haddam, Connecticut. In his review, critic Jack O'Brien cited the 1917 original:

> With a cast including Justine Johnson [sic], considered by connoisseurs of the era the most beautiful female ever to slink onto a stage. Headed for what seemed acting stardom with beauty, brains and talent, she opted instead for a most serious career in medical research: reports through the years noted her role in the development of many brilliant discoveries, for which she also refused publicly to take credit or bows of any sort.
>
> She'd be well into her 80s by now. Anyone know if Justine Johnson is still around? Probably she wouldn't even surface with that information. Her story's a dandy; worth at TV or big-screen movie.[7]

O'Brien was no doubt correct in assuming that if Justine knew he was asking about her, she wouldn't respond. He had done enough research on Justine to know that she had been a private person for more than forty years and had not been quoted for more than thirty.

Unfortunately, O'Brien had no way of knowing that nearly a year earlier, on September 3, 1982, Justine Johnstone Wanger had died at her Santa Monica home. She was 87.

Like her mother, Justine had developed a form of dementia. "My last visits with her," says Mr. Wanger, "were not happy. I believe she may have had Alzheimer's. She did not know who I was." The official cause of death was heart failure. Cremation took place on September 9, 1982, at the Chapel of the Pines Crematory, a facility that served many film industry clients. Her ashes were scattered at the crematory's Rose Garden.

Justine's sons cared for their mother's friend Stella until her death seventeen years later at age 99 at the Motion Picture and Television Country House in Woodland Hills. A memorial service was held, and Stella's obituary was carried in Los Angeles newspapers.

But there was neither memorial service nor obituaries for Justine. This was by design. "She wanted it to be nothing," says Mr. Wanger.

She knew what the obituaries would say. She would get the same treatment she'd had in Walter's obituaries, with references to the Justine that had been created more than seven decades earlier with the labels that she found so meaningless and so limiting. They might have recycled the inaccurate claim even that she had found a cure for syphilis. Whatever they said, it would have made good copy but would have had little to do with her.

They probably wouldn't have mentioned that she had defied categorization, managed her own career, survived any number of strikes against her, thrived in a male-dominated environment, was a major player in social causes, and raised two sons on her own. That was the real Justine, but she was for herself and those whom she loved.

Besides, she had already provided her own succinct synopses of her life. In the early 1940s, when news of her medical career was flurrying, journalists realized that a quote from her was so rare that they simply published her declines for interviews.

"My story is a very tame tale," she wrote to Henrietta Malkiel of *Harper's Bazaar*, "just the account of a person who made a shift in her interests. And what is more, I feel that perhaps I have enough resiliency to start again on something new."[8]

She told Laura Z. Hobson of the businesswoman's publication *Independent Woman*, "I'm about as interesting as a filterable virus."[9] The phrase was a throwback to her first major study of melanin. She was making a rather remarkable analogy to herself: something that can penetrate anything trying to stop it simply by being so small.

Miss Hobson had no idea what she meant. Justine explained simply, "I got by."

It was all anyone needed to know.

Chapter Notes

Preface

1. Mizener, Arthur. *The Far Side of Paradise.* Boston: Houghton Mifflin, 1949, p. 108.
2. Crosby, Edward Harold. "Under the Spotlight." *Boston Sunday Post*, January 5, 1919.
3. "Over the Teacups." *Picture-Play Magazine*, Vol. XIV, No. 2, March 1921, p. 54.
4. All quotes from Mr. Justin Wanger from telephone interviews with author, January 7 and April 27, 2017.
5. Wodehouse, P. G. *The Theatre Omnibus.* London: Hutchinson, 1994, p. 48.
6. Berger, John, et al. *Ways of Seeing.* London: British Broadcasting Corporation and Penguin Books, 1973, p. 47.
7. Underhill, Harriet. "In Spite of Her Beauty." *Picture-Play Magazine*, Vol. XIV, No. 3, May 1921, p. 25.
8. "Actress Caters to Palate of Patrons Who Dine Late." *Washington Herald*, February 3, 1918.

Chapter 1

1. Duckworth, J. Herbert. "Actress, at 19, Rules Broadway Because She is Natural." *Fairmont West Virginian*, September 10, 1917.
2. "Ambition to Become a Real Actress Inspires a Chorus Beauty to Start Again in the Country." *New York Herald*, June 22, 1919.
3. Stevens, Ashton. "When Justine Johnstone Was Natural." *Actorviews.* Chicago: Covici-McGee, 1923, pp. 237–238.
4. "A Long Walk Daily Is the Best Beauty Hint Justine Johnstone Knows." *Boston Sunday Post*, January 12, 1919.
5. Stevens, p. 238.
6. "A Long Walk Daily."
7. "Ambition to Become a Real Actress."
8. Ziegfeld, Florenz. "Behind the Scenes in Beauty Land." *Indianapolis Sunday Star*, August 21, 1921.
9. *Ibid.*
10. Stevens, p. 238.
11. *Ibid.*
12. Winchell, Walter. *Winchell Exclusive.* New York: Prentice-Hall, 1975, p. 28.
13. Kingsley, Walter. "Whence Comes Jass? Facts from the Great Authority on the Subject." *New York Sun*, August 5, 1917.
14. Merrill, Flor. "Walter Kingsley, 'King of Broadway' and Godfather to Struggling Actresses." *Brooklyn Daily Eagle*, October 26, 1924.

Chapter 2

1. Wheeler, Ralph. "Creating a Super Beauty." *Fort Wayne Journal-Gazette*, August 29, 1915.
2. "Stunning Hats for Young Women." *New York Evening Telegram*, December 30, 1910.
3. *The Theatre Magazine*, Vol. 13, January 1911, p. 64.
4. "Just a Few of the Newest Beauties on Broadway." *Pittsburgh Press*, Sunday Magazine Section, July 30, 1911.
5. "Being Beautiful Is These Girls' Business." *Boston Sunday Post*, July 26, 1914.
6. Review, "Plays of the Week: Folies-Bergère—Burlesque." *The Dramatic Mirror*, May 3, 1911.
7. Wolf, Rennold. "The Boy Who Revived Ragtime." *Green Book Magazine*, August 1913. Quoted in Sears, Benjamin, *The Irving Berlin Reader.* New York: Oxford University Press, 2012, p. 19.

8. Lasky, Jesse. *I Blow My Own Horn.* New York: Doubleday, 1957, p. 85.
9. Unknown clipping, interview with Justine, n.d. The Shubert Archive, E. R. Simmons production files, 1917–1929, b. 4, f. 6.
10. Adair, Margaret. "Truth About the Chorus Girl." *Evanston Press,* August 23, 1911.

Chapter 3

1. Johnstone, Justine. "How It Feels to Be 'The Prettiest Girl.'" *Pittsburgh Sun,* June 20, 1915.
2. "Eat and Grow Prettier: That Is the Rule and Practice of Miss Johnstone." *New York Sun,* January 6, 1918.
3. Stevens.
4. *Ibid.*
5. *Emma Willard School, One Hundredth Anniversary,* Catalogue, 1914–1915, Troy, New York, p. 14.
6. Stevens.
7. Iannucci, Nancy. "From Entertainer to Innovator." *Emma: The Alumnae Magazine of The Emma Willard School,* Vol. 65, No. 1, Winter 2007, p. 38.
8. "Review: The Crucible." *Canton Daily News,* January 3, 1915.
9. Ad: The Alviene School. *Cosmopolitan,* Vol. 53, June 1912, p. 24.
10. Magee, Jeffrey. *Irving Berlin's American Musical Theatre.* New York: Broadway Legacies, 2014, pp 34–38.
11. Review, "Watch Your Step." *New York Clipper,* December 19, 1914.
12. Review, "Watch Your Step." *The Theatre,* January 1915, Vol. XXI, No. 167, p. 9.
13. Caption. *Vanity Fair,* Vol. 3, Issue 3, March 1915, p. 29.
14. Note from Dillingham to Justine, January 25, 1915. The New York Public Library, Rare Books and Manuscripts, Charles B. Dillingham Papers, 1903–1931, b 16, f J–1915.

Chapter 4

1. "Minute in the Wings." *New York Times,* April 4, 1915.
2. Johnstone, "How It Feels to Be 'The Prettiest Girl.'"
3. "If She Could Choose." *Joplin Globe,* June 29, 1915.
4. *Ibid.*
5. Farnsworth, Marjorie. *The Ziegfeld Follies.* New York: Putnam, 1956, p. 131.
6. Ziegfeld, "Behind the Scenes in Beauty Land."
7. *Ibid.*
8. Ziegfeld, Florenz. "How I Pick Beauties." *Theatre,* September 1919, p. 158.
9. *Ibid.*
10. Higham, Charles. *Ziegfeld.* Chicago: Henry Regnery Company, 1972, p. 103.
11. Nathan, George Jean. *The World in Falseface.* Rutherford, NJ: Fairleigh Dickinson University Press, 1972, p. 104.
12. Ziegfeld, Patricia. *The Ziegfelds' Girl: Confessions of an Abnormally Happy Childhood.* New York: Little, Brown, 1964, p. 21.
13. Ziegfeld, "Behind the Scenes in Beauty Land."
14. Mantle, Burns. "The Players." *Everybody's Magazine,* Vol. XXXIII, No. 5, November 1915, p. 572.
15. *Ibid.,* p. 574.
16. Magee, p. 43.
17. Review quotes: "The First Night Calendar," *New York Times,* December 19, 1915; "Gaby Returns in Stop! Look! Listen!" *New York Press,* December 27, 1915; "Show Reviews: Stop! Look! Listen!" *Variety,* n.d., 1915.
18. Bergreen, Laurence. *As Thousands Cheer: The Life of Irving Berlin.* New York: Da-Capo Press, 1996, p. 131.
19. Johnstone, Justine (attributed). "Love and Art: Do They Mix?" Sydney Sunday *Times,* January 7, 1923 (but possibly taken from a U.S. article written years earlier).
20. *Ibid.*
21. Ankerich, Michael G. *The Sound of Silence: Conversations with 16 Film and Stage Personalities Who Bridged the Gap Between Silents and Talkies.* Jefferson, NC: McFarland, 2011, p. 77; quote from Billie Dove.
22. Wodehouse, P. G. "The Somber Sadness of Our Summer Shows." *Vanity Fair,* Vol. 6, No. 6; photo caption, p. 45.
23. Ommen van der Merwe, Ann. *The Ziegfeld Follies: A History in Song.* Lanham, MD: Scarecrow Press, 2009, p. 99
24. Mantle, Burns. "Mantle's News and Views of New York Stage." *Louisville Courier-Journal,* June 18, 1916.
25. "Follies Beauty Quits." *Syracuse Herald,* October 17, 1916.

Chapter 5

1. "Ambition to Become a Real Actress."
2. Ziegfeld, Florenz, letter to Bernie Sobel, July 27, no year. New York Public Library for the Performing Arts, Billy Rose Theatre Division, Flo Ziegfeld-Billie Burke Papers, 1907–1984, b. 3, f. 37.
3. Rubens, Paul Alfred, and Ross, Adrian. Lyrics. *Betty: A Musical Play in Three Act.* London: Chappel & Co., 1915.
4. "Review: *Betty.*" *New York Sun*, October 4, 1916.
5. "'Betty' Scores a Big Success." *Syracuse Herald*, September 19, 1916.
6. "Be Good and You'll Be Beautiful, Says Justine." *Boston Sunday Globe*, January 5, 1919
7. Johnstone, Justine. "How I Keep My Health, Complexion and Figure." Star Company feature syndicated in *Buffalo Courier News*, n.d., 1916.
8. *Ibid.*
9. *Ibid.*
10. Duckworth.
11. Wodehouse, P. G., and Bolton, Guy. *Bring on the Girls.* New York: Simon & Schuster, 1953. 57.
12. *Ibid.*, p. 58.
13. Wodehouse, P. G. *Yours, Plum: The Letters of P. G. Wodehouse.* Frances Donaldson, ed. New York: James H. Heineman, Inc., 1991, p. 220.
14. Wodehouse and Bolton.
15. Wodehouse and Bolton, pp. 60–61.
16. "Oh! Boy! You Win Permanent Home." *Brooklyn Daily Eagle*, February 22, 1917.
17. "New Plays." *New York Times*, February 18, 1917.
18. McCrum, Robert. *Wodehouse: A Life.* W. W. Norton & Company, 2004, p. 127.
19. "Heart Market 'Bulled' by $225,000 Verdict; Chorus Queens Chalk Up Cardiac Quotations." *New York Herald*, June 19, 1917.
20. "Notes of the Stage." *New York Herald*, March 9, 1917.

Chapter 6

1. Clipping from the New York *Evening Mail*, February 19, 1917. New York Public Library for the Performing Arts at Lincoln Center, Billy Rose Theatre Division, Walter J. Kingsley Papers, 1899–1935, Vol. 1.
2. Mordden, Ethan. *Ziegfeld: The Man Who Invented Show Business.* New York: St. Martin's Press, 2008, p. 88.
3. Letter from Justine in Washington, D.C., to Lee Shubert, August 19, 1917. The Shubert Archive, General Correspondence: 1910–1936, b. April 1917–March 1919, f. 1496.
4. MacIntyre, O. O. "New York Day by Day." *Reading Eagle*, November 28, 1934.
5. Fitzgerald, F. Scott. *The Beautiful and the Damned.* New York: Charles Scribner's Sons, 1922, p. 82.
6. "Eagerly They Pay $50 to Join Justine Johnstone's 'Little Club.'" *New York Herald*, April 14, 1917.
7. Unnamed article, n.d. The Shubert Archives. E. R. Simmons production files, 1917–1929. *Over the Top*, b. Justine Johnstone.
8. Wodehouse, P. G. "The Coming Theatrical Season, Which Is Likely to Be a Riot of Musical Comedy." *Vanity Fair*, Vol. 9, September 1917, p. 45.
9. "Broadway Dreams." *The New York Sun*, September 16, 1917.
10. "Life One Frock After Another." *Philadelphia Inquirer*, February 17, 1918.
11. Letter from Worm to Lee Shubert, April 11, 1917. The Shubert Archive, Correspondence: January, April, May 1917, b. 76.
12. Note from Justine to Worm, n.d., approx. mid–1917. The Shubert Archive. General Correspondence 1910–1926, b. 76: June 1917–March 1918.
13. "'Over the Top' Gets Over Jersey, Anyhow." *Philadelphia Inquirer*, February 19, 1918.
14. Memo from Worm to Lee and J. J. Shubert, "Re: *Over the Top* Opening," November 26, 1917. The Shubert Archive. General Correspondence 1910–1926, b. 76: June 1917–March 1918.
15. "'Over the Top' a Nine O'clock Show," *New York Times*, December 3, 1917.
16. "Drama." *Life*, Vol. 70, No. 2, December 20, 1917, p. 1011.
17. "Plays and Players." *Brooklyn Life*, December 8, 1917.
18. "Justine Johnstone, the Principal Beauty in Over the Top." *Theatre Magazine*, Vol. XXVII, No. 204, January 1918, p. 89.
19. White, Matthew, Jr. "The Stage." *Munsey's Magazine*, February 1918, p. 124.
20. "Justine Johnstone Opens New Theatre." *The Sun*, December 3, 1917.

21. "'Over the Top' at the Top of Triple-Decked Theatre." *New York Herald*, December 3, 1917.
22. Moderwell, Hiram K. "Shubert Patriotism in 'Over the Top.'" *Indianapolis News*, December 15, 1917.
23. Review of *Over the Top*, "Wynn," *Variety*, December 5, 1917, p. 15.
24. Review, "Over the Top," *Pittsburgh Press*, March 12, 1918.
25. "The Theatre." *The American Jewish Press Chronicle*, Vol. 4, No. 18, February 8, 1918, p. 393.
26. "Miss Justine Johnstone, a Star Above, a Caterer Below," *New York Herald*, December 9, 1917.
27. "Eat and Grow Prettier."
28. Ads, "Over the Top." *Washington Post*, February 8, 1918, and *Philadelphia Inquirer*, February 10, 1918
29. "Again the Cinderella Motive in Music Show." *St. Louis Post-Dispatch*, April 29, 1918.

Chapter 7

1. Stevens, pp 231–234.
2. *Ibid.*, p. 237.
3. *Ibid.*, p. 240.
4. *Ibid.*, p. 239.
5. *Ibid.*, pp. 235–237.
6. *Ibid.*, p. 239.
7. *Ibid.*
8. *Ibid.*
9. *Ibid.*
10. Letter from Justine in Buffalo, NY, to Lee Shubert, n.d. The Shubert Archive. General Correspondence: 1910–1936, b. April 1917–March 1919, f. 1476.
11. Letter from Lee Shubert to Justine, May 18, 1918. The Shubert Archive. General Correspondence: 1910–1936, b. April 1917–March 1919, f. 1476.
12. Letter from Justine to J. J. Shubert, June 2, 1918. The Shubert Archive. General Correspondence: 1910–1936, b. April 1917–March 1919, f. 1476.
13. Note from J. J. Shubert to Justine, June 3, 1918. The Shubert Archive. General Correspondence: 1910–1936, b. April 1917–March 1919, f. 1476.
14. "Frank Fay Scores Hit in 'Victory Girl.'" *Buffalo Evening News*, November 26, 1918.
15. Letter from Justine to Lee Shubert, n. d. The Shubert Archive. General Correspondence: 1910–1936, b. April 1917–March 1919, f. 1476.
16. Memo from A. Toxen Work to Lee Shubert, April 12, 1918. The Shubert Archive. General Correspondence: 1910–1936, b. April 1917–March 1919, f. 1476.
17. Letter from Justine in Philadelphia to Lee Shubert, February 4, 1919. The Shubert Archive. General Correspondence: 1910–1936, b. April 1917–March 1919, f. 1476.
18. Note from Justine to Lee and J. J. Shubert, February 18, 1919. The Shubert Archive. General Correspondence: 1910–1936, b. April 1917–March 1919, f. 1476.
19. Lahr, John. *Notes on a Cowardly Lion: The Biography of Bert Lahr*. E-book version. Open Road Media, 2013.
20. Article, New York *Evening Mail*, n.d. The Shubert Archive, E. R. Simmons Production Files, 1917–1929, b 4, f 6, box Johnstone, Justine.
21. *Ibid.*

Chapter 8

1. Kazan, Elia. *Elia Kazan: A Life*. E-book version. Knopf Doubleday Publishing Group, 2011.
2. Underhill, pp. 24–25; p. 93
3. "Heart on the Rialto." *Dramatic Mirror*, December 22, 1917.
4. Merkel, Henrietta. "Woman in White." *Harper's Bazaar*, July 1940, p. 82.
5. "Ambition to Become a Real Actress."
6. "Per Aspera," *New York Sun*, June 22, 1919.
7. "Ambition to Become a Real Actress."
8. "Per Aspera."
9. *Ibid.*
10. "Justine Johnstone Aspires to Act." *New York Tribune*, June 22, 1919.
11. Title unknown; clipping, *Vanity Fair*, September 1919, p. 57, from the collection of Mr. Justin Wanger.
12. "Legit." *Variety*, n.d., retrieved online, Fulton Postcards New York State newspaper archive.

Chapter 9

1. "Boo-Hoo, Pity the Sad Millionaires." *Burlington Gazette*, March 31, 1920.
2. Gordon, Ruth. *My Side*. New York: D. I. Fine, 1986, p. 308.

3. "Miss Johnstone, Stage Beauty, Walter Wanger Bride; to Be His Star in Balzac Play." *New York Herald*, September 14, 1919.
4. "'Make Own Clothes, Girls,' Beauty Girl Advises." *Detroit Free Press*. June 1, 1925.
5. Clipping, *Town Topics* magazine, April 1, 1920. New York Public Library for the Performing Arts, Billy Rose Theatre Division, Chamberlain and Lyman Brown papers, 1849–1961, Series II Correspondence 1858–1961, Sub-Series I–General, b. 55, f. 12, Correspondence, Justine Johnstone, 1946–1953, undated.
6. Baracks, Clarence A. "Growing Up in the New City in the 1920s." *South of the Mountains*, Historical Society of Rockland County, Tappen Zee Historical Society, Vol. 34, No. 1, January–March 1990, p. 10
7. "Class of 1915." Dartmouth *Alumni Magazine*, Vol. 13, Dartmouth Secretaries Association, 1921, p. 346.
8. "Husband and Career Both Satisfy Justine Johnstone." *Philadelphia Evening Public Ledger*, April 18, 1921.
9. *Variety Film Reviews: 1907–1920*. Vol. 1. R. R. Bowker, 1983; CD-ROM.
10. Photo caption for "Behind the Scenes in Beauty Land." *Muncie Star-Press*, August 21, 1921.
11. "The Importance of a Fine Back." *Vicksburg Herald*, April 15, 1921.
12. Review, "Blackbirds." *Variety*, December 10, 1920.
13. Review, "Blackbirds." *Dramatic Mirror*, n.d.; retrieved Old Fulton Postcards New York State newspaper archive.
14. Review, *Blackbirds*. *Wichita Daily Eagle*, December 30, 1920.
15. "Amusements." *Daily Republican*, Rushville, IN, February 26, 1921.
16. Ibid.
17. "Beauty Needs Not the Rouge Pots." *Philadelphia Inquirer*, April 17, 1921.
18. Underhill.
19. "Husband and Career Both Satisfy Justine Johnstone." *Philadelphia Evening Public Ledger*, April 18, 1921.
20. "Screen Gossip." *Ashland Weekly Tidings*, March 2, 1921.
21. Ibid.
22. Welsch, Tricia. *Gloria Swanson: Ready for Her Close-Up*. Jackson: University Press of Mississippi, 2013, p. 191.
23. Sherwood, Robert E. "The Silent Drama." *Life*, Vol. 77, No. 2009, May 5, 1921, p. 669.
24. Review, "Sheltered Daughters." *Wid's Daily*, May 22, 1921, Vol. XXI, No. 52, p. 19.
25. Sherwood, Robert E. "The Silent Drama." *Life*, Vol. 78, No. 2021, August 11, 1921, p. 22.

Chapter 10

1. Lasky, p. 196
2. "The Screen." *The Saratogian*, Saratoga Springs, NY, May 11, 1921.
3. Price, Lucy, Jeanne. "New York Letter." *Morning Herald*, Johnstown, NY, May 28, 1921.
4. *The Film Daily Year Book of Motion Pictures (Wid's Year Book)*, Vol. 4, 1921, p. 103.
5. "Wanger Out at Famous." *Variety*, May 20, 1921.
6. "Many Americans in Paris," *New York Clipper*, June 14, 1922.
7. "Les Films de la Semaine: Survivre." *Cinemagazine*, Vol. 4, No. 25, June 24, 1924, p. 503. Downloaded PDF from CineResources.net.
8. "Plays and Players." *Photoplay*, June 1921, p. 99. Retrieved on archive.org.
9. Graves, Charles. *The Price of Pleasure*. London: I. Nicholson, 1935, p. 367.
10. Brighten, Hilda. *No Bridge to Yesterday*. London: V. Gollancz, 1949, p. 147.
11. "Miss Johnstone to Produce Play in London." *New York Telegram and Evening Mail*, February 4, 1924.
12. Ibid.
13. "Last Night's Play: 'Polly Preferred." *The Observer*, London, April 4, 1924.
14. "Prefers Polly Preferred." *New York Evening Post*, April 7, 1924.
15. Review, "Polly Preferred." *Variety*, April 9, 1924.
16. "Feminine Celebrities from All Over the World." *Danville Bee*, Danville, VA, March 11, 1925.
17. Kaufman, S. Jay. "Round the Town." *New York Telegram and Evening Mail*, July 8, 1924.

Chapter 11

1. Woollcott, Alexander. "Plays and Players in These Parts: Justine's Johnstone's Part

as a Collaborator in 'Dancing Mothers.'" *New York Sun*, August 30, 1924.
 2. "In Vaudeville." *New York Times*, August 10 1924.
 3. "Vaudeville Reaches for Stage Stars." *Philadelphia Inquirer*, October 19, 1924.
 4. "Broadway Stars at White House." *The New York Sun*, October 17, 1924.
 5. Faine, Edward Allan. "The First Jazz Band at the White House." *Vintage Jazz Mart* online, retrieved January 14, 2017.
 6. Kaufman, S. Jay. "'Round the Town." *New York Telegram and Evening Mail*, January 2, 1925.
 7. Bernstein, p. 55.
 8. *Ibid*.
 9. *Ibid*.
 10. Roberts, Sam. Obituary, "Aileen Mehle, Gossip's Grande Dame Known as 'Suzy,' Dies at 98." *New York Times*, November 11, 2016.
 11. Bernstein.
 12. Obituary, "Anita Stewart, Silent-Film Star," *New York Times*, May 5, 1961.
 13. "Fine Vaudeville Bills." *New York Times*, December 8, 1925.
 14. "Vaudeville." *Variety*, August 19, 1925.
 15. "Justine Johnstone Is Keith Headline." *Philadelphia Inquirer*, December 15, 1925.
 16. Ad, *Oakland Tribune*, August 28, 1925.
 17. "Make Own Clothes, Girls."
 18. Johnstone, Justine. "Justine Johnstone Tells Way to Clear Up Skin Blemishes." *Minneapolis Daily Star*, July 20, 1925.
 19. Johnstone, Justine. "The Wide Open Spaces." *New York Times*, December 13, 1925.
 20. "Ousted from Play, Actress Sees Plot." *New York Times*, April 20, 1926.

Chapter 12

 1. "Another Gordon." *Brooklyn Daily Eagle*, February 22, 1925.
 2. Ad, *Hush Money. Bridgeport Telegram*, February 23, 1926.
 3. Review, *Hush Money. Variety*, March 3, 1926.
 4. Klayton, Alvin J. "In the Theatres on Broadway." *Brooklyn Daily Star*, March 26, 1926.
 5. Review, *Hush Money. Variety*, March 24, 1926.
 6. "'Hush Money' Crooks of a Familiar Sort." *New York Times*, March 16, 1926.
 7. "A Blonde, a Brunette, an Angel and Hush Money." *Indianapolis Star*, May 30, 1926.
 8. *Ibid*.
 9. *Ibid*.
 10. "Justine Johnstone Enters Firm Denial." *New York Times*, April 21, 1926.
 11. James, Rian. "Big Brothers to Broadway. 2: Abner J. Rubien." *Brooklyn Daily Eagle*, March 1, 1931.
 12. "Ousted from Play, Actress Sees Plot." *New York Times*, April 30, 1926.
 13. "A Blonde, a Brunette, an Angel and Hush Money."
 14. *Ibid*.
 15. "Justine Johnstone Enters Firm Denial."
 16. "A Blonde, a Brunette, an Angel and Hush Money."
 17. "Justine Johnstone Enters Firm Denial."
 18. "A Blonde, a Brunette, an Angel and Hush Money."
 19. "Injunction Suit by Actress Halts." *New York Times*, April 24, 1926.
 20. "Justine Johnstone Drops Injunction Proceedings." *New York Sun*, April 23, 1926.
 21. "Injunction Suit by Actress Halts."

Chapter 13

 1. Sperling, Cass Warner, and Millner, Cork, with Jack Warner, Jr. *Hollywood Be Thy Name: The Warner Brothers Story*. Lexington: University of Kentucky Press, 1998, p. 1981.
 2. Jablonski, Edward, and Stewart, Lawrence Delbert. *The Gershwin Years: George and Ira*. Cambridge, MA: Da Capo Press, 1958, p. 141.
 3. Lawrence, John. "London's Men and Women." *Brooklyn Daily Eagle*, September 27, 1926.
 4. Mencken, Henry Louis, Haardt, Sara, and Rodgers, Marion Elizabeth, eds. *Mencken and Sara: A Life in Letters: The Private Correspondence of H.L. Mencken and Sara Haardt*. New York: McGraw-Hill, 1987, p. 290.
 5. Letter from Justine to H. L. Mencken, n.d. New York Public Library Archives and Manuscripts: H.L. Mencken Papers, 1905–1956: microfilm r. 31.
 6. McIntyre, O. O. "In Li'l Old New York." Corning, NY, *Evening Leader*, July 19, 1926.
 7. McIntyre, O. O. "New York Day by Day." Steubenville, OH, *Star*, June 7, 1928.

Chapter 14

1. Hobson, Laura F. "Follies Girl to Scientist." *Independent Woman*, National Federation of Business and Professional Women's Clubs, Vol. 20, October 1941, p. 298.
2. Letter from C. C. Lieb to Justine and Walter, October 16, 1928. Wisconsin Center for Film and Theatre Research, Walter F. Wanger Papers, 1908–1967, Series: General Correspondence and Related Material, b. 27 f. 1.
3. Emma Willard, catalogue, p. 25.
4. Hyman, Harold. Autobiographical Manuscripts (Fragmentary / Incomplete), n.d. "Biographical Notes: Section XYZ." Papers of Harold Thomas Hyman, MD, 1894–1985, b. 1, f. 2, Archives and Records of the Icahn School of Medicine, Mount Sinai Hospital, New York.
5. *Ibid.*
6. *Ibid.*
7. *Ibid.*
8. *Ibid.*
9. Winchell, Walter. "Walter Winchell on Broadway." Glen Falls, NY, *Post-Star*, September 18, 1929.
10. McIntyre, O. O. "New York." *Lima Sunday News*, July 19, 1931.
11. Swann, Gilbert. Column. Cumberland, MD, *Evening Times*, March 17, 1932.

Chapter 15

1. Bordman, Gerald. *American Theatre: A Chronicle of Comedy and Drama, 1930–1969*. Oxford: Oxford University Press, 1996, p. 3.
2. Parsons, Louella O. "Marion Davies Returns to MGM Studio for Comedy." *San Antonio Light*, April 29, 1932.
3. Letter from Justine to Dr. James Bumgardner Murphy, July 31, 1932. American Philosophical Society Library, James Bumgardner Murphy Papers, Date: Circa 1918–1950, f. B M956.
4. Letter from Albert Einstein to the Leabach family, January 16, 1931, in *The Einstein Scrapbook*, Ze'ev Rosenkranz, curator. Baltimore: Johns Hopkins University Press, 2002 p. 122.
5. Keavy, Hubbard. "Picture Folks Cycle but It's Just a Mere Fad." *St. Petersburg Press*, April 14, 1933.
6. Parsons, Louella. Column. *Philadelphia Inquirer*, January 2, 1933.
7. Vieira, Mark A. *Irving Thalberg: Boy Wonder to Producer Prince*. Berkeley: University of California Press, 2009, p. 171.

Chapter 16

1. Winchell, Walter. "On Broadway." *Wisconsin State Journal*, July 3, 1933.
2. "Condition of House forms Basis of Suit." *San Bernardino County Sun*, June 12, 1935.
3. "Frogs Found in Swim Pool." *Nevada State Journal*, June 11, 1935.
4. "Swim with Frogs? Not My Husband!" *Pittsburgh Press*, June 11, 1935.
5. "Onus Placed on Gophers." *Los Angeles Times*, June 11, 1935.
6. Maas, Frederica. *The Shocking Miss Pilgrim: A Writer in Early Hollywood*. Lexington: University Press of Kentucky Press, 1999, p. 147.
7. Parsons, Louella. Column. *San Antonio Light*, September 4, 1932.
8. Massey, Raymond. *A Hundred Different Lives*. Toronto: McClelland and Stewart, 1979, p. 153.
9. Beauchamp, Cari. *Without Lying Down: Frances Marion and the Powerful Women of Early Hollywood*. Berkeley: University of California Press, 1999, p. 309.
10. *Ibid.*

Chapter 17

1. Marx, Harpo, with Rowland Barber. *Harpo Speaks!* Pompton Plains, NJ: Limelight Editions, 2002, p. 396.
2. Massey, pp. 155–156.
3. Mann, William J. *Kate: The Woman Who Was Hepburn*. New York: Macmillan, 2007, p. 184.
4. "Highlights of the Month in the Dramatic Onward March of Science, Pharmacy and Medicine." *American Druggist*, Vol.101 January–June 1940, p. 65.
5. Duboff, G., and Hirschfield, S. "Demonstration of an Enzyme-inhibiting Factor in the Serum of Cancer Patients." *Cancer Research*, Vol. 6, February 1946, p. 57.
6. Plenk, Henry P. *Medicine in the Beehive State, 1940–1990*. Utah Medical Association, 1992, p. 51.

7. Hirshfeld, Samuel. "Dysovulation." Read before the Southern California Medical Society on April 6, 1932. Published in *Cal West Med*, Vol, 42, No. 2, August 1935; retrieved online at PubMed Central, January 16, 2017.

8. Eyman, Scott. *Lion of Hollywood: The Life and Legend of Louis B. Mayer*. New York: Simon & Shuster, 2005, p. 193.

9. Marx, Samuel. *Mayer and Thalberg: The Make-Believe Saints*. New York: Random House, 1975, p. 225.

10. Parsons, Louella. Column. *Philadelphia Inquirer*, December 3, 1932.

11. Columbia University employment record, "Wanger, Justine Olive (Mrs. Walter F.)." Courtesy Stephen E. Novak, Head, Archives & Special Collections, Augustus C. Long Health Sciences Library.

Chapter 18

1. Several sources, including "Movie Producer, Wife Part." Belvidere, IL, *Daily Republican*, February 8, 1938.

2. Winchell, Walter. "On Broadway." *Reading Times*, June 2, 1936.

3. Among others, "Producer Divorced." AP story in *Chicago Daily Tribune*, April 16, 1938.

4. Bernstein, p. 165.

5. "Wife Divorces Walter Wanger." *Los Angeles Times*, April 16, 1938.

6. "Mrs. Walter Wanger Files Divorce Suit." AP story in *Bakersfield Californian*, February 1, 1938.

7. Parsons, Louella O. Column. *Amarillo Globe*, May 6, 1938.

8. Letter from Loyd Wright to Walter, January 11, 1940. Wisconsin Center for Film and Theatre Research, Walter F. Wanger Papers, 1908–1967, Series: Corporate and Financial Records, Personal and Family Financial Records, b 46, f 14.

Chapter 19

1. Kaempffert, Waldemar. "Science in the News: 5-Day Syphilis Treatment a Coordinated Campaign as to Wassermann Tests Discovery of 'Speed Shock' Effect on Blood Transfusions." *New York Times*, July 2, 1939.

2. Clipping. Harold Hyman Papers, Mount Sinai Archives, b 1, f 2.

3. "5-Day Treatment for Syphilis Found." *New York Times*, April 13, 1940.

4. Unreferenced clipping. "Johnstone [Wanger], Justine—Correspondence, Clippings, n.d." Harold Hyman Papers, Mount Sinai Archives, b 1, f 19.

5. Smits, Jeanette. "What the Follies Star Saw in a Test Tube." *Fresno Bee / Republican*, June 2, 1940.

6. "Former Student Here Revealed in Role of Scientist: Emma Willard Alumna, Once Follies Beauty, Helps Develop New Technique for Disease Cure." Troy, NY, *Times Record*, 1940, exact date unknown.

7. Winchell, Walter. "Walter Winchell in New York." *Cincinnati Enquirer*, May 28, 1943.

8. Mencken letter to editor St. Clair McKelway, November 30, 1940. *The New Mencken Letters*, Bode, Carl, ed. New York: Dial Press, 1977, p. 470.

9. Barlow, Robert. "Speaking of People." *Toledo Blade*, July 2, 1940.

10. Smits.

11. Hobson, Laura Z. "Follies Girl to Scientist." *Independent Woman*, magazine of the National Federation of Business and Professional Women's Clubs, October 1941, p. 319.

12. Hobson.

13. "Chatterbox." *Los Angeles Times*, September 16, 1941.

14. Parsons, Louella. Column. *Schenectady Gazette*, February 3, 1940.

15. Hopper, Hedda. "Retired Follies Girls Hungry for Spotlight." *Buffalo Courier-Express*, May 18, 1944.

Chapter 20

1. Malkiel.

2. Parsons, Louella. "Louella Parsons' Hollywood." *Albany Times-Union*, April 6, 1948.

3. St. John, Adela Rogers. "The Girls Who Glorified Ziegfeld." *Albany Times-Union*, June 30, 1946.

4. Hyman, Mount Sinai Archives papers.

5. Hyman, Harold Thomas, MD. "The Doctor Says." *The Saratogian*, August 14, 1960.

6. Undated letter 1 (1947) from Justine to Harold Hyman. "Johnstone [Wanger], Justine—Correspondence, Clippings, n.d." Harold Hyman Papers, Mount Sinai Archives, b 1, f 19.

7. Ibid.
8. Undated letter 2 (1947) from Justine to Harold Hyman.

Chapter 21

1. Roper, Mary Lou. "Fund Raising: A Report to Social Share Holders." *Los Angeles Times*, November 20, 1966.
2. Hopper, Hedda. "Hedda's Hollywood." *Salt Lake Tribune*, November 27, 1949.
3. "Meet the World Proves Impressive Stage Event." *Los Angeles Times*, March 31, 1950.
4. Advertisement section for Homes, *Los Angeles Times*, March 11, 1951.

Chapter 22

1. Justine letter to Walter, January 9, 1949, from 613 N. Hillcrest, Beverly Hills. Wisconsin Center for Film and Theatre Research, Walter F. Wanger Papers, 1908–1967, Series: General Correspondence and Related Material, b. 27, f. 1.
2. Gabler, Neal. *An Empire of Their Own: How the Jews Invented Hollywood*. New York: Anchor Books/Random House, 1989, p. 374.
3. Bennett, Joan, with Lois Kibbee. *The Bennett Playbill*. New York: Holt, Rinehart and Winston, 1970, p. 298.
4. Ibid., p. 300.
5. "Wanger Shooting Case." *Los Angeles Times*, December 16, 1951.
6. "Joan Bennett Sees Husband Shoot Agent." *Los Angeles Times*, December 14, 1951.
7. "Not Guilty, Plea of Wanger; Temporary Insanity Claimed." *Los Angeles Times*, January 8, 1952.
8. "Robert Mitchum, Durable Movie Star for 40 Years, Dies." Obituary, *Los Angeles Times*, July 2, 1997.
9. Bernstein.
10. "Walter Wanger Gets Out of Jail." *The Times*, San Mateo, September 13, 1952.
11. Hopper, Hedda. Column. *Los Angeles Times*, December 21, 1951.

Chapter 23

1. Williams, Shirley. "The Sage of Catfish Bend." *Louisville Courier-Journal*, December 28, 1980.
2. Gene Fowler letter to Ben Hecht, May 2, 1955. Hecht, Ben, *Letters from Bohemia*. Garden City, NY: Doubleday, 1964, p. 65.
3. Hopper, Hedda. "Hedda Hopper's Hollywood." *Lima News*, April 28, 1959.
4. Kilgallen, Dorothy. Column. *Cincinnati Enquirer*, August 7, 1959.
5. Hopper, Hedda. Column. *Chicago Tribune*, July 29, 1959.
6. Roosevelt, Eleanor. "My Day," March 13, 1959. From My Day column pages, George Washington website.
7. Hopper, Hedda. "Hedda Hopper's Hollywood." *Tucson Daily Citizen*, December 3, 1959.
8. Events blurb, no title, *Bath Independent*, Bath, ME, November 10, 1960.

Chapter 24

1. Guildes, Fred Lawrence. *Marion Davies: A Biography*. New York: McGraw-Hill, 1972, p. 369
2. All quotes from Justine Wanger Nutter, RN, telephone interview by author, January 4, 2017.
3. Clune, Henry W. "Seen and Heard." *Rochester Democrat-Chronicle*, July 19, 1960.
4. Houston, Levin. "Lavish, Stylish 'Irene' is Latest Nostalgic Hit." *Free Lance-Star*, Fredericksburg, VA, February 2, 1973.
5. Lyons, Leonard. "Lyons Den." *The Times of San Mateo*, February 16, 1971.
6. Morehouse, Ward. "Broadway After Dark." *Long Island Star-Journal*, October 19, 1964.
7. O'Brien, Jack. "The Next Hit." *Spartanburg Herald-Journal*, November 12, 1983.
8. Merkel, "Woman in White."
9. Hobson.

Bibliography

Basinger, Jeanine. *Silent Stars*. New York: Alfred A. Knopf, 2000.
Bergreen, Laurence. *As Thousands Cheer: The Life of Irving Berlin*. New York: Da Capo Press, 1996.
Bernstein, Matthew. *Walter Wanger: Hollywood Independent*. Berkeley: University of California Press, 1994.
Bordman, Gerald. *American Theatre: A Chronicle of Comedy and Drama, 1914–1930*. Oxford: Oxford University Press, 1995.
Bordman, Gerald, and Norton, Richard. *American Musical Theatre: A Chronicle*. Oxford: Oxford University Press, 2010 (Fourth Edition.)
Bordman, Gerald, and Hischak, Thomas S. *The Oxford Companion to the American Theatre*. New York: Oxford University Press, 2004. (Third Edition.)
Brideson, Cynthia, and Brideson, Sara. *Ziegfeld and His Follies: A Biography of Broadway's Greatest Producer*. Lexington: University Press of Kentucky, 2005.
Ceplair, Larry. *Dalton Trumbo: Blacklisted Hollywood Radical*. Lexington: University Press of Kentucky, 2014.
Dahl, Per F. *From Nuclear Transmutation to Nuclear Fission, 1932–1939*. Boca Raton: CRC Press, 2002.
Eyman, Scott. *Empire of Dreams: The Epic Life of Cecil B. DeMille*. New York: Simon & Schuster, 2010.
Farnsworth, Marjorie. *The Ziegfeld Follies*. New York: Putnam, 1956.
Gabler, Neal. *An Empire of Their Own: How the Jews Invented Hollywood*. New York: Anchor Books/Random House, 1989.
Golden, Eve. *Anna Held and the Birth of Ziegfeld's Broadway*. Lexington: University Press of Kentucky, 2013.
Guildes, Fred Lawrence. *Marion Davies: A Biography*. New York: McGraw-Hill, 1972.
Hamm, Charles. *Irving Berlin: Songs from the Melting Pot: The Formative Years, 1907–1914*. New York: Oxford University Press, 1997.
Hirsch, Foster. *The Boys from Syracuse: The Shuberts' Theatrical Empire*. Carbondale: Southern Illinois University Press, 1998.
Jablonski, Edward, and Stewart, Laurence Delbert. *The Gershwin Years: George and Ira*. New York: Da Capo Press, 1996.
Jason, David. *P. G. Wodehouse: Portrait of a Master*. London: Continuum, 1974.
Kellow, Brian. *The Bennetts: An Acting Family*. Lexington: University Press of Kentucky, 2004.
Kenrick, John. *Musical Theatre: A History*. London: Bloomsbury, 2010.
Koszarski, Richard. *Hollywood on the Hudson: Film and Television in New York from Griffith to Sarnoff*. New Brunswick: Rutgers University Press, 2008.

Marra, Kim. *Strange Duets: Impresarios and Actresses in the American Theatre, 1865–1914.* Iowa City: University of Iowa Press, 2006.
Marx, Harpo, with Rowland Barber. *Harpo Speaks!* Pompton Plains, NJ: Limelight Editions, 2002.
Massey, Raymond. *A Hundred Different Lives.* Toronto: McClelland and Stewart, 1979
McArthur, Benjamin. *Actors and American Culture, 1880–1920.* Iowa City: University of Iowa Press, 2000
McCrum, Robert. *Wodehouse: A Life.* New York: W. W. Norton & Company, 2004.
Mizejewski, Linda. *Ziegfeld Girl: Image and Icon in Culture and Cinema.* Durham: Duke University Press, 1999.
Mordden, Ethan. *Ziegfeld: The Man Who Invented Show Business.* New York: St. Martin's Press, 2008.
Nasaw, David. *The Chief: The Life of William Randolph Hearst.* Boston: Houghton Mifflin, 2000.
Page, William Adino, and Miller, Edward A. *Behind the Curtains of the Broadway Beauty Trust.* New York: Edward A. Miller Publishing Company, 1927.
Pizzitola, Louis. *Hearst Over Hollywood: Power, Passion and Propaganda in the Movies.* New York: Columbia University Press, 2002.
Plenk, Henry P., and McMurrin, Trudy, eds. *Medicine in the Beehive State, 1940–1990.* Salt Lake City: Utah Medical Association, 1992.
Proctor, Ben. *William Randolph Hearst: The Later Years, 1911–1951.* Oxford: Oxford University Press, 2007.
Riley, Kathleen. *The Astaires: Fred & Adele.* Oxford: Oxford University Press, 2012.
Rossiter, Margaret. *Women Scientists in America: Struggles and Strategies to 1940.* Baltimore: Johns Hopkins University Press, 1982.
Schary, Dore: *Heyday: An Autobiography.* New York: Little, Brown, 1979.
Sears, Benjamin, ed. *The Irving Berlin Reader.* Oxford: Oxford University Press, 2012.
Segrave, Kerry. *Actors Organize: A History of Union Formation Efforts in America, 1880–1919.* Jefferson, NC: McFarland, 2008.
Stagg, Jerry. *The Brothers Shubert.* New York: Random House, 1968.
Stanley, Autumn. *Mothers and Daughters of Invention: Notes for a Revised History of Technology.* New Brunswick: Rutgers University Press, 1995.
Thakkar, K. V. *Intravenous Therapy.* Bombay: R. R. Bakhale at the Bombay Vaibhav Press, 1944.
Travis, Doris Eaton. *The Days We Danced: The Story of My Theatrical Family from Florenz Ziegfeld to Arthur Murray and Beyond.* Seattle: Marquand Books, 2003.
Wainscott, Ronald Harold. *The Emergence of the Modern American Theatre, 1914–1929.* New Haven: Yale University Press, 1997.
Wilmeth, Don B., and Bigsby, Christopher, eds. *The Cambridge History of American Theatre, Volume II: 1870–1945.* Cambridge: Cambridge University Press, 1999.
Wodehouse, P. G. *Yours, Plum: The Letters of P. G. Wodehouse.* Frances Donaldson, ed. New York: James H. Heineman, 1991.
Wodehouse, P. G., and Bolton, Guy. *Bring on the Girls!* New York: Simon & Schuster, 1953.
Ziegfeld, Patricia. *The Ziegfeld's Girl: Confessions of an Abnormally Happy Childhood.* New York: Little, Brown, 1964.

Index

Numbers in ***bold italics*** indicate pages with illustrations

Abzug, Bella 190
Actors Equity Association 32, 74–76, 82, 112–113, 121, 179, 192
Actors' Fidelity League (FIDO) 75–76, 78
actors' strike of 1919 74–76
Adair, Margaret 18–20
Albee, Edward F. 99, 107; *see also* Keith-Albee vaudeville circuit
Allen, Dr. Bennet Mills 148–149
Allen, Billie 64, 159
Allenberg, Bert 142, 164, 169
Allenberg, Mildred ***142***, 155, 164, 169–170, 182–184
Alviene School of Stage Arts 23, 53
American Association for the United Nations 183; *see also* United Nations
American Federation of Labor (AFL) 74
American National Theatre Academy (ANTA) 183
Ames, Winthrop 9–10, 22
Anderson, Robert 183–184
"Ansco's Loveliest Woman" (photo contest) 26–27
The Apartment 175
Appleman, Dr. David 167–168, 179
Are You My Wife? 22
Arzner, Dorothy 87
Astaire, Fred, and Adele 23, 53, 55, 57, 58, 120; Adele 60; Fred 92, 93, 154, 162
Astoria Studio (Kaufman-Astoria Studios) 78, 87, 102, 110, 133
Atwell, Roy 22

Backus, Mr. and Mrs. Jim 187
Balanchine, George 26
Ball, Lucille 162
Bankhead, Tallulah 102–103
Bara, Theda 90
Barnes, T. Roy 53, 55, 58
Barrymore, Ethel 2, 27, 68, 73–75

Barrymore, John 22, 27, 52, 145–146
Barrymore, Lionel 27, 52
Bartholomae, Phillip 41, 64–65
Barton, Ralph 1, 118
Barton, Travis 120
Baxter, Warner 87, ***88***
Bayes, Nora 64, 68
Bel-Air Bay Club 143
Belasco, David 15
Bennett, Joan 149, 151–152, 154, 173–178, 189
Benny, Jack 105, 143, 169
Benny, Mary 143
Berger, John 3, 4
Bergman, Ingrid 174
Berlin, Irving 16–17, 24, 34, 91, 118; "Alexander's Ragtime Band" 17; "The Girl on the Magazine Cover" 34; "I Love a Piano" 34; "The Messenger Boy" 16–17; "Play a Simple Melody" 24; *see also* Watch Your Step; Stop! Look! Listen!
Berman, Pandro 184
Betty 38–40, 110, 192
Beverly Hills Hotel 141, 172, 191; "Hotel California" 191; Polo Lounge 141, 191
Biddle, Craig, Jr. 109
Blackberg, Dr. Solon Nathaniel 128–129, 131, 183
Blackbirds 81–82, 186
blacklist, Hollywood 173–174, 179–182
Blair, William 73
Blake, Eubie 93
Blake, Whitney 187
Blanchard, Nina 191
The Blue Bird (play) 9–12, 15, 20, 22, 38, 47; *The Blue Bird* (Famous Players–Lasky film) 53
Boardman, Queen Walker 141
Bolton, Guy 41–***44***, 45, 48, 69, 77, 94–96, 99, 133, 156, 193
Boughton, Helene 169, 187

207

208 Index

Bow, Clara 118, 140
Boyer, Charles 160
Bradbury, Ray 184
Brady, Alice 81
Brady, "Diamond" Jim 17
Braham, Gladys Feldman 192
Braham, Philip 93
Brice, Fanny 36, 109, 121, 162
Brighten, Hilda 93
Broadway Cares/Equity Fights AIDS 121
Broadway Theatre (Long Branch, NJ) 22
Broadway theatre district *see* "Great White Way"
Brooks, Louise 102
Brown, Horace 189
Bruns, Julia 65
Buchanan, Jack 92–93, 111, 154
Burke, Billie 31, 131, 146
Burke, Edwin J. 104
Burman, Ben Lucien 181
Burns, David 95
Burton, Richard 185
Butler, Hugo 180
Byers, John 141

California Institute of Technology (Caltech) 135–137, 139, 148, 163, 168, 185
Campbell, Craig 58
cancer studies 1, 123, 125–126, 128–129, 135–138, 147–150, 163, 165, 168; *see also* melanin
Cantor, Eddie 74, 133, 140
Capra, Frank 169
Castle, Vernon, and Irene 24, 51; Irene 70, 90–91, 121; Vernon 25
Cedars of Lebanon Hospital (Cedars-Sinai Medical Center, Los Angeles) 148, 163, 169, 183, 188–189; *see also* Mount Sinai Hospital (Los Angeles)
'Ception Shoals 67–68
Chalfin, Paul 77
Chandler, Jeff 170
Chaplin, Charles 102, 138, 143, 191
Chargin, Dr. Louis 158–159
Charisse, Cyd 162
Charles Frohman, Inc. 78; *see also* Frohman, Charles
Charlot, Andre 93, 99
Chatterton, Ruth 81, 118
Chayefsky, Paddy 183–184
Chevalier, Maurice 118
Chimot, Edouard 91
Christy, Howard Chandler 12
Churchill, Winston 143
Citizen Kane 39, 60, 156–157, 159
Claire, Ina 16, 32, 38, 110
Clark, Marguerite 3, 22, 24
Cleopatra (1962 film) 184
Clune, Henry W. 191
Cocoanut Grove 118, 157
The Cocoanuts 118, 120
Cohan, George M. 16, 36, 64, 74–75, 113

Cohn, Harry 134, 137, 139, 141
Colbert, Claudette 118, 143, 149, 154, 170
Columbia Pictures 133–134, 137
Columbia University 1, *124*, 131–132, 136, 145, 150, 162; College of Physicians and Surgeons 123–131, 134, 136, 144–145, 150
Comstock, F. Ray 40–43, 48, 67, 74, 94
Conant, Homer 53, 55
Conklin, Philip 26
Coolidge, Calvin 101–102, 143
Coolidge, Grace 102
Cooper, Gary 143, 145–146
Cosmopolitan Productions (Cosmopolitan Pictures) 76, 91, 99, 104, 133
Covent Garden 92
Coward, Noël 93
Crawford, Joan 143
Crews, Laura Hope 81
Crosby, Bing 156
The Crucible (1914 film) 22–23, 24

Daly, Arnold 100
Daniels, Bebe 81, 141
D'Anunzio, Gabriele 90
Darrach, Dr. William 126
Dartmouth College 67, 79, 125
Davies, Ethel (Douras) 34
Davies, Marion (Douras) 3, 34, *35*, 36, 38–40, *42*–44, 48, 50, 52, 62, 65, 70, 75–76, 91, 94, 99, *134*–136, 139, 141–143, 145, 156–157, 160, 163, 169, 184–185, 188–189
Davies, Rose (Douras, Van Cleve) 34, 91
Davis, Bette 143
de Forest, Lee 117
DeMille, Cecile B. 75, 87, 114, 172, 179
Deslys, Gaby 16, 34
Deuel, Dr. Harry 149
de Wolfe, Elsie 77, 91, 106
Dietrich, Marlene 103
di Frasso, Dorothy (Countess di Frasso) 145–146
Dillingham, Charles 24–25, *30*–32, 34–35, 38–39, 78, 101, 106, 120, 133
Dillon, Edward 87
Dillon, John (Jack) 81, 87
Disney, Walt 22, 138, 141, 176
Dolly Sisters 102
Donohue, Jessie Woolworth 109
Douglas, Kirk 182, 191
Douglas, Michael 191
Dove, Billie 135, 140
Dressler, Marie 74, 90
Drew, John, Jr. 27, 62, 101
Duboff, Dr. Gregory 148
Duff Gordon, Lady Lucile 32
Duke, Angier 50
Dunlavey, Donald J. 184
dysovulation 149

Earhart, Amelia 1943
Eaton, Mary 53, 55, 120–121

Ehrlich, Dr. Paul 129
Einstein, Albert 136–137
Emerson, Dr. Gladys 187
Emery, Dr. Clyde 135, 148, 168
Emery, Gilbert 161–162
Emma Willard School 3, 21–22, 31, 77, 127, 160, 172, 190
Englewood, New Jersey 5–6
Erlanger, A.L. 12, 46–47
Eyes of Youth 73

Fair and Warmer 72–73
Fairbanks, Douglas 1, 113, 143, 160
Famous Players Film Company 22–23, 75, 106; Famous Players–Lasky 75, 81–82, 87, 97, 99, 102, 104, 109, 117; *see also* Paramount Pictures Corporation
Fay, Frank 64
feminism 4, 27, 64, 106, 168, 190
Fenwick, Margaret (Peg) 169–170, 181
Ferguson, Elsie 3, 24, 78
FIDO *see* Actors' Fidelity League
Fields, Lew 51
Fields, W.C. 24, 32, 36, 118
Fisher, Harrison 26
Fiske, Minnie Maddern 26
Fitzgerald, F. Scott 1, 50
Fitzgerald, Zelda 1
Flagg, James Montgomery 12, 68
Fletcher Henderson Orchestra 64
Floradora 2
"Folies-Bergère Show" (Hell/Temptations/Gaby) 16–18, 20, 34, 59, 75
Folies-Bergère Theatre (Fulton Theatre, first Helen Hayes Theatre) 16, *17*, *18*, 20, 30, 34, 59, 80, 90, 94, 110, 154, 162
Follies (1971 Broadway musical) 192
Follies Club 192
Fonda, Henry 143
Ford, Harrison (silent film actor) 87
Forster, Maurice 91–92
Forsythe, John 183; and Mrs. Forsythe 187
44th Street Rooftop Theatre (Castles-in-the-Air) 51, *52*, 55, 64
Foster, Allan 53
Fowler, Gene 145, 147, 181
Freed, Arthur 162
Freed, Dr., and Mrs. Omar 187
Freedman, Flossie 92–93
Freeman, Jane Shields 187
Friedan, Betty 190
Friedlander, William B. 109
Frohman, Charles 22, 24, 27, 31, 47, 64, 78, 96; *see also* Charles Frohman, Inc
Frohman, Daniel 15, 22, 24
Fulton Theatre *see* Folies-Bergère Theatre
Furber, Douglas 92–93

Gable, Clark 143, 169
Gabler, Neal 174
Garbo, Greta 141, 143, 160

Garland, Judy 162, 169
Gayety Theatre (Hoboken) 7
Gentlemen Prefer Blondes (novel) 35, 42, 62, 135
Germania Garden (Hoboken) 7
Gershwin, George *118*–119, 143
Gest, Morris 74, 94
Giesler, Jerry 176
Gish, Dorothy 90
Glaenzer, Jules *118*–119
Glass, Everett 170, 177
Globe Theatre (Lunt-Fontanne) 34, 133
Going Hollywood 156
Goldstein, Leonard 164–165
Goldwyn, Sam (Goldfish, Gelbfisz) 20, 75, 93, 138–139, 141, 144, 174, 176
Gone with the Wind 81, 145
Good Samaritan Hospital (Los Angeles) 148, 150
Gordon, Kitty 17
Gordon, Max 99–100, 133, 162
Gordon, Ruth 77, 154
Gordon, Charles 109–117, 152
Gosnell, Evelyn 71
Grant, Cary (Archie Leach) 16, 143, 154
Granville, Bernard 32, 63
"Great White Way" (Broadway theatre district) 12–14
Green, Belle 5
Green, Johnny 184
Greenwood, Charlotte 101

Hairston, Jester 170
Hamilton, Margaret 170
Hammerstein, Arthur 125
Hammerstein, Oscar 125, 183
Hardwicke, Lady Mary 187
Harriman, Margaret 160
Harris, Henry B. 16, 20, 122
Harris, Reneé 20, 122
Hayes, Helen 98, 110
Hearst, Millicent 39, 134
Hearst, William Randolph 35–36, 39–40, 60, 70, 75–76, 91, 99, 104, 109, 118, 133, 134–135, 138, 142–143, 151, 156–161, 163–164, 183, 185, 188; San Simeon 135, 142–144, 188, 190
A Heart to Let 87
Hecht, Ben 145, 148, 165, 167, 181
Held, Anna 30–31, 47, 53
Helen Hayes Theatre *see* Folies-Bergère Theatre; Little Theatre
Helleu, Paul 161
Hennepin-Orpheum Theatre (Minneapolis) 105
Hepburn, Katharine 115, 146
Hi-Hat Restaurant 143
Hillcrest Country Club 141–142
Hirshfeld, Dr. Samuel (Sam) 123, 125–126, 128–132, 144–150, 155, 157–159, 160, 163, 165–169, 179, *182*, 183, 190
Hitchcock, Mr. and Mrs. Alfred 182

Hitchcock, Raymond 101
Hoboken, New Jersey 6–9, 22, 23, 31, 46, 71, 111, 142
Hobson, Laura 123, 194
Holmes, Rapley **80**
Holmes, Taylor 16, **80**–81, 90
Hope, Bob 142, 157
Hopkins, Miriam 118
Hopper, Hedda (Edna Furry) 16, 162, 166, 170, 174, 177–178, 182–185, 189
Horne, Lena 162
Horne, Marilyn 187
House Un-American Activities Committee (HUAC) 173–174, 179; see also blacklist, Hollywood
Houston, Levin 192
How He Lied to Her Husband 99–100, 102
Huffman, J.C. 53
Hughes, Howard 143
Hunt, Marsha 169, 179, 187
Hush Money (No Questions Asked, Back Fire) 109–115, 117, 139, 152; 1931 Fox film 152
Huston, Walter 138
Hutt, Henry 12
Hyman, Dr. Harold Thomas 125–**126**, 127–131, 146, 158–159, 161, 165–167, 181–183

Ince, Thomas 143
Inge, William 183–184
intravenous drug delivery (IV drip) 1, 130, 158

Jackson, Alfred G. 109–111
The Jazz Singer 117
Joan of Arc (1948 film) 174
Johnson, Gustav (father) 5–7, 9, 12, 17, 20, 23, 26, 39, 77, 98, 120, 190
Johnson, Owen 17
Johnson, Sophia Ommundson (mother) 5–7, 12, 20, 23, 26, 39, 51, 60, 63, 77, 98, 120, 154, 164, 190
Johnston, Julanne 1, 143, 160
Johnstone, Justine 1, 192
  agent, literary 179–182
  birth and childhood 5–8
  career ambitions, theatrical 21–23, 33–34, 36, 38, 58, 62–63, 69–74, 90–91, 94–95, 99, 108–110
  childhood ambitions 8, 21, 181
  children, adoption of 154–155
  children, views on 78, 106
  club see Justine Johnstone's Little Club
  death 193
  divorce 152–154, 170–171
  exercise 21, 23, 40, 83, 106–107
  feminism, views on 27, 33, 66, 90, 105–106, 190
  film 22–23, 80–90, 91–92, 104
  film production company 90–92
  golf 79, 86, 119, 141–**142**, 147–148, 155, 169–170, 187
  high school (Emma Willard) 20–22
  marriage, views on 36, 79–80, 86, 106
  marital problems 93, 102–103, 106, 151–154
  medical research—
    Los Angeles 135–137, 146–150, 154, 160–161, 163, 167–168, see also California Institute of Technology (Caltech), University of California at Los Angeles (UCLA)
    New York see Columbia University, School of Physicians and Surgeons
  model, child/teen 9 – 12, 191
  newspaper columns, authored 40, 106–108
  producer, theatrical 94–95, 170
  publications, scientific 131—
    "Influence of Velocity on the Response to Intravenous Injections" (with Hirshberg, Hyman) 129–131, 158–159
    "Melanuria" (with Blackberg) 128
    "Studies in Revivification—Organization or Resuscitation Measures" (with Blackberg) 129
  reading 7–8, 61, 119, 124, 181
  romances/gentlemen callers 17, 36, 44–45, 47–48, see also Bolton, Guy, Emery, Gilbert, Goldstein, Leonard, Hirshfeld, Samuel, Sadowsky, Jack, Wanger, Walter
  social and political activism 168–170, 172, 179–184, 187–188
  theatre—
    Broadway 9, 12–20, 24–29, 31–39, 41–44, 48, 51–59, 109–115
    London 92–96
    pre-Broadway 22
    tours (for Shuberts) 58–66
    vaudeville 99–108
  wedding 77
Jolson, Al 101–102, 117
Joplin, Scott 17
Joyce, Peggy Hopkins 65, 70, 121
Judy O'Grady 104–105, 107, 118
Justine Johnstone's Little Club (Castle Club, Club Alabam, Stage Door Canteen) 1, 47–48, **49**–52, 54, 58–59, 63–64, 112, 125, 159–160

Kaempffert, Walter 157–158
Kanter, Jay 175, 177
Karloff, Boris 104
Kaufman, S. Jay 96, 102
Kaye, Danny 184
Kazan, Elia 67
Keith-Albee vaudeville circuit 99–101, 104–108; Keith-Albee-Orpheum 146; RKO (Radio-Keith-Orpheum) 146
Keith's Temple Theatre (Detroit) 105
Kellas, Eliza 21, 77
Kellerman, Annette 105
Kellogg, William K. 135
Kelly, Gene 162

Kelly, Patsy 192
Kennedy, Joseph P. 90, 146
Kern, Jerome 41, 43
Key, Ellen 90
Kilgallen, Dorothy 183
Kingsley, Walter 9–12, 14–15, 22–26, 28, 46, 67, 71, 100
Kirchner, Raphael 39
Klaw, Marcus 12, 47
Knickerbocker Theatre 24
Knight, Goodwin Jess 153

LaGuardia, Fiorello 67
Lahr, Bert 66
Lake, Patricia Van Cleve 91
Lamarr, Hedy 1, 152, 160
Lang, Jennings 175–177
Lang, Pam 175, 177–178
Lasky, Bessie (Ginsberg) 103, 189
Lasky, Jesse L. 16–17, 20, 30, 75–76, 78, 90, 92–93, 96–98, 104, 113, 117, 119–120, 133, 138, 164, 189
The Last of Mrs. Cheyney 110–111
Laughton, Charles 183
Laurell, Kay 28, 32–33, 121
Lauritsen, Dr. Charles C. 135, 137
Lavery, Emmet 183–184
Lawrence, Gertrude 93, 99
League of Women Voters (Beverly Hills) 169–170, 172, 187–188, 191
Leifer, Dr. William 158–159
Lennon, John 191
Levy, Ethel 16
Lewis, Albert 99–100
Lewis, George 140
Lewis, Henry 187
Lewis, Monica 177
Lieb, Dr. Charles Christian ("C.C.") 125–128, 136
Lillie, Beatrice 93
Little Theatre (Philadelphia) 78
Little Theatre (second Helen Hayes Theatre) 94
Lonsdale, Frederick 38, 110
Loos, Anita 35, 42, 135
Lord, Marjorie 170
Lorraine, Lillian 31
Lorraine, Ted 56
Lusitania (RMS Lusitania) 77
Lyons, Leonard 192
Lytell, Bert 104

Maas, Frederica 141
MacDonald, Jeannette 118
Mack, Charles 56
Madame Sherry 12, 14–15
Maeterlinck, Maurice 9
Majestic Theatre (Columbus Circle) 9
Malkiel, Henrietta 163, 194
The Man Who Came to Dinner 181
Manor Girls' School 21

Mantle, Burns 33, 37, 116
Marbury, Elisabeth 40–41, 67, 70, 77, 106
March, Fredric 118
Marion, Frances 143
Marion Davies "Beach House" (Annenberg Community Beach House) **134**–136, 139, 143, 156, 163, 190
Marion Davies Children's Clinic (Marion Davies Children's Health Center, UCLA) 156, 163
Marion Davies Film Company 75; *see also* Davies (Douras), Marion
Markey, Gene 152
Marx, Dr. Walter 168
Marx, Groucho 133, 183, 189
Marx, Harpo 3, 118–119, 143, 145, 148, 155, 184, 189
Marx, Susan (Fleming; Mrs. Harpo) 145, 155, 184, 189
Marx Brothers 118, 141–143; "the four imposters" **118**–119
Mary's Ankle 71–**72**
Massey, Raymond 142, 145–146, 148
Matas, Dr. Rudolph 130
Maxine Elliott's Theatre 22
Maxwell, Elsa 118, 121
Maxwell, Helen 64
Mayer, Louis B. 118, 120, 138–139, 141, 143, 149–150, 174
Mayer, Margaret 149–150
Maytime 50, 54
McIntyre, O.O. ("Odd") 120, 131
McKelway, St. Clair 160
Meet the World 170–171, 177, **180**–181
Mehle, Aileen (Suzy Knickerbocker) 103, 116
melanin 125–128, 148, 168; *see also* cancer studies
Mencken, H. L. 1, 35, 119, 160
Metro-Goldwyn-Mayer (Metro Pictures Corporation, MGM) 43, 80, 92, 99, 104, 137–138, 159, 162, 174
Midnight Frolic 47, 50
Miller, Marilyn 64
Millikan, Dr. Robert Andrews 135–137
Ming Room 164
Minter, Mary Miles 81
Mitchum, Robert 169, 176–177
Moderwell, Hiram K. 57
Monroe, Marilyn 17, 164, 188
Moonlight and Honeysuckle 81
Moore, Denise (Dennie) 112–113, 115, 152
Morgan, Frank 118
Morgan, Julia 135
Motion Picture Relief Fund 189
Mount Sinai Hospital (Cedars-Sinai Medical Center, Los Angeles) 182–183, 189; *see also* Cedars of Lebanon Hospital
Mount Sinai Hospital (New York) 123, 125, 130, 158
Mudd, Dr. Seeley G. 135
Murphy, Dr. James Bumgardner 136

Murray, Mae 32, 121
Music Corporation of America (MCA) 175, 177, 179
Mussolini, Benito 151

Namara, Marguerite 44, 94
Nazimova, Alla 57, 61, 67
Never the Twain Shall Meet 104
New Amsterdam Theatre 12, *13*, 24, 33, 47, 133
New Theatre (Century Theatre) *9*, 38
Nicolson, Virginia (Welles) 157
Nielsen, Eveyn (Evvie) 6, 142
Nielsen, Lester 6, 111, 114
Nielsen, Peter, and Louise 6
Nilsson, Anna Q. 2, 118
Nixon, Richard 187
Nothing but Lies **80**-81
Novello, Ivor 93
Nutter, Justine Wanger (granddaughter) 190–191

Oakland Sisters 55, 58
O'Brien, Jack 193
Occidental College 172
Oh, Boy! 41–44, 46, 48, 65, 69, 94, 193
Oh, Mama! (Girl o' Mine, Victory Girl) 64
Oliver, Edna May 43
Ono, Yoko 191
Orpheum Theatre (Los Angeles) 105
Over the Top (Oh, Justine!, The Nine O'Clock Revue) 48, 52–59, 65, 68, 69, 93, 105, 112, 120; tour 59–62, 64, 118

Palace Theatre 11, 100, ***101***, 105, 107, 159
Palmer, Dr. Walter Walker 128
Paramount Building (1501 Broadway) 97, 133
Paramount Pictures Corporation 75, 87, 104, 117–118, 120, 131, 133, 138, 139; *see also* Famous Players Film Company; Famous Players–Lasky
Parsons, Louella 135, 137, 141, 143, 150, 154, 157, 161–162, 164, 166, 174, 189
The Patsy 156
Peck, Mr. and Mrs. Gregory 182
Perry, Antoinette 102
Peter Pan: play 96; Famous Players–Lasky film 96, 102
Petrova, Olga (Muriel Harding) 16, 90
Philibosian, Sirpuhe 187
Phillips, Coles 12
Pickford, Jack 121
Pickford, Mary 81, 90, 113, 121, 138, 143, 161, 189
Pidgeon, Walter 29
Pinero, Arthur Wing 62
The Plaything of Broadway ***84***, 87
Poli, Sylvester Z. 71
Poli stock company (Main Street Theatre, Waterbury, CT) 72–73
Poli's New Park Theatre (Bridgeport) 111

Polly Preferred 94–96, 98–99, 112, 156
Porter, Edwin S. 22
Powell, William 29, 162
Powers, Tom 43
Preminger, Ingo 179–182
Preminger, Otto 179, 182
Prince, Hal 192
Princess Theatre 40–42, 46–48, 50–53, 67, 74–75, 93, 133
Producing Managers Association (PMA) 74, 76
Purcell, Charles 50, 54

Ranlet, Ralph 17, 21, 77
Reagan, Nancy, and Ronald 182
Realart Pictures 81–89, 91–92, 99, 101, 109, 159, 164, 187
Red Channels 179
The Red Mill 24
Redford, Marion 94
Rice, Dr. John L. 158
Riviera Country Club 141
Robinson, Edward G. 169, 184
Rodgers, Dorothy 119
Rodgers, Richard ***118***-119, 125
Rogers, Buddy 143
Rogers, Ginger 102, 118, 143
Rogers, Will 36, 68, 141
Rolanda, Rosa (Rosalinda Cowan) ***49***, 53, 56
Romberg, Sigmund 53
Roosevelt, Eleanor 183
Roosevelt, James 187
Rossellini, Roberto 174
Rosson, Gladys 172
Rosson, Harold 172
Roth, Nat 58, 60
Rous, Dr. Francis Peyton 125, 128, 136
Royalton Theatre (London) 95
Rubien, Abner J. 113–114

Sacred and Profane Love 77–78
Sadowsky, Jack 45
St. John, Adela Rogers 164–165
Samuels, Dr. Leo Tolstoy 148–151, 167
San Simeon *see* Hearst, William Randolph
Sandow ("The Great Sandow") 30
Santley, Joseph 35, 38–39, 120
Sarnoff, David 146
Sawyer, Ivy 38–39
Schary, Dore 174, 183–184
Schenck, Joseph 139, 176
Selwyn, Archibald (Archie) 93, 98, 183
Selwyn, Edgar 93, 98, 122, 183–184
Selwyn, Rae 98, 183
Selwyn, Ruth 122
Selznick, David O. 81, 138, 143, 145–146, 148
Selznick, Irene 148
Selznick, Lewis 81
sexual harassment 102–103, 190
Sharrock, Harry, and Emma 56

Shaw, George Bernard 86, 99–100, 102, 143, 162
Shearer, Norma 143, 156
The Sheik 90
Sheltered Daughters 85, 87, **88**
Sherwood, Robert E. 87
Shipman, Helen 64
Show People 99, 156
Shubert, J.J. (Jacob) 46–48, 56, 62–63, 65–66
Shubert, Lee 1, 9, 22, 45–55, 62–66, 68, 106
Shubert, Sam 46–47
Shubert Academy of Dramatic and Musical Art 65
Shubert brothers 13, 15, 36, 40, 46, 47, 52, 53, 58–61, 63–66, 67, 71, 74, 93, 109, 118, 133, 154, 162
Simmons, Jean 184
Sinatra, Frank 169, 184, 191
Sissle, Noble 93
Slocum, John 64
Sloto, Evelyn **142**
Smith, Harold Jacob 180–181
Smith, Harry B. 34
Smith, Winchell 95
Smits, Jeannette 160–161
Sondheim, Stephen 192
Soulier's Lyric Theatre (Hoboken) 7
Stage Women's War Relief 67
Stanwyck, Barbara 64
Stassen, Harold 169
Steinem, Gloria 190
Stevens, Ashton 6, 60–62, 69, 157
Stevens, Morris 100
Stewart, Anita 104
Stewart, Mr. and Mrs. James 182
Stieglitz, Alfred 26
Stop! Look! Listen! 34–36
Storey, Bobbie 93, 121
Streisand, Barbra 141
Survivre 91–92
Swanson, Gloria 81, 87, 90, 143, 146, 189
Swift, Kay 143
syphilis studies 1, 129–131, 157–161; "five-day syphilis treatment" 157–159
Szold, Bernard 170

Taylor, Elizabeth 182, 185
Taylor, Laurette 68, 72
Tedrow, Irene 170
Tell, Alma 65
Tenney Commission 179
Thalberg, Irving 137–138, 143
Theatrical Syndicate 12, 46–47
Thienes, Dr. Clinton 149
Thomas, Olive 32, 52, 121, 129
Thomson, Kenneth 109, 112, 114–115, 139
Three for Today 183–184
Times Square Theatre 93
Toni 92–93
Tourneur, Maurice 104
Travis, Doris Eaton 121

Trocadero 143
Trumbo, Dalton 180, 182
20th Century–Fox 141, 164, 185

Ulric, Lenore 121
Underhill, Harriet 83, 85
Unger, Gladys 38
United Artists 81, 138, 170
United Nations 169–170, 183; UNESCO 170; Freedom from Hunger campaign 187–188; *see also* Meet the World; Three for Today
Universal International 164, 181
University of California at Los Angeles (UCLA) medical research: 148–149, 156, 163, 167–168, **171**, 179, 185, 187; *see also* Meet the World
University of Southern California (USC) 149, 172
Urban, Joseph 31–32, 36, 104

Valentino, Rudolph 90, 120
Van Cleve, George 91
Very Good Eddie 40–41
Vidor, King 99
Vitaphone 117

Wanger, Beatrice (Nadja; Walter's sister) 77
Wanger, Henry (Walter's brother) 173
Wanger, Justin (son) 4, 116–117, 154–**155**, 163–165, 169, 171, 173–174, 177, 183, **188**, 190, 193
Wanger, Stella (Walter's mother) 67, 77
Wanger, Walter 67–71, 74–76, **77**–81, 83, 85–86, 90–95, **96**, 97–99, 102–103, 106, 110, 112–113, 116–120, 122–123, 125–126, 131, 133–134, 137–145, 150–155, 157, 159–160, 164, 170–171, 173–179, 185–186, 189–190, 193
Wannamaker, John 50
Warburg, Jimmy 143
Warne, Clore 179
Warner, Jack 174; and Mrs. Warner, 182
Warner Brothers (studio) 117, 139; producers 139, 143
Warrick, Ruth 192
Warschaw, Carmen 187
Wasserman, Edie 182
Wasserman, Lou 182
Watch Your Step 24–26, 34, 70, 91, 121
Wayburn, Ned 23, 36
Wayne, John 160
Wayside Honor Rancho 176–177
Webb, Clifton 164
Weiner, Willard 184
Welles, Orson 60, 156–157, 170
Wenzell, A.B. (Albert Beck) 12
West, Mae 20
Wheaton, Anna 43
"When the War Is Over, I'll Return to You" (Dudley/Watson) 66
Whipple, Dr. Allen Oldfather 128
White, George 32
White, Matthew, Jr. 56

White Memorial Hospital (Los Angeles) 148
White Studio 14–15, 71, 74
Whitney, Payne 50
Wickes, Mary 184
Wilde, David 189
Wilder, Billy 175
Wilding, Michael 182
William Morris Agency 169
Williams, Bert 32–33, 36
Williams, Rhys 170
Wilson, Michael 180
Wilson, Richard Alan 170
Winchell, Walter 131, 139, 141, 151, 160, 189
Windsor Theatre (Bronx) 111
Winter Garden Theatre 36, 53, 56, 63, 154, 159
Witherspoon, Cora 129
Wodehouse, P.G. (Pelham Grenville) 3, 36, 4–44, 133, 193
The Women 115
women's suffrage 70, 106
Wood, Dr. Francis Carter 136
Woods, A.H. (Albert Herman) 12, 71

Woodward, Joanne 185
Woollcott, Alexander 98, 119
Worm, A. Toxen 49–51, 54–55, 58–60, 64–65
Wynn, Ed 32, 58, 61, 64, 74, 101, 154, 162
Wynn, Keenan 162
"Wynn" (*Variety* critic) 57

Young, Loretta 169
Young, Nedrick 180–181

Zanuck, Darryl 141, 176, 183
Ziegfeld, Florenz 2–3, 8, 10, 14, 24, **28**–32, 36–38, 47–48, 53, 56, 58, 74, 106, 120–121, 131, 133, 146, 162; "glorification" (objectification) of women: 2–3, 28–32, 37
Ziegfeld, Patricia 31
Ziegfeld Follies of 1915 **29**, 31–34
Ziegfeld Follies of 1916 **29**, 36–37, 67
"Ziegfeld walk" 36
Zucco, George 188, 190, 193
Zukor, Adolph 22, 75, 79, 81, 120, 133, 141